Globalization

Policies, Challenges and Responses

Edited by
Shereen T. Ismael

Detselig Enterprises Ltd.

Calgary, Alberta, Canada

Globalization: Policies, Challenges and Responses
© 1999 Shereen T. Ismael

Canadian Cataloguing in Publication Data
Main entry under title:
Globalization

Includes bibliographical references.
ISBN 1-55059-169-X

1. International economic relations--Social aspects. 2. International finance--Social aspects. I. Ismael, Shereen T.
HF1359.G58 2000 337 C99-911255-4

Detselig Enterprises Ltd.
210-1220 Kensington Rd. N.W.
Calgary, Alberta T2N 3P5
Telephone: (403) 283-0900/Fax: (403) 283-6947
e-mail: temeron@telusplanet.net
www.temerondetselig.com

We acknowledge the financial support of the Government of Canada through the Book Publishing Industry Development Program (BPIDP) for our publishing activities.

Globalization was produced with the support of the Eastern Mediterranean University Press.

ISBN: 1-55059-169-X
SAN: 115-0324
Printed in Canada
Cover Design by Dean Macdonald

Table of Contents

Contributors . . . . *v*

Preface . . . . *vii*

Introduction . . . . *viii*

I. GLOBALIZATION IN WORLD AFFAIRS *17*

First World, Third World, Globalizing World:
Where is the Middle East?
    Enid Hill 19

Globalization: Established Fact or Uneven Process?
    Ray Kiely 45

Against the Globalist Paradigm
    Philip Marfleet 65

II. REGIONAL RESPONSES *85*

Developmental Stalemate in the Eastern Mediterranean:
Some Conceptual Tools for the Understanding of
Contemporary Problems
    Ivan Ivekovic 87

The Dynamics of Trade Liberalization and Poverty in Africa
    Danbala Danju 109

Globalization and Traditional Authority in Africa:
Investment, Security and Land in Ghana
    Donald I. Ray 125

"Internationalization" and "Localization" in the
Chinese Search for Human Justice
    Ronald Keith 143

Globalization: Aid, Trade and Investment in Egypt,
Jordan and Syria Since 1980
    Paul Sullivan 169

Marginalized Violent Internal Conflict in the
Age of Globalization: Mexico and Egypt
    Dan Tschirgi 217

Egypt in the Space and Time of Globalism
  Raymond William Baker 243

*Globalization and Turkey: From Capitulations to
Contemporary Civilization*
  Seymen Atasoy 257

*Globalization, Identity and Social Work Practice:
Insight from Working with Bedouin Arab Peoples*
  Alean Al-Krenawi & John R. Graham 271

Contributors

Seymen Atasoy is Associate Professor and Chair of the Department of International Relations, Eastern Mediterranean University.

Raymond William Baker is Professor of International Politics at Trinity College in Hartford, CT, and Adjunct Professor of International Relations at the American University in Cairo. Professor Baker is currently on sabbatical, working on a study of Islamic centrists and their role in civil society, having completed a term as Dean of Faculty at Trinity. *Sadat and After: Struggles for Egypt's Political Soul* (Harvard University Press, 1990); *Egypt's Uncertain Revolution Under Nasser and Sadat* (Harvard University Press, 1978).

Danbala Danju is Assistant Professor in the Department of Economics, Eastern Mediterranean University.

John R. Graham, PhD RSW, is Associate Professor, Faculty of Social Work, University of Calgary, Alberta, Canada. Longstanding collaborator with Alean Al-Krenawi, their recent publications on cross-cultural and international mental health/social work practice appear in numerous journals

Enid Hill is Professor and Chair, Department of Political Science, American University in Cairo. *Al-Sanhuri and Islamic Law: The Place and Significance of Islamic Law in the Life and Work of Abd al-Razzaq Ahmad al-Sanhuri, Egyptian Jurist and Scholar, 1895-1971; Mahkama! Studies in the Egyptian Legal System: Courts & Crimes, Law & Society.*

Shereen T. Ismael is an Assistant Professor of Social Work at the University of Northern British Columbia in Canada. She specializes in international and Canadian social policy, participatory action research and population health.

Ivan Ivekovic is Professor of the Department of Political Science at the American University in Cairo.

Ronald Keith is Professor and Chair, Department of Political Science, at The University of Calgary in Calgary, Alberta, Canada. *Energy, Security and Economic Development in East Asia* (ed.); *Comparative Political Philosophy: Studies Under the Upas Tree* (ed.); *China's Struggle for the Rule of Law: The Diplomacy of Zhou Enlai.*

Ray Kiely is Professor, Department of Cultural Studies, University of East London, and has published widely in numerous journals in recent years on developmental issues. *The Politics of Labour and Development in Trinidad* (Kingston: The Press University of the West Indies, 1996); *Sociology and Development: The Impasse and Beyond* (London: UCL Press, 1995).

Alean Al-Krenawi, PhD, is Lecturer, Department of Social Work, Ben Gurion University of the Negev, Beer Sheva, Israel. He is a long-time collaborator with John R. Graham.

Philip Marfleet is Lecturer, Development Studies; and Director, Refugee Studies Program, University of East London. *Globalization and the Third World*, co-edited with Ray Kiely, Routledge, 1998.

Donald I. Ray is a professor of Political Science at the University of Calgary, Calgary, Canada. His work has been published in North America, Europe and Asia. His research focuses on the relationship between traditional authority and the state in Africa, especially Ghana. He is also the International Coordinator of the Traditional Authority Applied Research Network (TAARN) which draws together researchers and policy practitioners from Ghana, South Africa, Botswana, Calgary and elsewhere.

Paul Sullivan has been teaching courses on the Middle East and Central Asia at the American University in Cairo since the fall of 1993. His research and writing have been almost exclusively on the economics and political economy of the Middle East and Central Asia. Recently, however, he has begun writing on US diplomacy in the Middle East, especially US policy towards Iraq. The economies of Iraq, Palestine/Israel, Syria, Jordan and Egypt are his main foci.

Dan Tschirgi is Professor, Department of Political Science, American University of Cairo, *Development in the Age of Liberalization: Egypt and Mexico*, American University in Cairo Press, 1996, editor; *The Arab World Today*, Lynne Rienner Publishers Inc., 1994, editor; *Origins and Development of the Arab-Israeli Conflict*, with Ann Mosely Lesch, Greenwood Publishing Group, 1998; *The American Search for Mideast Peace*, Praeger Pub., 1989.

Preface

An international conference, Globalization: Socio-economic, Business and Political Dimensions, was held under the auspices of the International Center for Contemporary Middle Eastern Studies (ICCMES), at the Eastern Mediterranean University (EMU), in the Turkish Republic of Northern Cyprus (TRNC), from November 19-21, 1998. The papers in this volume were selected from the conference proceedings. I would like to thank the contributors for their participation and Hayriye Kahveci and John Measor for assisting me in putting this book together.

Shereen Ismael

University of Northern British Columbia

Introduction

Globalization may be viewed as a new stage in international relations that draws into question the primacy of the state system as the foundation of world order. In a "post" Cold War world, it serves as a restructuring paradigm, which is evidenced in the "compression of time and space" through the development and adoption of advanced communications technology and the accessibility of rapid global transport. Finally, it exhibits a reconstruction of the foundation of knowledge and power, the dawning of the "information age," through the mass use of computers and information technology. However, globalization's technological base should not hide its ideological dimensions. The advance of technology has been enshrined within the ability of market forces to structure human relations in a manner amenable to neo-liberal and predominantly Western (mainly American) values and hierarchies. The impulse towards privatization and liberalization of world economies, and the advancement of *laissez-faire* – promoting the ideal of minimal government involvement – has not allowed for greater input from citizens, but has instead hindered social activism. The enshrinement of the international economic system, as advanced by the institution of Bretton Woods, has forced developing nations to adopt neo-liberal goals without examining other potential paths of development.

This consensus has resisted the build-up of institutions at the international level, except for those which facilitate trade and economic growth. Performance is assessed solely in economic terms, to the exclusion of human, social and environmental dimensions. Societies not conforming to this paradigm are seen as illegitimate and dangerous, often acquiring the appellation "rouge states." The advance of technology has widened the gap between strong and weak states, especially in the sphere of military strength, and has altered geopolitics from a balance of power system to placing a select few Western states in a hegemonic role in world affairs. The role of the "private sector," most notably through the mass media's portrayal of the benefits of a consumerist society, has further advanced the view that government involvement is not necessary. It has engendered a wedge between state structures and monetary forces, lending credence to the notion of government's inability to manage the economy.

Three types of regional reaction to this "globalization from above" have appeared. First, organized labor, which has lost much of its credibility as individuals are encouraged to see themselves as economic engines rather than workers with the shift from industrial to electronic methods of money-making. Second, religious extremism, which is portrayed as a fragmentary and often ultra-nationalist force. Third, grassroots populism, which is both local and transnational, though often focused upon principled issues such as human rights or environmentalism. Though meeting with varying degrees of success, these forces cannot, at the present time, assume the role of a countervailing force to neo-liberalism. They are not broadly enough based, and success stories of the past – whereby government energy was focused by these groups – will no longer be easily organized as governments learned that they could not harness and direct these movements.

In the first chapter, Enid Hill argues that the present "global" economy does indeed encompass the globe and that the importance of the advanced, industrial countries to this globalization is central to its continuation. However, these same countries account for only a portion of the world that is ostensibly part of the global system. Asking what is to become of other countries, the so-called developing world or Third World, she concerns herself particularly with that part of the developing world that we call the Middle East, and its place within the globalizing system. The argument put forth is based upon the proposition that the globalizing system is primarily capitalist. Thus there is first a brief discussion of globalizing capitalism, in the First World and in the Third World, discussed by reference to regulation theory. The chapter then turns to situating the Middle East within the globalizing capitalist system. By reference to selected statistics of the World Bank, the more industrially-advanced countries of the Middle East are compared with each other and are located in relation to industrializing countries in Asia and Latin America. Inferences are drawn as to what this indicates about the position of the Middle East in the world economy.

In chapter 2, "Globalization: Established Fact or Uneven Process?" Ray Kiely examines the role of local actors. Postulating that despite their enormous differences, political economy and cultural theory are too often guilty of exaggerating the degree of mobility of both capital flows and media cultural images, he goes on to describe the often wild conclusions reached when too much weight is placed upon them, such as the death of the nation state or the end of meaning. Through a theoretical and empirical critique of such hyper-globalization theses, his chapter argues that the global has not destroyed the local and that local and national spaces remain, often of crucial importance. The argument is given more specific consideration through an examination of the "local and the global" in the late 1990s recession in East Asia.

Phil Marfleet, in chapter 3, "Against the Globalist Paradigm," asks if globalization is a developmental solution – or a problem. He examines the arguments that partisans of globalism have presented, namely the presentation that this is a "global era" and period of liberating economic change, during which there can be an advance towards more general prosperity world wide. Those hostile to the idea have depicted a world in which capitalism races unregulated across the globe, often with negative outcomes. But both proponents and detractors have largely accepted the globalist paradigm as an appropriate description of the contemporary world. Marfleet argues that the paradigm itself is false. Much recent evidence suggests that although some aspects of the world system demonstrate genuine integration, others do not; that although some patterns of economic activity make for high levels of coherence, others are productive of asymmetry, fragmentation and even disintegration. The pattern of change is towards contradictory outcomes – not towards the holistic models advanced by theorists of globalization. Marfleet's chapter considers these contradictions, especially the uneven character of changes in world trade, in finance and in investment. It asks why the globalist model is so often invoked in order to describe such changes and advances an alternative view of contemporary development in which human agency – largely absent in globalist theory – plays a key role.

Chapter 4, "Developmental Stalemate and Political Violence in the Middle East and North Africa," by Ivan Ivekovic, examines the stalled development of mass industrial society in the Eastern Mediterranean. Ivekovic surveys the Eastern Mediterranean and examines its historical industrial development as a three-stage process. Each stage or progressive level of technological development, Ivekovic argues, is characterized by a specific social structure of accumulation (SSA). Practically all of the nation-states of the Eastern Mediterranean are seemingly trapped between the first stage and the second. Stage one is characterized by the development of a modern bureaucracy, the legalization and consolidation of private property, agricultural reform, monetization of the economy and the standardization of laws and institutions which then correspond to the international states system. Stage two is associated with a protectionist state, its classic form being European mercantilism, which in the 20th century can take the form of models of import substitution. Economic self-sufficiency as a precondition for national independence has been a policy pursued by a diverse selection of developing states in the 20th century, the Soviet Union and South Africa, Kemalist Turkey as well as Arab nationalist governments. The third stage of the process of modernization, mass industrial society in association with the processes of globalization, is not yet in evidence in the states of the Eastern Mediterranean. As the industrial powers of Europe expanded throughout the 19th and 20th centuries, appropriating the markets and raw materials of colonial empires, they managed to transform entire regions into free-trade zones, initiating a distorted capitalist development corresponding to the first stage of development. Latin America, China, modern Persia and the dismantled Ottoman empire all provided areas in which European economies could expand unimpeded. The peripheral free-trade model has evolved into the neo-liberal model of development promoted today by a web of international financial institutions as implemented by the World Bank and IMF. However, none of the states of the Eastern Mediterranean has advanced to the third stage of development. Such modernization requires technological innovations that in turn require continuous adaptation of the domestic SSA to both internal and external influences. This stall in development and inability to adapt to changing circumstances has led to an increase in political violence initiated both from above and below.

The African reaction is examined in chapters 5 and 6, beginning with Danbala Danju's "The Dynamics of Trade Liberalization and Poverty in Africa." Danju examines the structural adjustment programs adopted in several African countries since the early 1980s. Often adopted more due to external pressure than internal policy conviction, the programs are designed to reverse economic decline and poverty. A key component of the adjustment programs involves the reform or liberalization of a country's trade regime. The dynamics of trade liberalization and its impact upon poverty in Africa is explored, and Danju argues that limited trade liberalization has been undertaken by African nations relative to other regions of the globe. Macro-economic evidence suggests, contrary to the advocates of liberalization, an increase in poverty levels in those states adopting the programs since the 1980s. Although necessary, trade liberalization alone will not be a sufficient condition for the eradication of poverty in Africa.

In chapter 6, "Globalization and Traditional Authority in Africa: Investment, Security and Land in Africa," Donald Ray examines the effect traditional leaderships have on the diffusion of globalization in a developing nation. In late 1982, the government of Ghana had begun to adopt a variety of measures that increased the opening up of its economy to the processes of globalization. During the 1980s and 1990s, many sectors of the Ghanaian economy were drawn into the dynamic of globalization, but land remained on the whole under customary tenure, controlled by traditional authorities, be they chiefs or extended family leaders. The conceptual tools of divided sovereignty and divided legitimacy are used to examine the interaction of the Ghanaian state and traditional authority over the state's attempts to change the system of land tenure in response to globalization pressures. These traditional leaders still had the ability to contest, politically, socially and even economically, the expansion, penetration and diffusion of globalization, which needs to take into account traditional authority wherever it exists in Africa.

In chapter 7, "Internationalization and Localization in the Chinese Search for Human Justice," Ronald Keith argues that the international censure of Chinese human rights performance has not provided an adequate basis for a comprehensive analytical understanding of the contemporary adaptation to human rights categories and concepts in new legislation and jurisprudence inside the PRC. Keith sees this adaptation as not merely a matter of a closed "cultural relativist response" to the presumably civilized dimensions of "globalization" or "Westernization." Rather it legitimately reflects a local desire to insure that human justice and related law are appropriately anchored in a rational and meaningful response to local society and culture. At the same time this adaptation reveals a largely unrecorded, but nonetheless robust pattern of "internationalization," defined in China in terms of an international developmental process in law which facilitates the search for human justice in mutual learning and conceptual convergence across cultures and state jurisdictions.

In chapter 8, "Globalization: Aid, Trade, Investment and Development in Egypt, Jordan and Syria," Paul Sullivan focuses on the period 1978-1996 in Egypt, Jordan and Syria. He first tries to answer the question: are these countries developing? Then the major trends in foreign aid, trade and investment are presented. For aid, these are the amounts of aid, the sources and where the bulk of the aid was directed in the host country. For trade, these are the amounts of trade between the target countries and some of its major trading partners, including the types of goods traded. For investment, these trends are in foreign direct investment, foreign portfolio investment and in the overall development of the financial markets in the countries as represented by proxy figures. Then these trends are analyzed separately to see their globalization content, and to see how they connect up with overall development in the three countries. The chapter concludes with lessons learned about the impacts of globalization on aid, trade and investment in the three countries – and how these impacts have either aided or hindered development.

In chapter 9, "Marginalized Violent Internal Conflict in the Age of Globalization: Mexico and Egypt," Dan Tschirgi compares the conflicts launched in Mexico (in Chiapas) and Egypt (largely in Upper Egypt) respectively by the *Zapatistas* and the *Gama'a al-Islamiyya* in the 1990s. It argues that despite significant differences in their manifestations, these conflicts share fundamentally similar dynamics and – moreover – that their distinctive unfoldings are explicable through the application of an analytical framework that sheds light on how and why different stimuli had different impacts in each case. These conflicts are labelled as "Marginalized Violent Internal Conflict" (MVIC), their hallmarks being a violent clash between governments and rebellious protagonists who neither seek separation from the state, nor challenge the state's essential validity, nor find their basic objectives in particularistic ethnic, tribal or regional demands. Insurrection is mounted in the name of the state itself and of its entire population. The polity's "true" values are claimed to be those of the insurrectionists. The existing government, or the existing political system in its entirety, is charged with betrayal of those values. Ethnicity, while possibly a practical factor in insurrectionary mobilization, is overshadowed by insurrectionary invocations of broader values within the state. Yet in contrast to civil wars, conflicts of this sort do not produce relatively balanced warring parties who share the perception that a critical and decisive military struggle has been joined. Instead, the armed challenge to state authority emanates almost exclusively from mobilized elements of the most marginalized sectors of national society. The imbalance of power so overwhelmingly favors state authorities that the rebels armed crusade fails to present a credible military threat. Authorities can therefore characterize the marginals' struggle as an irritating and misguided aberration of little consequence to the normal functioning of the state. Thus, the conflict is doubly linked to "marginality," pitting elements of the functionally superfluous against national governments in a struggle that is itself officially marginalized. There is, however, an important caveat to this: although the insurrectionary marginals have opted to reject the existing political process, their objectives are largely shared and supported – at least morally – by important dissenting actors within the political system.

While the conflicts in Egypt and Chiapas correspond to this schematization, differences in their manifestations are explained through an analytical framework that merges historical, sociological, ideological and economic analysis. Specifically, the analysis focuses on historically-derived socio-political-economic dynamics that have shaped the context of the conflicts' origins, linkages between these and the national political systems, linkages between both the former and civil society in each state, and finally, political and economic linkages between all of the above and the international environment. The analysis of these elements pays particular attention to the role of religion – especially of syncretistic folk religions – in political mobilization. The chapter concludes that identifiable processes of globalization can, under identifiable circumstances, act as catalytic agents for MVIC and that this carries the implication that "as globalization touches the 'Wretched of the Earth' in the world's most remote backwaters it may help trigger violent reactions from people who will not be dissuaded by even the most overwhelming objective evidence of the hopelessness of armed struggle."

In chapter 10, "Egypt in the Space and Time of Globalism," Raymond Baker sees the most urgent task for the new century to be to foster peaceful networks of trans-national co-operation in the planetary and human interest. The dominant globalism of the US hegemony and corporate capitalism dampens the hope for such humane global politics. At the same time, transportation and communication networks have created an enabling space-time compression that makes what was once a utopian dream of responsible global citizenship a reality within reach. Prophetic minorities with a global consciousness have spontaneously arisen, committed to the peaceful remaking of themselves, their own societies and the global economic system. Such groups are the vanguards of grassroots globalism. In their ranks are those with Egyptian names and identities shaped by their commitment to the universalistic values of Islam, interpreted for the late modern world.

This chapter highlights two aspects of Egyptian politics: first, the emergence of Islamic centrist groups that are recognizable as potential partners in the efforts of an emerging network of trans-national social movements struggling to bend globalism to humane and principled ends; second, the negative role of US policy in Egypt in failing to support and press for democratic reforms of the Egyptian regime, necessary to sustain such groups. The chapter concludes with specific policy recommendations to advance the democratic agenda both in Egypt and as part of the larger effort to strengthen civil society around the world.

In chapter 11, "Globalization and Turkey: From Capitulations to Contemporary Civilization," Seymen Atasoy examines the impact of globalization in the republic of Turkey. "Globalization" served as a key concept of the dominant political discourse and as a guiding principle of macro-economic reform in Turkey throughout the 1980s and 1990s. The import-substitution based industrialization strategy pursued since the early 1930s had led to formidable economic bottlenecks in the 1970s, thus forcing the adoption of an export-promotion orientation. Yet, economic circumstance alone does not suffice to explain why Turkey has whole-heartedly embraced globalization. Historical experience and political culture seem to have significantly shaped the Turkish approach. Having defended their independence against European colonialism during the last two centuries through the use of military, administrative and technological models borrowed from Europe, Turks have developed a pragmatic political culture towards the West which is unique in the Middle East. As a phenomenon mostly emanating from the West, globalization was facilitated during the last two decades by the Western-oriented political culture of the country. The long term cost-benefit balance of such rapid globalization remains to be seen.

In chapter 12, "Globalization, Identity and Social Work Practice: Insight from Working with Bedouin-Arab Peoples," Alean Al-Krenawi and John R. Graham begin by making the case that social work epistemology remains a largely Western conception, but is nonetheless beginning to add space for non-western voices and perspectives. The next section analyzes three culturally specific facets of Bedouin-Arab life – blood vengeance, polygamy and traditional healing – that can well enhance social work's efforts to understand and act upon differences between Western and non-western peoples. A concluding section considers the common ground that exists between social work and important leaders in Bedouin-Arab communities; principles for integrating social work professionals, and non-western, cultural ways of looking at social work intervention; and the significance of these facets to globalization.

Globalization in World Affairs

First World, Third World, Globalizing World: Where is the Middle East?

Enid Hill

How, then, should we think of the contemporary "global" economy? Unprecedented in most respects, it has only the barest similarity to historical economic experiences. Even if we accede to Andre Gunder Frank's latest thesis that the expansion of trade world wide during the four centuries prior to 1800 constituted a "global" economy (Frank, 1998), the fact remains that the European industrial revolution changed the nature of production, and with it economic relationships and institutions. Pre-industrial centres of production and of economic life may have been connected by long distance trading of merchants and intermittent travels of adventurers, but the societies themselves were not structurally connected. Nor is today's global economy simply another form of imperialism, although the centres and institutions of finance capital wield enormous influence. It is a "world system" certainly, but industrialization in some parts of the periphery belies those theories which posit inevitable dependency and unrelenting underdevelopment as the lot of a "periphery."

The most prominent characteristic of today's global economy is that it is capitalist. Its most visible participants come from, and also are, capitalist national economies and multi-national firms. Its contours derive from capitalist economic institutions and the behavior of finance capital – nationally regulated, internationally largely unfettered. Certainly globalization owes its origin to the growth and spread of capitalist relations of production from its developed centres. It also owes much to advances in technology that allow instantaneous communication and movement of financial assets around the globe, and the capacity to transport large numbers of people and amounts of material across large distances quickly. This kind of technology was pioneered within the advanced industrial economies that continue to be almost exclusively its producers.

The centrality of advanced industrial capitalist economies to the presently developing global economy is indisputable. However, such states account for a minority of the world's peoples and occupy geographic areas of limited extent. What of other countries and peoples, those called the Third World, which are pulled into the global economic orbit? The connotation of "global" encompasses inclusion.

First we will introduce the theory of *regulation* developed to understand periods of capitalist growth and crisis in the industrialized centres. Then we will discuss the spread of industrialization to the periphery as the *regulationists* analyze it, including reference to the Middle East generally and to Egypt. Finally we show where the Middle East fits into the global capitalist order.

"First World" Capitalism

The heartland of capitalism, where industrial and finance capital developed, the so-called "developed" world, otherwise spoken of as the centre of the world system, is the place where capitalism first appeared and from whence it spread outwards to far corners of the earth. Capitalist development in the centre is not, however, uniform. Cycles of growth intersperse with recessions that at times become crises. The latter have stimulated attempts to theorize and explain, to try to mitigate the effects and to figure out how to reverse the downward spirals of capitalist accumulation. In the 1970s, when a new recession became undeniable, new theories and hypotheses appeared.

Of particular interest for this paper is the theory of *regulation*. Formulated by French researchers in the 1970s, it was initially concerned with the empirical, historical situation of economic crisis in the United States and France. They sought to understand the nature of structural change that brought the downturn of growth and crisis in industrial capitalist economies. Subsequent work expanded to include a number of Third World states as well as global relationships.

Regulation translates into English as "regulation" only in the broad sense of social ordering, the "regularization" of those relationships that underpin the social order (see Jessop, 1997: 519). For *regulationists* the most important relationship is that of capital and labor, as it is the primary contradiction of capitalism.

This theory works with two main concepts: "mode of *regulation*" and "regime of accumulation." A "mode of *regulation*" refers to those individual and collective actions that reproduce fundamental social relations of a given historical-institutional context, allowing decentralized economic decisions to maintain the system. A "mode of *regulation*" produces a "regime of accumulation" where the established regularities insure orderly accumulation (Boyer and Saillard, 1995: 546, 547). From this base the theory elaborates other concepts and ways of analyzing structural relations of periods of rapid growth in capitalist economies. It is also "a theory for troubled times." The authors claim the *regulation* approach treats problems of economic crisis "many others have treated badly" (pp. 11, 12).

Problems analyzed include unemployment deriving from differences between growth of the economically-active population and a slow-down in the creation of jobs. Such disjunction is seen as connected with the persistence of forms of organization which, although inadequate for new social and economic conditions, remain deeply rooted in existing institutions and state policies. Institutions that inhibit the utilization of new technologies to restore gains in productivity need reforming. Also needed is an understanding of the market as "a form of coordination of economic activities much more organized and sophisticated than neoclassical theories suppose." While the market is "incapable of self-institutionalization," it can work "with great efficacy and appear to be self-regulating" once it is situated within "a web of rules and legal constraints" (p. 14).

The first generation of *regulationist* writers formulated their theory by direct reference to the historical experiences of the United States and France with capitalist growth (i.e., accumulation) and crisis (i.e., recession). They sought to explain why accumulation faltered in these countries at the end of the 1960s and continued in recession. They conceptualized the inter-war period and the post-war years (to the late 1960s) as one of increased accumulation through assembly line production, pioneered by Henry Ford in the 1920s, greatly increasing labor's productivity. Thus the era was one of "intensive" accumulation which *regulation* theory calls "Fordism." Fordism's characteristic feature is a form of institutionalized labor-management relations whereby, through institutionalized modes of adjustment, wages are kept at a level that allows the labor force to become mass consumers of their mass production. Thus capital accumulation and investment continues, and the system grows. However, not all regimes of mass production produce mass consumption. While mass consumption began in the United States during the inter-war period, it did not occur in France until after 1945.

Another concept developed by *regulationists* is "Taylorism," both predecessor and contemporary of Fordism in the historical progression of industrialization of the first world. The name derives from the inventor of "scientific management." In *regulation* theory it refers to the tasks of organization of the labor process being separated from their execution on the shop floor (Lipietz, 1995: 348). Its hallmark is "direct control by the management of the activity of workers" (p. 352). Its relation to Fordism? Fordism is "Taylorism plus mechanization" (p. 348). Adapted to conceptualize situations of Third World development, they become "peripheral Fordism" and "primitive" or "bloody" Taylorism.

Fordism's transformation of industrial production through the assembly line means division of industrial activities into (1) conception, organization, engineering; (2) skilled manufacturing; and (3) unskilled (perhaps more accurately, semi- or low-skilled) assembly (Lipietz, 1987: 71). "Taylorism" is used by the *regulationists* to refer to increased accumulation achieved through greater exploitation of workers, as occurred in the industrialized centres before the age of Fordism. It is now showing a comeback with newly-devised forms of work force "flexibility" and "hierarchical direct control" in the wake of the restructuring and the demise of Fordist labor-management regulation in, notably, England and America. "We are back to some form of Taylorist organization of the labor process without the social counterparts of Golden Age Fordism" (Lipietz, 1995: 348, 353). It happens because labor's position is considerably weakened vis-a-vis capital and the compensating features of complimentary levels of production allowing mass consumption have been eroded. Lipietz coined the term "neo-Taylorism" to mean the return to forms of exploitation of labor in the "post-Fordist" North that are unmitigated by Fordist levels of capacity to consume, and with employment unprotected.

With the expansion of capitalist production and the distribution of commodities around the world, the notions of the *regulationists* become relevant to the global context. But there is great variation between and among economies in the "globalized" world. There are world market factories where industrial production of the centre countries is moved overseas but kept within the control of centre industrialists. There is piece-work and various forms of partial assembly moved out of the centre to the periphery, leading to variants within the new international division of labor (see Froebel et al., 1980). But there has also been industrialization, properly speaking, within the periphery. In some countries it has been recent, while other countries have had historical experiences extending back for considerable periods of time. How, then, are we to understand the present position of the periphery within globalization?

The Third World

Regulation theory was derived from case studies of advanced industrial capitalism at the centre but its conceptual apparatus concerns *capitalism* as such. Since capitalism has spread world wide, it is not surprising that *regulationist* theorists began to analyze socio-economic development in the Third World. A proliferation of persons using *regulation* theory for case studies in the Third World appear among the contributors to recent collections (Boyer and Saillard, 1995; Schor and You, 1995; Aglietta et al., 1994). The basic perceptions as to how *regulation* theory applied in the periphery were set forth in Lipietz, 1987, 1986; Boyer, 1990; and Boyer et al., 1986. The earliest case studies of the Third World in *regulationist* perspective were of Chile (Ominami, 1980) and Venezuela (Hausmann, 1981). Ominami (1986) looked at the crisis of capitalism in relation to the Third World specifically and Mistral (1986) considered Third World development in relation to the global economy.

"Peripheral Fordism" means that whereas the organization of production is Fordist in the sense that there is mechanization and a combination of intensive accumulation and a growing market for consumer durables, the skilled manufacturing and engineering levels are still mainly outside these countries. This external location of the higher levels of the production process includes the machines that are used for industrial production. "Primitive Taylorization" includes the transfer of specific and limited segments of manufacture to states with high rates of exploitation and the exportation of the production back to the centre (Lipietz, 1987: 78-79). It also includes the exploitative sweat shops and garment factories in some newly-industrialized countries (NICs).

It is incontrovertible that, since its invention, industrialization has been the motor of vast economic growth. In the 18th century the per capita margin of variation of national product was 1 to 1.5. From the first third of the 19th century, the variation began to increase significantly between rapidly industrializing countries and others. As of the early- to mid-1980s and "excluding extreme examples," the variation was 1 to 20 (Mistral, 1986: 173). Not knowing what "extreme examples" Mistral eliminated, we cannot calculate change. However, taking $1000 per capita GNP as the low end (thus eliminating Sub-Saharan Africa and South Asia) and Sweden and France at the high end (ranking 10th and 11th) at slightly over $26 000 GNP per capita income, one can readily see that the ratio is at least 1:26 using figures from the same source (World Bank, 1998/99: 190-191). Both this ratio and undoubtedly that of Mistral concern countries in the more "developed" part of the periphery, many with industrialization.

The claim is made that Fordism, even if it is in crisis, still dominates. This means a close link between the valorization of capital invested in the production of commodities and the realization of profit through their sale. "The logic of the international diffusion of Fordism . . . presupposes the simultaneous expansion of productivity and real wages," that is, an increase in disposable income to purchase the increase in commodities. The Fordism of the centre provided increased purchasing power through higher wages to workers, resulting in mass consumption. In the Third World this condition tends to be met by increased income in the middle class "provided that class is sufficiently large" (Lipietz, 1987: 102). Foreign direct investment in industrial projects in the Third World today often seeks markets in those countries for the commodities produced there, perhaps in the process getting around import barriers and high import tariffs. That is, foreign direct investment may involve other considerations besides finding cheap labor to produce commodities for central markets.

Amounts of direct investment by multi-national corporations (MNCs) are, however, less than the amounts of commercial borrowing by the countries themselves. Peripheral Fordism began to expand in the 1960s through borrowing for capital investments from international banks. After the first oil shock in 1974 came an explosion of available liquid assets that banks were eager to lend and the amount borrowed rapidly increased (see Sampson, 1988). There were also export credits to import capital goods. Amounts borrowed from banks rose from 10 to 145 billion between 1971 and 1980. In the same period borrowing against issues of debentures increased from 4 to 15 billion, while export credits to import capital goods went from 25 to 110 billion. Direct investment abroad rose from 53 billion to 120 billion in this period. All this borrowing meant "a heavy debt servicing burden" as well as the repatriation of profits by the multinationals. Thus "in terms of transferring value from the periphery to the centre, the new system is as efficient as the old" (Lipietz, 1987: 106-107). Nevertheless, this did mark the "end of classic dependency" (Lipietz, p. 107) and a number of countries of the South did develop substantial industrial activities, albeit unevenly. They were often of the "primitive Taylorist" variety. The four Tigers (Singapore, Hong Kong, Korea and Taiwan) accounted for 60% of exports from the South (1980s figures), while if Brazil and India are added, this rises to 70% (p. 95).

A home market is obviously developing in some of these NICs. There is also, says Lipietz, a "common market" of middle class demand that is fueling trade between (some) countries of the periphery. While few countries have become export-based industrial powers, capital goods account for 41% of this "common market" trade (for example, cheaper professional equipment and engineering products), as against 31% of the total export trade from NICs to the North. (p. 97). Third World industrialization is more widespread and occurred earlier than one might think. Singapore was a NIC already in the early 1960s (p. 95).

Regulation theory has identified three possible economic strategies for Third World states. The first is the traditional one of the exportation of primary products. Then there is that of import substitution industrialization, and lastly "export substitution," which means substituting manufactured products in place of primary products. Choices, it is emphasized, are largely political, "bound up with the internal class struggle" involving "classic ruling classes" and their struggles to maintain or regain control of the state (p. 78).

We are reminded that "the economic constitution of nations is not geographic but historical" (Mistral, 1986: 176). Many Third World countries find themselves in an impasse as regards industrialization that "depends more on internal forces than on pernicious international influences." Mistral recounts the experiences of Australia and Argentina. Both embarked on a process of rapid growth in the mid 19th century, exporting the same range of agricultural food products, and with a revenue per capita at the beginning of the 20th century that was "the most elevated in the world." The principal external influence at that time was British, "at least as great in Australia as in Argentina." In Argentina, however, there was "an old class of powerful landed proprietors that Australia did not have." By contrast, political life in Australia "was sufficiently influenced by urban milieus to engender the development of industrial activities" (p. 178).

What then can be said of modes of *regulation* in the Third World? Presently, "the Third World looks like a constellation of special cases." There are "vague regularities" and "elements of a logic of accumulation," but the variation is much more compelling. Korea exports one third of total output while Brazil exports relatively little (Lipietz, 1987: 98-99). Historically, the diffusion of the industrial revolution also occurred in an unequal manner. Internal forces are also referred to as an explanation for unequal development then also. Industry depended on agriculture and it was also affected by the concentration of power in a landed aristocracy.

Lipietz calls for concrete analysis, "the study of the economic and social history of each specific country, for the study of the modes of regulation, their forms of class alliance and their successive hegemonic systems" (p. 99). This has been done now for several countries. Latin America figures prominently. The Middle East is notably absent.

The Middle East

Prior to the massive influx into Middle Eastern markets of European machine-made goods during the 19th century, the Ottoman Empire not only produced cotton and silk textiles and yarn to meet domestic needs but also exported considerable amounts to France. By 1825 Ottoman industry began to be "exposed to the crushing competition of the Manchester factories" (Issawi, 1966: 48) from which it was not to recover for a century.

Egypt had an early period of industrialization with Muhammad Ali's military factories established to serve his construction of a modern army, as well as those serving the domestic market. He established cotton spinning and weaving mills, factories for cloth production, woolen and linen factories, refineries for sugar. He had establishments that manufactured glass, paper, tanneries, sulphuric acid and other chemicals, a foundry that produced 1000 tons per annum and an arsenal in Alexandria that "launched seventeen warships and five steam vessels" in the 1830s (Issawi, 1966: 389). Following the defeat of his army and the Treaty of London in 1840 he was obliged to close the military factories and to open Egypt to foreign commerce. Muhammad Ali also began the production of long staple cotton. During the American Civil War in the 1860s the world market demand for cotton rose sharply and Egypt became a vast cotton plantation serving the mills of Lancashire. Cotton exports continued to rise until the turn of the century, when cotton and cottonseed then became 90 percent of Egypt's exports (pp. 416-

417). Egypt's next phase of industrialization began following the first World War, the results of which became nationalized between 1956 and 1961 into a public sector.

Middle East/North African countries (MENA) have very disparate economic characteristics. "Only Turkey is clearly a fullfledged NIC," say Richards and Waterbury (1990: 78). This assertion is curious given current figures and definition of the NIC (see below). Egypt is clearly moving ahead with industrial development, as will be outlined below. Morocco also was exporting industrial products at a creditable percentage of its exports in 1985 (40%) with industry producing 17% of GDP, and employing 25% of its work force. In addition to these actual and proto-NICs are the "oil industrializers" (Iran, Iraq, Algeria and Saudi Arabia). They have used their large revenues from oil exports to develop industry. A group of smaller countries with limited natural resources (Israel, Jordan, Tunisia and Syria) have concentrated on "exporting skill-intensive manufactures" and have "made major efforts to educate their people" (p. 78).

In recent years Turkey has moved ahead with industrialization in the region. In 1985 the country had a manufacturing share of GDP of 25%, the highest in the MENA, a percentage equal to France and above average for OECD countries and the United States (Richards and Waterbury, 1990: 69). This percentage went down to 18% around 1987 (World Bank, 1998/99: 213) (further discussion below). In terms of growth of GDP (1980-85), Egypt is highest with 5.2 percent. From 1970-1980 it was 7.4 percent, explainable as the great boom of economic activity that followed the economic opening (*infitah*) of 1974. Algeria had a rate of growth of 7.0 for 1970-80, but it dropped to 4.9 in 1980-85 (and has dropped further since). Rates of growth for Turkey were 5.9 percent for 1970-80 and 4.5 percent in 1980-85 (p. 70, using figures from the World Bank, *World Development Report*).

A better picture of "sustainable structural change" is to be had from manufacturing and manufacturing value added (MVA) than using the industrialization category, as the latter includes the petroleum sector. Comparative figures for this category show clearly how the region is lagging behind other industrializing parts of the Third World: The total MVA in the region is approximately that of Brazil. Turkey and Iran have the same number of people as Italy, but Italy's MVA is five times that of Turkey and ten times that of Iran. Turkey and Iran account for 48% of all manufacturing in the region. Saudi

Arabia and Algeria account for another one-fifth. Adding Egypt "brings the total share of manufacturing for the five countries with the largest manufacturing sectors to over two-thirds of the total" (Richards and Waterbury, 1990: 73). This concentration of manufacturing in five countries in terms of MVA is a graphic indicator of the condition of the rest of the countries in the area. The labor force also shows the nature of economies. From one-quarter to one-third of the labor force is employed in industry in MENA and "well over one-half of these workers are small establishments with fewer than twenty people." The informal sectors of many of these countries are extensive. This figure also shows that industrial growth has been insufficient "to provide enough decent jobs for the rapidly growing labor force," perhaps the region's most pressing issue (p. 73).

Whereas Egypt has yet to create the conditions for industrial employment to deal with its sizeable number of unemployed, an acceleration of investment in modern private sector industry has clearly taken place in recent years.

Egypt

Since 1981 there has been a policy in Egypt to push productive enterprise. That was also the year when the new Company Law was issued, greatly facilitating the establishment of companies of all kinds. In 1989 a new "consolidated" investment law was passed which increased tax holidays and other incentives for projects in specified fields that were high priority for development, and located in an industrial zone of one of the "new communities" established in the desert. In 1991 came the Public Business Sector Law that would be the vehicle by means of which public sector companies were prepared for privatization. It has been written and said by many that Egypt's only hope for the future is to industrialize. Samir Amin wrote in the early 1960s: "The only solution possible, outside of massive emigration, is rapid industrialization in a few decades such that demographic growth . . . would not neutralize it" (Riad, 1964: 191). Whereas one cannot characterize the present growth as "rapid industralization," there has been a remarkable increase in industrial establishments during the past two decades.

Statistics of the Ministry of Planning and CAPMAS (quoted in Soliman, 1998) show the following: The share of industry (except petroleum) in GDP increased from 13.5% (1980/81) to 18.1% (1996/97). The rate of growth of industry (except petroleum) was above that of the GDP in the 1980s and 1990s: 7.5% industry in contrast to 5.4% GDP (1982-95 average). The rate of value-added in the manufacturing sector rose from 26.6% in 1975 to 37.2% in 1990. The share of industry in private sector investments moved from 15.9% in 1981, to 34.7% in 1990, to 45.9% in 1995. (In 1995 – as the major push to privatize was beginning – investment in industry in the public sector was 4%.). The share of industry in total private sector product was 9.1 in 1981 and 17.3 in 1995/96. The rate of growth of private industrial product was 10.3% in 1995/96.

Industry is the fastest job generator in the private sector. Its share in private employment in 1983 was 7.3% and in 1992 it was 11.8%. Increase in the share of intermediate and capital goods industries in 1980/81 was 9.6 and in 1994/95 it increased to 11.8. There are (at last count) 13 foreign vehicle companies in Egypt with 15 plants capitalized at 6.1 (perhaps more since the latter figure relates to a previous count of 9 car manufacturing companies). Similarly potentially underestimated, the figure of 133 factories of feeder industries was given in the local press. The new vehicle manufacturing sector is reported to have created 100 000 new jobs and is growing. And the number of larger enterprises (100+ workers) has steadily risen (Figure 1):

Figure 1

No. of Workers	1976	1986	1996
1000+	2	8	30
500-999	9	25	69
100-499	161	237	621

Source: Soliman (1998).

Locating the Middle East in the Globalizing World

Examining states of the region as regards key factors of importance to capitalist economies, compared among states of the region and with selected states in the First and Third Worlds, can give an overall view of the relationship of the Middle East to the globalizing world. For this we use the World Bank statistics as supplied each year in their *World Development Report*. One caution: The WB figures are only as accurate as those reporting give accurate figures, but they give some idea in broad outline.

Relationship #1. Size of Economies and Per Capita Incomes.

The six largest economies today in order of magnitude of GNP are the United States, Japan, Germany, France, United Kingdom and Italy, but then the developing countries appear. China ranks seventh, Brazil eighth, Korea 11th, India 15th, Mexico 16th and Indonesia is 22nd. As regards the Middle East:

Figure 2: The Nine Largest MENA Economies (in order of size of GNP)

Ranking by GNP per capita	$ billion GNP
1. Turkey ranked 23rd	199.5
2. Saudi Arabia ranked 30th	129.9
3. Iran (not ranked)	113.5
4. Israel ranked 37th	87.6
5. Egypt ranked 41st	71.2
6. Algeria ranked 49th	43.8
7. UAE ranked 50th	42.7
8. Kuwait (not ranked)	35.0
9. Morocco ranked 51st	34.4

Source: World Bank (1998/99: 190-191, 232).

These figures indicate remarkable development in the erstwhile "periphery," namely capitalist growth, making theories about the centre keeping the periphery in an underdeveloped condition questionable. It has not been only the "miracle" economies of the little tigers of Asia that have been industrializing and whose economies have grown dramatically in recent years. The nine states of the Middle East above are presently in the upper one-third of the world economies' GNP. Among them are the region's most populous states (Turkey with 64 million, Iran with 60.9 million and Egypt with

60 million). The populations of Algeria and Morocco together amount to another 57 million.

Several states have had remarkable growth rates since 1970. Note the large increases from 1970 when the recession began in the industrial economies and their crisis in capital accumulation appeared (Figure 3).

Figure 3: Growth of MENA Economies, 1960-1997

Rate of growth (GNP) 1960-97	GDP in billions of $ (rounded)					
		1997	1991	1980	1970	1960
8.1%	Turkey	181.5	95.8	68.8	11.4	8.8
4.9%	Egypt	73.4	30.3	23.0	6.6	3.9
2.0%	Algeria	46.0	32.7	42.3	4.5	2.7
-2.7%	Morocco	33.3	27.7	18.8	4.0	2.0
11.5%	Tunisia	19.1	11.6	8.7	1.2	0.8

Source: World Bank (1998/99: 190-191, 212-213; 1995: 242-243; 1982: 114-115)

However, composite figures of 1997 (GNP) place the Middle East/North Africa region above only south Asia and sub-Saharan Africa. Regions above them are:

Latin America	1916.8 billion $
East Asia	1707.3 billion $
Eastern Europe/Central Asia	1105.8 billion $
<Middle East/ North Africa	582.7 billion $>

(World Bank, 1998/99: 191)

Turkey's $199.5 billion GNP is not included in MENA as the World Bank classifies it with Europe. High levels of oil production in some countries give the region a special significance in the world economy. The region has also produced some of the highest per capita incomes in the world, although not the highest. Kuwait is the top per capita income in the region at $ 22 110. Next is the UAE with $17 360. In contrast, the present world leader, Switzerland, is at $44 320, followed by Japan ($37 850), Norway ($36 090), Singapore ($32 940), Denmark ($32 500) and the USA ($28 740). Israel had a per capita income of $15180. Lebanon was highest among the other states of the region with $3350 in 1997. Turkey was next with $3130. These are in contrast to some of the highest per capita incomes of the more-rapidly developing states in Latin America and Asia (Figure 4).

Figure 4: Per Capita Income, 1997, of Selected States of Latin America and Asia

Korea	$10 550
Argentina	$8570
Chile	$5020
Brazil	$4720
Malaysia	$4680
Mexico	$3680

Source: World Bank (1998/99: 190-191)

The oil economies are linked to the industrialized parts of the world with a special relationship. They supply the industrialized world not only with oil, but also provide their financial institutions with petro-dollar deposits which exponentially increased after 1993. Industrializing Third World countries took advantage of this by borrowing heavily from these deposits. At the same time, Middle Eastern oil-exporting states provided markets for industrial goods, including capital goods, and services from the First World.

Relationship #2. Manufacturing and the Export of Manufactures.

To estimate something of the nature of the growth of these economies, we can take a look at the percentage of value added by industry and manufacturing to the GDP in the high growth countries. Manufacturing does not include petroleum, but it comes within the industry category.

The value-added share of manufacturing in Turkey rose from 14% of GDP to 18% from 1980 to 1997. Industry rose 22% to 28% over that time. The industry category includes mining, manufacturing, construction and electricity, gas and water. Not being an oil-producing economy, Turkey does not have petroleum extracting as part of its industry. Agriculture dropped in the same period from 26% to

17%. The share of manufactures in merchandise exports in 1997 was 74%.

Value added in Egypt's manufactures rose from 12% in 1980 to 25% in 1997. Industry (which in Egypt's case does include petroleum extraction) fell during the same period from 37% to 32%. Agriculture also fell from 18% to 16%. Egypt's share of manufactures in merchandise exports in 1997 was 32%.

Tunisia's share of value added by manufacturing grew from 12% to 18% and in industry declined from 31% to 28%. Agriculture was static at 14%. Share of manufactures in merchandise exports was 80%.

In Morocco manufacturing has been static over the period at 17% value added and industry was static at 31%. Contrary to the above states, agriculture in Morocco *increased* from 18% to 20%. Algeria also has been static in manufacturing, which in any case is not large (9%), and industry fell from 54% to 51% while agriculture there also increased from 10% to 12%.

The OECD (Organization of Economic Cooperation and Development) defines NICs as countries where manufactured products represent 25% of GDP and at least 50% of exports. None of our industrializing states in the Middle East, including Turkey, quite meet this criteria (Figure 5), contrary to the assertion of Richards and Waterbury (1990) using earlier figures (see above).

Figure 5: Manufacturing, 1997

	% in GDP	% in Exports
Turkey	18%	74%
Egypt	25%	32%
Tunisia	18%	80%
Morocco	17%	50%

Source: World Bank (1998/99: 212-213)

Only Egypt meets the OECD requirement in percentage of manufactures in GDP (25%), having risen from 12% in 1980, but it does not have a developed export market to the size specified. Both Turkey and Tunisia have well over the 50% requirement for the percentage of manufactures in exports, but both are under the 25% for percentage of manufactures in GDP. Morocco also has reached the magic number of 50% for share of manufactures in exports, but is below the GDP percentage. Thus none of these are, according to OECD criteria, NICs.

Comparative figures are instructive (Figure 6).

Figure 6: Comparative Experiences, Manufacturing, 1997

	Value added as % of GDP	% of Manufactures in Exports
Israel	—	91%
Brazil	23%	54%
Mexico	20%	78%
Korea	26%	92%
Malaysia	34%	76%

Source: World Bank (1998/99: 212-213)

All of these industrializing Third World states have well over the 50% required to be an NIC in the percentage of manufactured goods in their exports, but only Korea and Malaysia have more than 25% of valued added to GDP and thus are NICs! It would seem that this designation of "NIC" given to the industrializing Asian economies heavily leans to include those with manufacturing largely for the world market. For a real world economy to develop, however, the purchasing power of the labor forces in these countries needs to increase. High percentages of manufactured goods as exports in developing countries almost certainly points to primitive Taylorism, especially when coupled with relatively low proportions of value added. By contrast, the low percentage of manufacturing in exports in Egypt combined with the relatively high percentage of manufacturing in GDP indicates a developing home market. Egypt may not have a developed capital goods sector, but the expansion of the domestic market is a necessary condition of balanced (as opposed to peripheral) forms of capitalist growth.

Relationship #3. Labor Forces and Total Populations

Turkey has a large labor force in proportion to total population, as does Tunisia. Thus it is no surprise that they also have among the largest percentages of females in the work force. Morocco surprisingly also has a large percentage of women in the work force, which may indicate a high rate of migration of males and/or point to world market manufacturing (Figure 7).

Figure 7: Labor Forces in the Largest MENA Populations

(In order of the size of the work force)

	Population (millions)	Labor force (millions)	Av. Annual growth rate (1990-97)	% of females in labor force
Turkey	64	29	2.2	36
Egypt	60	22	2.8	29
Morocco	28	11	2.5	35
Algeria	29	9	4.1	26
Saudi Arabia	20	7	3.2	14
Yemen	16	5	4.9	28
Tunisia	9	4	3.0	31
Syria	15	4	3.3	26

Source: World Bank (1998/99: 194-195)

Of the seven countries listed, minus Turkey, the labor force is only 32% of the population, which bears out what is known otherwise, that the populations of the region are generally speaking young, substantiated below (Figure 8). Adding Turkey takes the labor force up to 40%. The work forces in other listed states (Jordan, Lebanon, UAE and Oman) are stated as one million each but all figures are rounded.

Comparisons of the percentage of the population who are between the ages of 15 to 64 by regions is instructive. In the Middle East/North Africa, this part of the population is lower than Latin America and both are much lower than East Asia. The Middle East reports the least amount of women and children in its labor force. Both Latin America and East Asia report substantially more. Even given the admitted unreliability of labor force figures, it would seem that a much smaller part of the total MENA population is economically active.

Figure 8: Labor Force Composition by Region

	Pop. Aged 15-64 (millions)	Labor force (millions)	% pop. 15-24 in labor force	% women in labor force	% children in labor force
MENA	162	92	57%	26%	5%
Latin America	306	206	67%	34%	9%
East Asia	1155	979	85%	44%	10%

Source: World Bank (1998-99: 194-195)

Relationship #4. Financial Flows and Exports

Turkey and Egypt both show increases in net private capital flows between 1980 and 1996. In Egypt they doubled and in Turkey they increased three-fold. Of the next largest, Lebanon showed an increase from a very low level, but still obviously was not recovered from the war. Tunisia moved from a negative position to being the fourth largest.

Turkey shows a small increase in foreign direct investment for the period, while Egypt actually had a decrease. As indicated above, foreign capital was not the motor of Egypt's great spurt in industrialization in the last decade. While Lebanon shows a large jump in foreign direct investment in this period, it is still low, substantially less than even Tunisia. Capital flows in Tunisia are the big surprise, moving from a negative position to where Egypt was in 1980 (Fig. 9).

Figure 9: (millions of $)

	Net Private Capital Flows		Foreign Direct Investment	
	1980	*1996*	*1980*	*1996*
Turkey	1782	5635	684	722
Egypt	698	1432	734	636
Lebanon	12	740	6	80
Tunisia	-122	697	76	320

Source: World Bank (1998/99: 230-231).

However, financial flows within MENA, even including Turkey (and/or Israel), are dwarfed beside those of the major developers in Latin America and in East Asia (Figure 10a).

Figure 10a: Financial Flows (millions of $)

	Net Private Capital Flows		Foreign Direct Investments	
	1980	*1996*	*1980*	*1996*
Algeria	-422	-72	349	4
Egypt	698	1434	734	636
Jordan	254	-119	38	16
Lebanon	12	740	6	80
Morocco	337	388	165	311
Oman	-259	69	141	67
Syria	18	77	71	89
Tunisia	-122	697	76	320
Yemen	30	100	-131	100
Total	**526**	**3314**	**1449**	**1623**
+Israel	—	—	101	2110
Total	—	—	**1550**	**3072**
+Turkey	1782	5635	684	722
(- Israel)				
Total	**2308**	**8949**	**2113**	**2345**

Source: World Bank (1998/99: 230-231)

There is a problem with the figures supplied by the World Bank. My computations from figures for all the individual countries of MENA given in the World Bank tables are detailed in Figure 10b, with totals shown beside those of the composite figures for MENA given by the World Bank in the same table.

Figure 10b: Financial Flows (millions of $)

	Net Private Capital Flows		Foreign Direct Investment	
	1980	*1996*	*1980*	*1996*
MENA*	526	3314	1449	1623
+Israel	—	—	1550	3072
+Turkey	2308	8949	2234	3794
MENA**	646	1979	2757	614
Latin America	12 601	95 569	8188	38 015
East Asia	18 443	101 272	10 347	58 681
South Asia	2173	8743	464	3439
Sub-Saharan Africa	195	4376	834	3271

Source: World Bank (1998/99: 230-231)

*Totals computed in Figure 10a from countries for which figures are given by World Bank, not including Turkey, which is classified by WB with Europe. Israel is classified as Middle East, but no figures are given for net private capital flows for 1980 and 1996.

**Composite figures for MENA given by the World Bank are significantly different from any combinations including/excluding Turkey and Israel, for which the variations are computed in Figure 10a. Figures which should be comparable are highlighted.

The net capital private flows in the MENA region were substantially less than South Asia in both 1980 and 1996, unless Turkey is included, in which case they are roughly similar. In 1996 MENA without Turkey even lags behind Africa. Both Latin America and East Asia are huge in both net capital flows and foreign direct investment by comparison.

As regards *increases* in net capital flows between 1980 and 1996, my figures show a six-fold increase in MENA compared to a five-and-a-half increase in East Asia, and over seven-fold in Latin America. South Asia shows only a four-fold increase, but Africa, starting very low, jumped 22 times in net capital flows.

The MENA increased very little in foreign direct investment (FDI). If Israel is included, FDI doubles. That is by contrast with Latin America, where FDI increased four-and-a-half times, and East

Asia, where it increased five times. Starting much lower, FDI to South Asia increased seven-and-a-half times and to Africa, four times. Overall the picture given by such statistics shows the Middle East/North Africa as a region not keeping pace with net capital flows and foreign direct investment elsewhere.

Relationship #5. "Export Substitution"

In *regulationist* theory the term "export substitution" is coined to indicate the shift away from the export of primary products to that of manufactured goods. Below is shown the amounts and percentage increases in five countries of the area where this phenomenon would seem to be developing (Figure 11).

Figure 11: Merchandise Exports (In descending order of percentage of manufactures exported in 1996)

	1980		1996	
	Millions of $	*% of manufactures*	*Millions of $*	*% of manufactures*
Tunisia	2234	36%	5517	80%
Turkey	2910	27%	23 045	74%
Morocco	2403	24%	4742	50%
Jordan	402	34%	1466	49%
Egypt	3046	11%	3534	32%

Source: World Bank (1998/99: 228-229)

Turkey shows a phenomenal jump since 1980 in both value of merchandise exports (eight times) and percentage (more than two-and-a-half times). Tunisia and Morocco both doubled the value of merchandise exports. Tunisia has a very high percentage of manufactured goods in exports, a suspicious indication of the phenomenon of world market factories. Turkey also has almost as high a percentage of manufactures in total exports. As shown above, Egyptian manufacturing has grown greatly in the past ten years, but manufactures still are barely one third of exports.

Egyptian manufactured commodities are obviously absorbed to a large degree by the home market. The relatively small change in the total *value* of manufactures exported, read against what we know of the increase in domestic manufactures, bears out the contention that Egypt's increased production is largely absorbed by the home market. The three-fold increase in value of *imports* between 1980 and 1996 (from $4860 million to $13 020 million), read against the GNP growth rate (1996-97) of 4.9% and the growth rate for GNP per capita of 3%, suggests a further increase in domestic consumption. Such aggregate figures do not indicate where in the social/class structure these increases are occurring.

Comparisons with countries that export substantial amounts of manufactured goods, that are also above 50% of exports, shows Malaysia, Mexico and South Korea have higher percentages of manufactures in exports than Turkey. Thailand has just about the same, 73% as opposed to 74% for Turkey. The increases of all these countries since 1980 (except South Korea) is phenomenal. All would seem to be embarked on "export substitution." South Korea, of course, not a primary exporter previously, was at 90% of exports being manufactures in 1980, rising to 92%. In 1996, Argentina, with 30% of exports in manufactures, is similar to Egypt's 32%. However, the value of Argentina's manufactured exports is nearly seven times that of Egypt.

Because we referred to a comparison above between the situation of Argentina and Australia in the 19th century, it is interesting to make a comparison with 1996 figures in this context. Australia, with 30% of its exports as manufactures in 1996, is slightly less than that of Egypt with 32%. The total value of manufacturing exports is more than double for Australia over Argentina (with Egypt's value of exports more than six times less than Argentina's). Such comparisons indicate "peripheral capitalism," if not also peripheral Fordism.

Conclusion

When applied to countries of the Third World, *regulation* theory points to the phenomenon of industrialization that has occurred now in a number of parts of the so-called periphery, and identifies characteristics of economic development that accompany it. Although the MENA region is noticeably absent in *regulation studies*, the concepts are clearly applicable.

Turkey (if we still accept it as being Middle Eastern after it was classified as European by the World Bank) is the most advanced state of the MENA region industrially. It has the largest population and is now in a league with other industrializing economies of the periphery, although by some criteria it does not quite qualify as a NIC. (The OECD definition of a NIC is that manufactures are 25% of GDP and at least 50% of exports.)

Egypt has made a substantial jump in the last few years, but is still dragged down by its large, underemployed, impoverished urban and rural masses, and has not become an urbanized industrialized population. The Egyptian Central Agency for Public Mobilization and Statistics (CAPMAS) joyfully announced in 1976 that for the first time, the decennial census showed the urban population of Egypt to have reached 50%. The World Bank, however, puts Egypt's urban population at 45% in 1997, up 1% from 1980. High illiteracy (36% males, 61% females as of 1995) (World Bank, 1998/99: 192) further mitigates against the creation of a skilled labor force (The contrasting figures for Turkey are 8% and 29%). Other states show interesting developments, for example Tunisia, with its quite extraordinary statistical indications of recent economic growth. Israel figures prominently, with a sizable per capita income ($15 810), second only to the UAE in the region, above both Spain and Greece and ranking 22nd in the world. In World Bank statistics, its population is listed as 6 million with a GNP of $87.6 billion (p. 190). The OPEC oil exporters are also in a category to themselves. They produce proportionally large per capita incomes – although not the highest globally. The largest have significant GNPs, but again they are dwarfed by the developed industrial countries. Nor do they have the highest GNPs in the region. That position belongs to Turkey with $199.5 billion.

Such examples underscore the great differences in economic base and development of states that are geographically located in the MENA. At the same time, political situations vitiate the contributions to economic development and integration of substantial populations of the region into the globalizing economy. The erratic shifts in the financial flows shown in Figure 10a are testimony to real and imagined political disturbances periodically in the region.

Nevertheless, what we are seeing in the Middle East in the era of "globalization" is the advancement of industrialization in Turkey and Egypt in ways that seem to be surmounting the "dependency" syndrome. Their home markets have obviously expanded.

The economies of the developed capitalist countries exert strong influences – that is undeniable – but at the same time the developed capitalist economies were forced to change. Two things happened historically. One was the crisis of central capitalism, beginning in the late 60s, fully recognizable in the 1970s. The second was change in the political economies of several states in diverse parts of the globe. For those who wish to see humans as the makers of their own destinies, such developments are vindication. Indeed, human agency did take advantage of propitious conditions for industrialization in the periphery, in a number of places in the MENA.

Regulationist theory captures some essential features of these changes. Viewing capitalist economies as "regimes of accumulation," *regulationists* are interested in those states where the kind of accumulation that industrialization allows takes place. That this theory of capitalist development has interested itself in the industrializing states of the periphery is itself a demonstration of the significance of present industrial development in the Third World. The recently emerged "regimes of accumulation" are also shown to have "modes of *regulation*" that define the way accumulation takes place. Obviously unsolved, however, in many states, is the incorporation of large sections of populations into the more productive forms of activity.

This is a particularly acute problem in Egypt, given its large population of rural, unskilled labor, without any solution in evidence. It bears restating that the capital-labor relation is the most important of the several relations that "modes of *regulation*" must accommodate in ways that do not hinder and preferably advance accumulation. In developing the home market, however, Egypt has certainly made a beginning in the development of a regime of mass consumption, necessary if heightened productivity and therefore increased earnings can occur.

At the same time, evidence of the particular forms that capitalism on the periphery takes, as described by Ominami and Liepitz *inter alia*, are evident in the MENA region. A feature of "peripheral Fordism" is the dependence on central capitalism for complex machinery. It is not the case in Egypt, however, that industrialization depends on design and production planning abroad. Only in very limited areas (notably the recent establishment of automobile factories) has Egypt hosted multinational enterprises where production is based on foreign conception and planning. In the industrial areas of the Gulf oil-producing states, this feature of peripheral Fordism is ubiquitous.

"Primitive Taylorism" of low-paid assembly by low-skilled, low-paid labor is not in evidence in the region. Tunisia is where the figures suggest it may be occurring. Poor working conditions and low salaries for manual labor are of historical origin, long before the globalization of production took place. Most of this production does not enter the world market except as handicrafts for the tourist trade in Egypt and the smaller states of North Africa and Jordan.

With the great diversity of populations and production regimes in the Middle East, "globalization" is shown to have affected this region in widely divergent ways.

References

Aglietta, M. 1976. *A Theory of Capitalist Regulation*. London: New Left Books.

Aglietta, M., et al. 1994. *École de la Régulation et Critique de la Raison Économique*. Paris: Éditions L'Harmattan

Boyer, R. (ed.). 1986. *Capitalismes Fin de Siècle*. Paris: Presses Universitaires de France.

Boyer, R. 1990. *The Regulation School: A Critical Introduction*. New York: Columbia University Press.

Boyer, R. & Saillard, Y. 1995. *Théorie de la Régulation: L'état des Savoirs*. Paris: Éditions La Découverte.

Frank, A.G. 1998. *Reorient: Global Economy in the Asian Age*. Berkeley: California University Press.

Froebel, F., Heinrichs, J. & Kreye, O. 1980. *The New International Division of Labour*. Cambridge: Cambridge University Press.

Issawi, C. 1966. *The Economic History of the Middle East 1800-1914*. Chicago: The University of Chicago Press.

Jessop, B. 1997. "Twenty Years of the (Parisian) Regulation Approach: The Paradox of Success and Failure at Home and Abroad." *New Political Economy, 2*, 503-526.

Lipietz, A. 1987. *Mirages and Miracles*. London: Verso, New Left Books.

Lipietz, A. 1995. "Capital-labor relations at the dawn of the twenty-first century." In Schor and You, (eds.), *Capital, the State and Labour*. Aldershot, UK: UN University Press.

Mistral, J. 1986. "Régime internationale et trajectoires nationales," in Boyer (ed.) *Capitalismes Fin de Siècle*. Paris: Presses Universitaires de France.

Ominami, C. 1986. *Le Tiers Monde dans la Crise*. Paris: Éditions La Découverte.

Riad, H. (Samir Amin pseud.). 1964. *L'Égypte Nasserienne*. Paris: Éditions de Minuit.

Richards, A. & Waterbury, J. 1990. *A Political Economy of the Middle East*. Boulder: Westview Press.

Sampson, A. 1988. *The Moneylenders*. London: Hodder and Stoughton.

Schor, J. & You, J. (eds.) 1995. *Capital, the State and Labour: A Global Perspective*. Aldershot, UK: United Nations University Press.

Soliman, S. 1999. "State and Industrial Capitalism in Egypt." *Cairo Papers in Social Science 21*(2). Cairo: The American University in Cairo Press.

World Bank. 1998-99. *World Development Report*. New York: Oxford University Press.

Globalization: Established Fact or Uneven Process?

Ray Kiely

Introduction

Globalization has become a key word of the 1990s. Within the academy, sociology, economics, geography, politics, international relations, and cultural and media studies have increasingly debated the globalization thesis. Politicians too have used the term, often to show the constraints faced by elected national governments.[1] There is, however, a striking lack of clarity over the term, and often a reluctance to bring the debates down to an empirical level. Moreover, the idea that we now live in a global economy or global society is often assumed, as if no proof was needed.

This chapter challenges some of the key assumptions of the globalization thesis, particularly the notion that globalization is a self-evident fact. The main argument of this chapter is that, though the concept of globalization may point to some real changes in the global order over the last 30 years, these are strictly limited and that above all, globalization does not mean the end of "local" spaces, including the nation state. This is illustrated by focusing on two areas – the global political economy and global media culture. Although the focus, and indeed the theoretical assumptions, are markedly different in these two fields, the "strong globalizers" in both share an exaggerated claim that the extent and speed of global flows is so great that local spaces have been destroyed. This position is rejected.

My argument is outlined in four sections. First, a brief overview of the notion of globalization is introduced. Second, the arguments of strong globalizers, which advocate the "end of the local," are outlined. Third, these positions – in both political economy and media culture – are rejected through a theoretical and empirical critique. Finally, I examine the implications of the East Asian recession for my argument.

1. The globalization thesis: a brief overview.

The best broad definitions of globalization can be found in the works of David Harvey (1989) and Anthony Giddens (1991). Their work refers to globalization in two ways. First, ever increasing parts of the globe are drawn into a global system and so are increasingly affected by events which occur elsewhere. Second, these events are happening at an ever greater pace – what Harvey (1989: 240) calls "time-space compression."

The first definition could refer to the fact that the current recession in East and South-East Asia has already had an effect in the rest of the world – for example, the closure of some East Asian-owned production sites in Britain. The impact of this recession may have only just started and there is a possibility that it may trigger a world slump. The second definition could refer to the growing importance of new communications technologies which change our sense of space and place. So for example, the development of satellite television means that faraway events can now be experienced, not as distant or recent historical events, but as live events broadcast in our living rooms. Similarly, the development of cheaper transport and communications systems and more efficient systems of supplying goods (discussed below) has meant that many of us now experience a bewildering variety of goods in our shops, each of which may lead to a changing sense of space and place.

These two uses of the term globalization are not without their contentious points. For example, we may ask: how new is the experience of being affected by events elsewhere? For much of the so-called Third World, this experience was central to the slave trade and colonialism (Kiely, 1998). In terms of the second usage: do new global flows (be they productive or financial capital, media images or popular cultural forms[2]) reach and affect everybody in a similar way? This is a key point in my criticisms of the strong globalization thesis, and I will return to it in due course.

Their weaknesses notwithstanding, the two definitions are useful as entry points into the globalization debate. However, rather than address the globalization thesis at such a general level, I will now focus on two areas, and in criticizing these I will by implication be re-addressing the two definitions described so far.

2. The strong globalization thesis: political economy and media culture.

(i) Political economy.

Proponents of the view that there is now a truly global political economy rest their case on two positions. First, that the development of trans-national corporations (TNCs) has reached such a level that they are more powerful than nation states in determining economic growth rates within countries. Second, that the enormous flows of financial capital have made fiscal control by nation states an irrelevance. In other words, the mobility of capital is so great that it has transcended the immobility of the nation state. Thus, for Nigel Harris (1990: 124), "in an important sense capital has no location."

The growth of the TNC has indeed been considerable. Some companies, such as Royal Dutch Shell, General Motors, Exxon and Mitsubishi all have assets which compare with the GNPs of some developing countries. By 1996, the largest 100 TNCs (based on size of foreign assets) owned $1.7 trillion worth of assets in their foreign affiliates and controlled about one-fifth of global foreign assets (UNCTAD, 1997: xvii). But it is the *qualitative* change that TNCs represent which is deemed to be of such importance. An international economy, based on trade between nations (or colonies), is hardly new. A global economy is said to be different, as it is "one in which the stress is placed upon the erosion of national barriers and the movement of economic activities across national boundaries" (Allen, 1995: 59). The key argument is that investment flows are so mobile that national boundaries are effectively ignored. Economic activity can easily shift from one part of the globe to another.

Neo-liberals welcome these developments. For Kenichi Ohmae (1993: 78), the nation state "has become an unnatural, even dysfunctional unit for organizing human activity and managing economic endeavor in a borderless world." The move to a global free market is welcome as it ensures that all nations will compete in a world economy, as opposed to monopolistic states protecting inefficient industry within their own domestic economy. Such competition will force countries to be efficient, and thereby exercise their comparative advantage. Mobile capital will thus be free to roam the globe, moving to areas of capital scarcity, such as the so-called Third World. This is broadly the explanation for the rise of East Asia – these countries succeeded by allowing market forces to operate and so discovered their comparative advantage in cheap labor through open competition (Balassa, 1981; *The Economist*, 1994). The structural adjustment of so-called Third World societies is thus seen as productive because it incorporates nation-states into a competitive global economy through market-friendly policies (World Bank, 1993).

Some writers on the left share the belief that there is now a global free market economy, but disagree with neo-liberals concerning the implications. A global economy means the intensification of the exploitation of the Third World as mobile capital takes advantage of cheaper labor, poorer work conditions and lower rates of taxation. This leads to what Gunder Frank (1981) long ago called the super-exploitation of workers in the Third World. The result is that all nation-states must downgrade in order to attract investment. The growth of Export Processing Zones since 1965, in which TNCs enjoy tax holidays, limited or no unions and few labor standards, is one example of this downgrading. For Peet (1987) the rise of the East Asian newly-industrializing countries (NICs) can be explained in this way.

The implications for the "advanced" capitalist countries are similarly negative. Relocation to low-cost areas is said to have led to de-industrialization and unemployment in the First World. So, in the face of a hyper-mobile global capital, which has no commitment to any particular country, the working class faces super-exploitation in the Third World and unemployment (or lower standards) in the First (Lang and Hines, 1993). Frobel et al. (1980) have argued that there is some grounds for optimism as workers throughout the globe share a common interest – to resist capital flow as it leads to unemployment or super-exploitation. However, this argument is unconvincing as – if we accept for the moment the claims made – it is just as likely to encourage racist scape-goating by workers in the First World, and workers in the Third World may be so desperate for a job that they accept anything (Jenkins, 1987: ch. 5). On the whole then, the left-wing position leads to a political pessimism, which is hardly surprising given that it starts from the assumption that (national) labor is passive in the face of a hyper-mobile global capital.

Advocates of the strong globalization thesis make similar and even stronger claims for the hyper-mobility of financial capital. Facilitated in part by the development of new communications technologies (O' Brien, 1992), financial capital moves rapidly around the globe, undermining the capacity of nation states to regulate the "national economy," through, for example, balancing budgets, mobilizing revenue for public programs and controlling national currencies. Certainly, since the move away from fixed exchange rates from 1971-3 and the subsequent liberalization of exchange controls, the flow of financial capital has grown at an unprecedented rate; from 1980-90 the volume of cross-border transactions grew from $120 billion a year to $1.4 trillion,[3] and international bank lending stock rose from $324 billion to $7.5 trillion (Hoogvelt, 1997: 78-80). At the time of the British Sterling-Exchange Rate Mechanism crisis in September, 1992, the daily turnover in currency was US $900 billion a day (Wade, 1996: 73).

The growing mobility of financial capital is said to have led to the undermining of the capacity of national governments to carry out neo-Keynesian macro-economic management. National economic planning is said to be a thing of the past.

(ii) Media culture.

Many cultural and media theorists have little interest in political economy. Baudrillard (1981) has even claimed that political economy no longer exists in a society dominated by images, or "signs." Much of what is outlined above is of little interest to the likes of Baudrillard and Lyotard, as the cultural sphere is said to be so great that it has effectively subsumed the political/economic sphere. The likes of Harvey (1989) have attacked "postmodernists" on precisely these grounds. Debates in cultural studies often focus on the centrality of political economy versus culture (McGuigan, 1992; Storey, 1997; Garnham, 1998; Grossberg, 1998). Moreover, there is little in the work of Baudrillard and Lyotard that explicitly addresses the question of globalization.

Nevertheless, despite very different theoretical approaches, there is something shared by both Harvey and Baudrillard which relates to their implicit account of globalization. For Harvey, globalization is primarily about a new period of capitalism characterized by an increase in the amount and intensity of capital flows (political economy). For Baudrillard and Lyotard, globalization (implicitly at least) is about an increase in the amount and intensity of media image or popular culture flows (culture).

Baudrillard argues that new communications technologies have promoted a global culture of instant but meaningless communication, in which time and space horizons have collapsed. The new social order is said to be based on the dominance of signs rather than material production – the "metallurgic" society has given way to a "semiurgic" society (Baudrillard, 1981: 85). In this totally mediated society there is no distinction between image and reality as there is no longer any space in which we can ground ourselves and gain a better understanding of the world. Where once signs may have been representational (they referred to a reality beyond the sign), they now refer only to other signs. Baudrillard (1993: 17) argues that "we manufacture a profusion of images in which there is nothing to see. Most present day images . . . are literally images in which there is nothing to see."

It is for these reasons that Baudrillard (1991) denied that the Gulf War took place. His position was not simply that the war was presented by the media in a sanitized way, because this critical approach to the war suggests that there were more truthful or meaningful accounts that could have been presented. Rather, he suggested that the war was so thoroughly mediated that – beyond it being a war game simulation of nuclear war – it became a meaningless event.

Given that he believes that we live in society in which there is no meaning, Baudrillard shows little concern with linking his approach to a theory of globalization. However, there does seem to be an implicit theory based on the centrality of new communications technologies. Baudrillard appears to be suggesting that it is the visual immediacy of these new technologies – and in particular satellite television (Caldorola, 1992) – which had the effect of denying the viewer any historical perspective on the event, so reducing the war to a meaningless event.

This focus on the end of meaning is also present in the work of Jean-François Lyotard. The trend towards greater global interdependence has led to fragmentation, difference, but above all an emphasis on the transient, fleeting and ephemeral. This takes place across national boundaries, resulting in the undermining of national identity, but without any meaningful replacement. Lyotard (1984: 76) argues that "Eclecticism is the degree zero of contemporary general culture: one listens to reggae, watches a western, eats McDonald's food for lunch and local cuisine for dinner, wears Paris perfume in Tokyo and 'retro' clothes in Hong Kong: knowledge is a matter for TV games."

This "global post-modern" (Hall, 1992: 303) condition suggests that as social life becomes increasingly mediated by global marketing, new media technologies and international travel, so new identities become detached from specific times and places. Cultural identity is thus in crisis as people increasingly lose any sense of place, and older cultural traditions become part of a meaningless "global supermarket."

3. A critique.

(i) Political economy.

In this part I will suggest that there are important limitations to the strong global political economy thesis. My focus will be on the global operations of TNCs, debates over national versus global determinants of economic growth and the limitations of financial capital. I will also suggest that theories of globalization have focused too much on the role of dominant groups as the agents of globalization, and that some attention must be paid to struggles between dominant and dominated.

Although direct foreign investment (DFI) increased ten-fold between 1970-2 and 1987-9 (Moran, 1998: 62), this figure presents only part of the picture. In fact, most TNCs continue to concentrate their operations in their home region. Of the top 100 firms in the world in 1993, 82 held the majority of their assets in their country of origin (Wallace, 1996: 24). The proportion of sales of TNCs in their home country remains extremely high and has sometimes increased: German manufacturing TNCs sold 75 per cent of their goods in their home market in 1993, compared to 72 per cent in 1987; Japan sold 75 per cent, compared to 64 per cent in 1987; while the USA sold 67 per cent in 1993, compared to 70 per cent in 1987. In terms of assets, the figures are similarly high: Japanese manufacturing TNCs held 93 per cent of their assets in Japan in 1992-3; the US 73 per cent, and even for Britain the figure was as high as 62 per cent (Hirst and Thompson, 1996: 96). It is estimated that TNCs employ 65 million people worldwide, and of these 43 million are in their country of origin (Moran, 1998: 62-3).

Moreover, foreign investment flows are highly concentrated in certain parts of the world. In 1996, "less developed countries" (including the East Asian NICs) received around 34 per cent of direct foreign investment (DFI) flows (UNCTAD, 1997: xvi). This is a sharp proportionate decline from 66 per cent for the developing world in 1938 (Moran, 1998: 65). The United States, as well as being the main foreign investor, is also the largest recipient. Most of the US' DFI goes to European Union countries (around 40 per cent), while "developing countries" as a whole receive 30 per cent. Figures on European Union DFI have been complicated by the recent move to a single market, but most goes to North America, followed by the richer nations of Asia. Similarly, Japanese investment focuses mostly on the United States, richer parts of Asia and to some extent the European Union, although there has been some decline in the latter in recent years (UNCTAD, 1997: xix-xx). So, DFI is actually first and foremost concentrated *within* First World countries, and not, as is commonly assumed, between First World countries investing in the Third World (where the latter is said to have a super-exploited, or a comparative advantage in, a cheap labor force).

Moreover, the small proportion which does go to the Third World is concentrated in a few countries. In the early 1990s, just ten nations accounted for 68 per cent of DFI in the "developing world" (*New Internationalist*, 1993: 19).[4] In the early 1990s, Africa received 1.7 per cent of total DFI; Latin America and the Caribbean 9.8 per cent; West Asia 0.8 per cent; and East, South and South East Asia 18.8 per cent (UNCTAD, 1995: 12). These proportions have changed slightly in the last three years, with some increase for Latin America in particular, but also continued decline in Africa (UNCTAD, 1997: xx-xxi), and so the continued concentration of DFI in certain regions of the world continues. Moreover, the boom in DFI in Latin America appears to be over as Brazil is (in 1998) entering a new recession.

Global trade patterns reinforce this picture. The share of exports as a proportion of the GDP of "advanced" capitalist countries rose steadily from the 1950s to the 1980s, but by the late 1980s this proportion was still lower than it had been in 1913. Latin America and Africa's share in world trade in 1990 had actually declined since the 1950s: from 12.4 per cent to 3.9 per cent for the former; and from 5.2 per cent to 1.9 per cent for the latter. Both the "developing world" as a whole and Asia's share slightly increased in this period, but this was accounted for by the rise of the four East Asian tigers, who together accounted for around half of all the manufacturing exports from the "developing world" in 1990 (Kiely, 1998: 50; Glyn and Sutcliffe, 1992: 79, 90-1).

Clearly then, the pattern of DFI and trade in the world economy does not conform to the picture presented by the "super-globalizers," discussed in section two above. Capital is not significantly moving away from the high cost (in labor and taxation) First World to the low cost Third World. Capital has continued to concentrate in the advanced capitalist world because these countries continue to maintain distinct competitive advantages. Early developers enjoy a *relative* advantage over later developers as they secure economies of scale, utilizing methods of production which allow them to produce many more goods both more cheaply and efficiently than later developers. These advantages include the use of mass production techniques, access to cheap credit, access to inputs from nearby suppliers, sophisticated infrastructures, skilled labor and research and development facilities (Kiely, 1998: chs. 5 and 8). Neo-liberal "super-globalizers" believe that a global free market is a progressive development because it promotes a level playing field in which all countries exercise their comparative advantage and therefore achieve economic growth. But "this assumption ignores the fact that there are formidable entry barriers for developing countries attempting to move up the ladder of the international division of labor – because of cumulative causations in technological progress . . . imperfect domestic and international financial markets . . . a lack of marketing skills and infrastructure, and so on" (Chang, 1995: 215).

This process of concentration is reinforced by the <u>partial</u> move towards new, post-Fordist experiments in industrial organization. Although the advocates of a new post-Fordist era of capital accumulation often overstate their claims (Amin and Robins, 1990; Kiely, 1998), it is the case that some sectors and some companies have attempted to introduce more flexible systems of production in order to increase efficiency. This may involve the use of flexible technologies which enable firms to switch product lines in accordance with demand; flexible labor which may involve a core of skilled workers whose tasks rotate according to the goods being produced and a periphery of workers who supply the final producer with various inputs; and flexible markets, which are based on increased information concerning consumer demand and which therefore partly eliminate waste and reduce the turnover time of capital (Lash and Urry, 1994). Such a political economy of post-Fordism is often linked to a culture of post-modernism, based on an increasing (and increasingly meaningless) range of consumer goods, discussed above.

The argument that we now live in post-Fordist times is problematic. A rigid separation of a Fordist era, based on the mass production of standardized goods, from a post-Fordist one, based on flexible production of niche, customized goods (see Harvey, 1989: pt. II), exaggerates the rigidity of Fordism and the flexibility of post-Fordism. General Motors (a larger company than Ford) produced cars for a a wider market than Ford during the Fordist era. Similarly, the argument that once a market is exhausted in the post-Fordist era, a company can easily switch flexible computerized machinery to producing another good is a gross exaggeration (Williams et al., 1987).

Nevertheless, there have been some moves towards greater experiments with flexible, post-Fordist accumulation.[5] Thus in retailing, market leaders have developed a computerized system (the "barcode") which supplies information about customer demand which is intended to overcome the problems of under-production (which may lead to loss of market share) or over-production (which leads to wasted stock). Through computerized accounting of stocks in shops, leading retailers can reduce market uncertainty by allowing supply to coincide with demand (Murray, 1989: 42-3). Such technology also allows suppliers to cater to niche markets, on the basis of age, income, occupation, lifestyle (the "post-modern consumer" discussed above). The Italian clothing company Benetton has extended this principal furthest, selling its products (themselves largely made by sub-contractors) through franchise agreements. A computer at company headquarters links every shop, and detailed information of sales is transmitted on a regular basis. In this way Benetton "can control without *owning* because of its possession of the information vital for both successful production and successful retailing" (Elson, 1989: 103).

This principle can also operate in the relationship between core firms and suppliers. Thus Toyota has attempted to implement the "retail model" so that its supplies are ordered on the basis of daily need, and so components are produced on the same day that they are assembled. Thus, the passage of products through the factory system has become far more rapid. Waste is eliminated as components arrive "just-in-time" for final assembly, and so manufacturers' demand coincides more closely with supply. Toyota therefore relies on a complex system of "independent" (but subordinate) suppliers, with around 230 first tier suppliers, who themselves sub-contract work to around 5000 second tier suppliers, who in turn sub-contract to a further 20 000 suppliers (Ruigrok and van Tulder, 1995: 53). Although some have seen potential in this for more equitable systems of work organization (Piore and Sabel, 1984), in fact profits (and wages) tend to decline the lower one's place in the hierarchy.

Most crucially for our purposes here, the move towards post-Fordist industrial practices has the effect of increasing the concentration of capital. This is because if companies are to rely on receiving final inputs just in time for final assembly, or if they are to send finished products to their final market quickly, *then there must be close proximity to both suppliers and final markets.* If goods (either as inputs to the final producers or as finished goods to the retailers) are being supplied on something like a daily basis, then it makes no sense to rely on production thousands of miles away. The effect is therefore a greater concentration of production and a further marginalization of parts of the Third World.

There are some exceptions to this rule and in some industries, the Third World continues to be attractive to TNCs. Reasons may include access to particular raw materials or access to domestic markets. Low labor costs are also sometimes important. TNCs may employ cheap (often female) labor in world market factories, operating in special Export Processing Zones (EPZs) where labor costs are low and unions barely exist. Alternatively, TNCs may sub-contract production activities out to local companies – a common practice among clothing companies such as Nike and The Gap (Donaghu and Barff, 1990; Mitchell, 1992).

While such practices show that TNCs can and do exploit cheap labor, their global significance has been exaggerated. Around 200 EPZs in the world today currently employ approximately 2 million workers – although this does not include the Special Economic Zones in China (Gereffi and Hempel, 1996: 22). Employment in these zones rarely accounts for more than 5 per cent of total industrial employment within individual countries, and in most cases less than 10 per cent of total manufactured exports originate from EPZs. Moreover, local capital is just as likely to take advantage of EPZs as foreign capital (Jenkins, 1987: 132). Similarly, the practice of sub-contracting has made little difference to the share of industrial goods exports from Third to First World. Figures on such practices are hard to find, partly because they are so difficult to quantify. However, a statistically significant increase could be found through examining the First World's share of industrial imports coming from the Third World. In fact, in the late 1980s, the EEC's share of industrial imports coming from the Third World was just 2.83 per cent; for North America the figure was 3.42 per cent; and for Japan it was just 1.43 per cent (Jenkins, 1992: 34).

The evidence presented so far suggests then that the argument that – in terms of productive capital at least – global forces are now so great that they have entirely destroyed nation states is a gross exaggeration. Given that in 1990, 98 per cent of Japanese savings remained in Japan, 96 per cent of US savings stayed in the United States and 83 per cent in Britain, it is more accurate to claim that "MNCs are not the driving force of the world economy – nationally determined growth rates are" (Moran, 1998: 60, 66). Similarly, the rise of East Asia cannot be explained by the relocation of foreign capital attempting to take advantage of cheap labor (see Frobel et al., 1980; Peet, 1986) because until the 1980s, Taiwan and South Korea imposed strong restrictions on foreign capital and industrialization was the product of local capital investment strongly supervised by a developmentalist state. In Taiwan, for example, foreign firms accounted for only 5.5 per cent of capital formation in the miracle years from 1962 to 1975 (Wade, 1990: 149). The South Korean and Taiwanese states were both heavily protectionist, precisely because the global economy is not the level playing field that the super-globalizers imagine it to be. Industrial policy was designed to promote exporters attempting to break into the world economy and to protect them from cheap foreign imports within the domestic economy (Amsden, 1989; Wade, 1990; Kiely, 1998: chs. 7 and 8). In other words, contrary to the claims of the super-globalizers, the *nation-state was central to the rise of the East Asian NICs.*[6]

Even in the case of financial capital, there are limits to the process of globalization. If global financial integration was "complete," there would be greater price uniformity, with firms drawing on foreign as well as domestic finance. In fact the price differential for both loan and equity capital remains high (Wade, 1996: 75). Moreover, there are still large differences in savings and investment rates between countries, including in the advanced capitalist world. In the OECD countries, rather than drawing on other countries' savings, the bulk of domestic investment is still mainly financed out of domestic savings. Thus there remains a close link between domestic savings and investment rates, as countries on the whole do not draw freely on other countries' savings. Although there has been a recent fall in the OECD savings-investment correlation, this may be due to a massive drop in the national savings of the United States, and its consequent reliance on other countries' savings, rather than a straightforward closer integration of financial markets (Weiss, 1998: 178-9).

Moreover, the development of these financial markets is not as global as is sometimes claimed, as most parts of the world are simply left off the map. The real global cities are the likes of London,

New York and Tokyo and not Calcutta, Port of Spain or Lagos. The Third World's share of international bank lending declined to about 11 per cent at the end of the 1980s, and this was concentrated in the (at the time) booming Asian economies. Greater financial integration has impacted in the "developing world" as it has eased the process by which national financial elites can export capital to the dominant centres. In this way, global financial integration may have deepened, but it has not widened (Hoogvelt, 1997: 80). The argument that new communications technologies have made location an irrelevance to global finance (O'Brien, 1992) ignores "the geography of information that is embedded in the provision of specifically financial products" (Clark and O'Connor, 1997: 90). Locally specific information is crucial to the monitoring of the financial and investment performance of firms. Financial centres are therefore not indifferent to local spaces as they are simultaneously centres of information collection, exchanging specialized knowledge.

Finally, the globalization thesis completely ignores the role of labor and class struggle. As Moody (1997) points out, when labor is mentioned, it is usually as a passive victim of social forces entirely beyond its control. However, the (partial) globalization of financial and productive activity is in part a response to struggles between capital and labor. Thus, global financial deregulation in Britain from the mid-1980s occurred only after the defeat of organized labor, while the threat of TNC exit from, for example, Sweden has been used as a weapon to restructure class relations (Moran, 1998). The successes of Taiwan and South Korea from the 1960s to mid-1990s were facilitated in part by radical class struggles for land in the immediate post-war period, which paved the way for land reform and a successful process of "primitive accumulation" of capital emanating from the countryside (Kiely, 1998: ch.7).

Thus, in terms of political economy, the super globalizers exaggerate the degree of capital mobility. Instead, it is the continuing tendency of capital to concentrate in certain locations, and thereby marginalize others, which has led to an intensification of uneven development. Established centres of capital accumulation (the European Union, North America and Pacific Asia – although there is uneven development within these regions too) are attracting the lion's share of capital investment. The result is an intensification of global inequalities. In 1900, the gap between the richest and poorest nations was around 8:1; by the late 1980s it was 36:1 (Freeman, 1991: 155). In 1960, the richest 20 per cent of the world's population received 70 per cent of global income, while the bottom 20 per cent received 2.3 per cent; the corresponding figures for 1989 were 82 per cent and 1.4 per cent. The ratio of rich to poor income earners thus increased in this period from 30:1 to 59:1 (*New Internationalist*, 1996: 19).

In Marxist terms, this situation is best characterized by marginalization rather than global exploitation. Clearly, some local spaces remain central to capital accumulation, while others do not.

(ii) Media culture.

Baudrillard suggests that (post-)modern society is so thoroughly dominated by media images that there are no longer spaces in which we can form meaningful identities. The information we draw upon to construct our identity is thoroughly mediated. Two immediate objections can be made to this argument. First, it simply is not the case that face to face interaction has ceased to exist in the modern world. Our immediate contacts with family, friends, co-workers and so on "continue to shape our sense of who we are and our subjective outlooks on the world" (Moores, 1997: 239). Second, and related to the first point, this interaction in part serves to allow us to critically reflect on the media images that are presented to us. Such critical reflection in itself gives meaning to events, no matter how mediated.

For example, if we take the Gulf War, it is undoubtedly true that the Gulf War was experienced by most of the world as a solely informational event, and indeed that much of the media presented the war in a heavily sanitized way. But it was precisely because the reporting of the Gulf War was so questionable "that we may point to the possibility of representational news being produced about it, and to the possibility of discriminating between types of coverage to indentify the more reliable from the less" (Webster, 1995: 188; Norriss, 1992). In arguing that the Gulf War was a meaningless event because it was so mediated, Baudrillard reduces us to being robotic extensions of new media technologies. Clearly, for those who actively supported or actively opposed the war, it had some meaning.

Baudrillard's argument that "the social" has given way to a meaningless society of signs is similarly problematic. If it is the case that we have entered a new kind of society, then there must be some (historical and social) causal factors that have created this situation. One possible explanation is to be found in the argument that postmodernism coincides with a new stage of post-Fordist capitalism (see above; also Harvey, 1989; Lash and Urry, 1987, 1994; Jameson, 1991), but this would suggest that there is a deeper meaning beyond immediate appearances, something that Baudrillard will not allow. It is therefore unclear how we have moved from a "metallurgic" to a "semiotic" society.[7]

Moreover, both Baudrillard and Lyotard are guilty of totalizing theories, assuming that the post-modern condition applies equally to everybody. The quotation from Lyotard above concerning the eclecticism of consumer styles may apply to some people, but this will partly depend on ("old fashioned") social questions concerning income and access. As Slater (1997: 201) argues, "(i)f post-modern experience depends on access to consumer goods or, more generally, on the ability to construct one's life along the model of the consumerist lifestyle, then money and power quite directly restrict access to post-modern culture." Los Angeles is often cited as the archetypal post-modern city. If we takes this to mean a city based in part on diversity, greater reliance on the service sector, more consumer choice for the middle classes, but also greater social inequalities and more intensive policing (rather than public provision) of associated social problems, then this is an accurate description (Davis, 1990). If post-modern in this context means "the end of the social," then we are left with a political position of arrogant indifference.

So, for example, Malcolm Waters (1995: 124), clearly influenced by Baudrillard, argues that that "material and power exchanges in the economic and political arenas are progressively becoming displaced by symbolic ones, that is by relationships based on values, preferences and tastes rather than by material inequality and constraint." Given the figures on growing global inequalities cited above, this assertion is breathtakingly banal. Such indifference brings us back to Baudrillard on the Gulf War, for his over-emphasis on the mediated experience of the Gulf War *for those in the West* leads him to downplay the fact that for those thousands of people killed in the war, and the friends and families that they left behind, the war was far less of a mediated experience (Norriss, 1992). The "cutting edge" theorizing of Baudrillard thus betrays a (media) technological determinism along with Eurocentrism.

As I have stated already, political economists and cultural theorists often disagree sharply with each other. What I have tried to demonstrate is that despite these disagreements, there is sometimes common agreement based on the implicit assumption that globalization has arrived and it stands above social relations or spatial structures. Put more concretely, both positions *exaggerate mobility*, be it of capital or media images. The result is that we are left accepting globalization as uncontested, a fact of life beyond our control and subject only to the "logic of capitalism" or an infinite process of meaningless signs. Both positions therefore agree that globalization has dissolved space – thus capital has no location, communications technologies or finance capital have resulted in the end of geography, so every space is mediated and so meaningless.

My critique suggested that in fact, local spaces remain a central component of the global order. But this has not led to a flattening of hierarchies. Insofar as we have entered a new era (of globalization, post-Fordism, post-modernism or whatever), we are witnessing an *intensification* of "geographical difference and diversity. Geography matters in this instance, precisely because global relations construct unevenness in their wake and operate through the pattern of uneven development laid down" (Allen and Hamnett, 1995: 235; also Castells, 1996: 102-3). Thus, there continue to be divisions between centres and peripheries (Lash and Urry, 1994: 28-30), not in the Frankian sense (which was always of very limited use) of the former exploiting the latter, but simply in that certain areas enjoy competitive advantages, access to wealth and income and so on, over other parts of the world.

4. The East Asian crisis: the end of the nation state?

In July 1997, the Thai currency, the *baht*, was devalued. This was the beginning of a currency crisis that spread throughout the region, and threatens worldwide recession. According to some economists, this recession spells the end of Asian state capitalism and the full move to a free market system.[8] Thus, the Chair of the US Federal Reserve Bank, Alan Greenspan, has argued that "(t)he current crisis is likely to accelerate the dismantling in many Asian countries of the remnants of a system with large elements of government directed investment, in which finance played a key role in carrying out the state's objectives" (cited in Wade, 1998: 1536). The justification for this argument is that state intervention is inherently inefficient and only a global free market can allocate resources efficiently. The crisis thus can be said to represent the final triumph of the global market against national governments. Thus, for the purposes of this chapter, the implication is that while the above arguments concerning the continued relevance of space were correct, it is likely that events since 1997 will make them out of date. "Globalization" may not have occurred in the late 1960s, but is an inevitable outcome of the events of 1997.

However, a careful consideration of the evidence suggests that the crisis was caused by a *lack of state regulation.* In the case of south east Asia (Thailand, Indonesia and to some extent Malaysia), the move to recession has been caused by "the absence of investment coordination to ensure that resources are directed to more productive ends" (Weiss, 1998: xi). In Thailand the private sector invested without restriction in the unproductive property market in the context of rising debt and appreciating currencies (tied to the US dollar). The property market crash of 1996 affected the whole financial sector, including the foreign exchange market, as foreign investors realized that domestic borrowers were unable to meet their debt service obligations (Wade, 1998). The crisis was thus in part caused by the failure of the state to regulate capital, both in terms of borrowing and investment (see further below).

In the case of South Korea, where the state has historically been very active, there was considerable deregulation in the 1990s. Controls on foreign borrowing were relaxed, there was no state control of the exchange rate and industrial policy was reduced. As Chang (1998: 1559) points out, "(l)ack of investment coordination led to overcapacity, which resulted in falling export prices, falling profitability due to low capacity utilization, and the accumulation of non-performing loans in a number of leading industries." This shift away from deregulation was in part caused by international pressure (especially from the Organization of Economic Cooperation and Development, which Korea joined in 1996), but was also a product of the growing domestic power of the *chaebols* (an economic system composed of conglomerates of numerous companies centred around one holding company).

The IMF medicine for the region predictably promotes increased deregulation to allow for greater capital mobility. But this approach is based on a fundamental misunderstanding about the specificity of East Asian capitalism.[9] Much of the region has a high level of domestic savings, facilitated partly by a relatively equal distribution of income. These savings are deposited in banks and then loaned to business. Thus, "the system is biased towards high ratios of debt to equity in the corporate sector . . . Firms with high levels of debt to equity are vulnerable to shocks that disturb cash flow or the supply of (bank or portfolio) capital – for debt requires a *fixed* level of repayment while equity requires a *share* of profits" (Wade, 1998: 1540). Thus, the higher the debt to equity ratio, the more likely any depressive shock will lead to default and bankruptcy. What is therefore needed is close bank/firm/government cooperation as protection against systemic shocks. It is this close collaboration that neo-liberals describe as "crony capitalism," and which, they argue, needs replacing by a genuinely free market. But this medicine is likely to make matters worse, as it was poor financial regulation that led to the crisis in the first place.

The immediate consequence has been recession and suffering for many people. In the long run, at least the countries with stronger economic foundations, such as South Korea, are likely to recover. However, these strong foundations may be partially undermined as the high-debt/high growth "model" gives way to a western approved system of lower debt, lower growth capitalism.

On the other hand, there is the possibility that the crisis – both within the region and worldwide – will reinforce the growing notion that free market capital is the problem and not the solution, and so the case for regulation will be revived. IMF medicine is likely to make things worse, thereby intensifying uneven development. Even without countervailing forces, this inequality will again demonstrate the continued relevance of local spaces. But just as likely is a nationalist backlash in the region, which may include an increase in the role of the state.

The recession in East Asia does not therefore mean the end of local space and the confirmation of the hyper-globalization thesis. The causes of the recession must be located in the absence of adequate regulation mechanisms, and so the medicine of abolishing regulation wholesale is likely to make matters worse. This may lead to a reconfiguration of core-periphery relations between parts of the West and parts of East Asia (especially south-east Asia). In this case local spaces thus remain of crucial significance. However, the crisis is equally likely to call into question the ideology of those committed to a global free market. In this case, local spaces, and above all the nation state, are likely to increase in significance.

Endnotes

[1]Tony Blair has, for example, used the constraints of globalization argument to argue that national governments can play only a limited domestic

role. See Today, BBC Radio 4, 30/9/98. Extracts can be found in *Marxism Today*, Nov/Dec 1998.

[2]Media images and popular cultural forms are of course capital too, a point important to my later arguments about the limitations of globalization.

[3]These are US figures for billion and trillion.

[4]These were Singapore, Mexico, Brazil, China, Hong Kong, Malaysia, Egypt, Argentina, Thailand and Taiwan.

[5]These experiments are discussed in detail – with considerable attention to the automobile, semi-conductor and clothing industries – in Kiely (1998: ch. 9; 1998).

[6]This is not to say that there is an easily replicable model of state-led capitalist development. Crucial here is the question of state capacity, which in turn is linked to state-civil society relations. See further Kiely, 1994; 1998: ch. 8; 1998; Evans, 1995; Weiss and Hobson, 1995; Weiss, 1998.

[7]As Strinati (1992: 78, n.8) puts it, "if the 'real' has 'imploded', as Baudrillard argues, then what 'real' evidence can we refer to in order to show that it has done so. If we could find this evidence then the point would be disproved, but if we couldn't then we wouldn't know if it had or it hadn't."

[8]Though where this leaves the neo-liberal argument (World Bank, 1993) that East Asia developed through market-friendly intervention is unclear. It seems that neo-liberals argue that the miracle was caused by market-friendly policies while the recession was caused by market-unfriendly policies. This is a perfectly acceptable position if evidence was presented to show how the East Asian countries moved from a simulated free market to an over-regulated state, but none is forthcoming. For a critique of the World Bank's position on the miracle, see Kiely (1998).

[9]Using the notion of a singular East Asian capitalism is itself too much of an over-generalization, and one needs to be sensitive to the specificities within the region. This point actually reinforces the point that I am making in the text, namely that globalization does not mean the end of international or national differences.

Against the Globalist Paradigm

Philip Marfleet

Is globalization a developmental solution – or a problem? Partisans of globalism have presented the "global era" as a period of liberating economic changes during which there can be an advance towards more general prosperity. Those hostile to the idea have depicted a world in which capital races unregulated across the globe, with negative outcomes. But both proponents and detractors have largely accepted the globalist paradigm as an appropriate description of the contemporary world. This chapter argues that the paradigm is false.

Since the late 1980s, globalization theory has exerted enormous influence. In a review of the globalist literature, Waters concludes that it constitutes "a key idea by which we understand the transition of human society into the third millennium" (1995: 1). At its core is the idea of world integration by means of powerful capital flows. This development is said to be novel and unstoppable: such a fundamental change that economic and social relations as a whole must be understood within the new globalist context. Spybey, for example, concludes that "political, economic and cultural institutions have been globalized. Today there is virtually no one on the planet who can participate in social life without reference to globalized institutions" (Spybey, 1996: 9). Global influences, it is argued, are ubiquitous: we are all of the global condition and are increasingly constrained to see ourselves as such. In observations which are typical of much academic comment, Shaw (1994: 9) suggests that recent changes challenge conceptions about the very nature of society, the state and civil society.

Underlying the perspective is an assumption that the world is being integrated positively by forces of the market, with flows of capital crossing old boundaries to produce an encompassing whole. In management theory and among business strategists this often produces a view that world integration is accomplished or largely complete. One leading corporate executive has commented that major companies no longer debate the existence of globalized conditions but are preoccupied by their challenges – those of "a 'global village' of diminished borders, internationalism and free trade" (FitzGerald, 1997: 741). Even those most critical of the impacts of perceived integration insist it is a reality all must confront, especially if they are concerned with the fate of the Third World or the South. Robinson, who identifies globalization as "a war of the global rich and powerful" against the mass of humanity, suggests that political radicals face a struggle to come to terms with what he calls "the fundamental dynamic of our epoch: capitalist globalization" (1996: 13). Those who wish to stand with "the global poor – [a] dispossessed and outcast majority" – must recognize the realities of the system.

> In my view, activists and scholars alike have tended to understate the
> systemic nature of the changes involved in globalization, which is
> redefining all the fundamental reference points of human society and
> social analysis, and requires a modification of all existing paradigms
> (Robinson, 1996: 1).

In a similar vein, Gray cautions those sceptical of the paradigm that they must recognize the scale and novelty of recent changes. He maintains that those who question the bases of globalization theory – world integration, the power of capital flows, and changes in the status of the nation-state – are unwilling to confront a new reality. Although hostile to some impacts of globalization, he suggests that "globalization sceptics are trading in illusions" (1998: 67).

Robertson, who has been among the architects of globalist theory, argues that a substantial critique of globalization is meaningless. He suggests that "there can be no foreseeable retreat from globalization and globality" (1992: 10). Human existence is now shaped by the condition of globalism, he maintains, and "anti-global gestures" are merely "encapsulated within the discourse of globality" (1992: 10). On this account the human condition *is* that of a globalized world and those who question the notion are engaged in a tortured, unproductive struggle to escape from an embracing reality – what Robertson calls "globality" or "unicity."

But the case for a world integrated on the globalist model has *not* been made. At the level of economic change, much recent evidence suggests that although some aspects of the world system demonstrate genuine integration, others do not; that although some patterns of economic activity make for high levels of coherence, others are productive of asymmetry, fragmentation and even disintegration. The pattern of change is towards *contradictory* outcomes – not towards the holistic models advanced by theorists of globalization. Nor is there convincing evidence that globalizing tendencies are autonomous or that they not susceptible to human intervention. Vast numbers of people *do* attempt to change their circumstances in ways which violate the globalist perspective. Are they "encapsulated" within globality and merely reflect the global condition, or do their aspirations and actions help to inform us about the inadequacy of the globalist paradigm?

The global economy

Markets and consumers

For many academic theorists, professional economists and business people, globalization *is* the expansion of economic forces worldwide. FitzGerald, for example, asserts that it is "simply the latest phase in the evolution of international business and the integration of the world economy" (1997: 741). This observation is important, suggesting as it does a naturalistic development – "evolution" – of economic activities towards a high phase. It is consistent with a globalist orthodoxy that associates world integration with positive assertion of market forces. It is also inseparable from wider developments: from the aggressive activity by dominant states and transnational financial organizations, which for 20 years have attempted to impose neo-liberal economic strategies, especially upon states of the Third World. This period in fact correlates with the "global era" celebrated by globalization theory, during which capital flows have allegedly transformed the world order towards singularity.

The most widely cited globalist text, Ohmae's *Borderless World*, celebrates the perceived achievements of this period of change (1990). It depicts a planetary unity in which freely flowing capital has at last made for a properly functional system. As old political frontiers become meaningless, Ohmae argues, uninhibited capital movement brings to life a world system which has in effect been awaiting animation. New centres of economic activity come into being, drawn by "the deft hand of the market" (Ohmae, 1993: 78). The progress towards globalism brings a flowering of market forces – development towards a higher state in which elements of the system can at last operate in harmony. On this view, the nation-state – with its tariffs, preferences, protectionism and attempts to control capital flows – is an irrational irruption into the market system. It is dysfunctional, for it violates natural links between local economic activities and the global market.

There are loud echoes here of classical economics – of Adam Smith's injunction in *The Wealth of Nations* that "all systems of preference or restraint" in business should be withdrawn, in order that "the obvious and simple system of natural liberty establishes itself of its own accord." All interventions in economic activity which inhibit entrepreneurialism and associated "natural liberty" violate an order which should develop "of its own accord." Ohmae and his co-thinkers reproduce this 18th century creed as a modern prosperity doctrine. They argue that as the world system sheds the inhibitory influences of the state, the whole global body can approach good health. In their account the role of the early entrepreneur has been taken by trans-national financial institutions and multi-national companies (MNCs). Moving capital across old boundaries, they allow the market to re-emerge as the natural context for economic activity. The state retreats – not merely as a redundant structure but as an inappropriate one – as a violation of the "natural" system of profit-seeking which brings general prosperity. States and their ideological irrationalities can at last be set aside: as Negroponte suggests, with increased globalization, "there will be no more room for nationalism than there is for smallpox" (Gray, 1998: 68).

There is a further reference to classical economics in the globalist argument for an integrated world of investors and consumers. This is especially important, as it links globalist economic theories with influential notions of a "global society" and of "globalized" culture. Smith, Ferguson and the early political economists saw a world in which rational individualism shaped economic life – in which the market was composed of many decision-makers among whom the most energetic and acute were able to accumulate rapidly, progressing society as a whole. In the late 20th century, the key role is allocated to banks, finance houses and MNCs, which are seen as energizing the world system. At the same time, there is a renewed role for individuals. Bryan and Farrell write: "Increasingly, millions of global investors, operating out of their own economic self-interest, are determining interest rates, exchange rates and the allocation of capital, irrespective of the wishes or political objectives of national political leaders" (Gray, 1998: 68). In a similar way, individual consumers make countless decisions which are said to shape a global market. With global capital offering an unprecedentedly wide range of goods and services, consumers are able to think and act "globally," their aggregated choices making what has been called "the culturized economy" (Waters, 1995: 95). Summarizing recent work in socio-cultural analysis of globalization, Waters comments that in these circumstances, "The economy becomes so subordinate to individual taste and choice that it becomes reflexively marketized and, because tokenized systems do not succumb to physical boundaries, reflexively globalized" (1995: 95). The outcome is a world economy shaped by "consumption, lifestyle and value commitment" (1995: 95). On this view, global capital and the global consumer operate in a happy liaison.

Corporate vision

Some of these ideas have recently been criticized as misrepresentations of globalizing processes, what Held and others have described as "hyper-globalization" (Held, 1997; Gray, 1998). They suggest that Ohmae's global market is indeed based upon a model of perfect competition: that it correlates the world economy with a neo-liberal utopia. Gray warns that this is an "illusive vision," that the notion of economic actors operating rationally across the world market is "a corporate Utopia, not a description of any present or future reality" (1998: 68). But these ideas *are* the key reference points for most approaches to globalism and influence profoundly even global "revisionists" such as Gray. Reviewing literature in economics, business and across the social sciences, Axford comments upon their very widespread influence. He notes the impact of ideas of "complete 'globalization' of economic relations" and "an unquestioning certainty about the existence of a truly global economy" (1995: 9). Hirst and Thompson also conclude that among academics and management thinkers, "it is widely asserted that a truly global economy has emerged or is emerging" (1996: 195). They identify a consensus that powerful capital flows have rendered meaningless nation-states and "national economies":

> *The world economy has internationalized in its basic dynamics, is dominated by uncontrollable global market forces, and has as its principal actors and major agents of change truly trans-national corporations (TNCs), which owe allegiance to no nation state and locate wherever in the globe market advantage dictates. (1996: 195)*

Even in more reserved accounts of globalization, in which these changes are yet to be accomplished, there is a conviction that they are a developmental conclusion of current processes and should shape interpretations of the contemporary world. They are especially influential in determining economic policy and business strategy. Axford describes "a global mentality" that has developed across industry, finance and commerce. Elaborated between executives and managers at a formal and informal level, this stresses the emergence of a liberated world market and a "global rationale" for corporate activity. Axford comments that "the global corporation" may be more myth than reality but that "it is one which now exercises a powerful hold over the strategic vision as well as the management styles of large corporations with international connections and markets" and that "the rhetoric of global management informs much of their discourse" (1996: 98). Hoogvelt points out that the idea of a "global market discipline" has profound consequences: she comments on "the *awareness* of global competition which constrains individuals and groups, and even national governments" (1997: 124). Such consciousness of a global reality, she argues, is being internalized in the behavior of economic agents (1997: 124).

By the late 1990s this perception of world affairs had become increasingly general. Only the shock of economic crises associated with the South-East Asian and Russian "meltdowns" gave some globalists pause for thought. Noting widespread fears that the global marketplace might collapse, the *Financial Times* (8 January 1998) asked "Who's afraid of globalization?" As Latin American economies faced mounting difficulties, it warned that the whole strategy for world development was at risk: that what it called the "Washington consensus, the idea that economic modernization is best performed by liberalizing goods and capital markets" could be called into question (*Financial Times,* 12 August 1998). Commenting upon growing anxiety among academics, analysts and investors, *The Economist* (5 September 1998) observed that "panic" was abroad, together with what it called a dangerous suggestion, "that it is not merely the international capital market but the basic principles of capitalist economics that need to be questioned." This is stark recognition of the problems of the whole neo-liberal account from journals which have played a leading role in articulating globalism.

In fact, the gap between the globalist vision and the global reality has long been immense, and during the "global era," it has been widening. While mainstream economics and development theory has urged adherence to neo-liberal/globalist doctrines as a means to wider prosperity ("there *is* no alternative"), the mass of the world's people have been witness to a different reality. Even by the mid-1990s, only 21 of 147 "developing" countries achieved the 3 per cent increase in annual growth that is the United Nations' benchmark for reduction of poverty (UNDP, 1998); meanwhile, in scores of national economies, there was a *contraction* in economic activity. Rather than embracing prosperity, their populations face a more relentless struggle for survival. Over half the countries for which statistics are available do not have enough food to maintain basic nutritional standards for all their populations (Caulfield, 1998: 332). Across Africa, the average household consumes 25 per cent less than in the early 1970s (UNDP, 1998); in South-East Asia (home of the neo-liberal "miracle") the World Bank points out that poverty and inequality are becoming far more general (*The Guardian*, 28 August 1997). While ideologues of globalism continue to urge Third World countries to embrace the free market and receive the reward of prosperity "for decades to come" (*The Economist*, 4 September 1998), the United Nations Development Programme (UNDP) comments on a world of "shortfalls and gaping inequalities" that has rendered some regions "economic wastelands" (UNDP, 1997; 1998).

This difference – between the globalist vision and the experiential world of billions of people – is so significant that the globalist paradigm as a whole must be described as an *ideological* perspective, one at odds with another reality but which is elaborated primarily by those for whom it provides a specific rationale. Notwithstanding anxieties about recent market instabilities and political upheavals, most globalists are therefore unwilling to confront this discrepancy. Most academic, professional and business opinion continues to describe the world as positively integrated by market forces – a vision of the world as neo-liberalism *wishes it to be*. The attempt by a minority of globalization theorists to rescue the paradigm from alleged "hyper-globalizers" will not do: the concept as a whole is flawed.

Contradiction

There has, of course, been change in the world economy, but it has not tended towards generalized growth or towards consolidation of an harmonious global system. The most striking example of *contradictory* patterns of development is in the contrast between changes in world finance, in world trade and in investment.

In providing evidence for a globalized world, much is made of the trans-nationalization of finance. The increase in volume of financial transfers is very striking: between 1976 and 1993, borrowing on international capital markets, for example, increased from less than $100 billion to $818 billion (Hirst and Thompson, 1996: 40). By 1995 the *daily* volume of transfers on world currency markets had reached $1500 billion – a figure more than the annual domestic product of all but three national economies (*The Independent*, 30 June 1998). The change in scale of activity has been accompanied by a change in means and speed of transfer. In the 1970s, there was still a system of national financial centres linked by a relatively small number of operators who bought and sold credit. By the 1980s this had been replaced by a global network of dealers linked by digital communications systems. In the new context, comment Stopford and Strange, physically separate national markets have been able to function "as if they were all in the same place" (1991: 40). This development is often seen as testimony to the development of a globalized system in which "elimination of space has accomplished the conquest of time" (Waters, 1995: 88). Axford comments that: "The underlying logic of the unfettered capital market in the borderless world is seen more clearly in global financial transactions than anywhere else," making such changes "the most unequivocal indicator of the globalization of economic affairs" (1996: 107-8).

The changes are indeed very significant. They are associated with the introduction into the world financial system of a large number of national markets in Africa, Asia and Latin America, which were hitherto relatively isolated from world financial centres. Banking centres established during the colonial era, such as Shanghai, Sao Paulo, Cairo, Istanbul, Beirut, Johannesburg and Jakarta, have been given increased importance. At the same time, a number of new markets have been established, the role of which is precisely to conduct business within the global networks. These include disparate and physically distant cities – Harare, Nairobi, Abidjan, Lima, Quito, San Jose, Kingston, Karachi, Dacca, Saigon, Hanoi and many others. Their emergence is often taken as evidence that all economies may now participate fully in the world system.

There is a widespread assumption that the technology associated with such trans-nationalization is itself constructing a globalized world. Gray, for example, concludes that "We are not masters of the technologies that drive the global condition: they condition us in many ways we have not begun to understand" (1998: 206). A similar determinism is evident in Cerny's assertion that the power of such technologies and the financial flows they facilitate means that today "the world order follows the financial order" (1993: 18). But greater interconnectedness of world finance has not produced the positive developmental outcomes depicted in globalist accounts. Most financial activity continues to take place within and between established centres of world finance in North America, Europe and Japan. Activities which do involve the new financial centres are often predatory ventures: plays upon local currencies or tradeable securities undertaken by Western banks and finance houses which are able to move vast amounts of money against the prospect of quick speculative gains. The "meltdowns" of 1997 and 1998 provided stark evidence of the extent to which integration of world money markets emphasizes extreme unevenness of the world system, precipitating headlong falls in currencies and securities, especially those associated with weaker economies. In addition, interconnectedness of such markets has transmitted local crisis with great speed across the world system. These developments *do* speak of genuine integration – but not an integration accompanied by the positive outcomes celebrated in globalism.

These difficulties are much more pronounced in the areas of trade and of investment. The neo-liberal agenda for trade, aggressively pursued by the World Bank and the International Monetary Fund (IMF), insists upon de-regulation as the catalyst for economic growth, especially among states of the Third World in which there have been strong state-centred development policies. Hoogvelt comments that for 20 years, the Bank and the IMF have targeted the "development state" as "the real cause of Third World poverty and underdevelopment" (1997: 169). Under immense pressure from these institutions, national governments in Africa, Asia and Latin America have dismantled trade controls and protectionist measures. But after a generation of reform, most Third World countries are placed *less* advantageously within the world system. Various calculations show that although world trade has grown steadily, sometimes spectacularly since the 1960s, the proportion associated with developing countries has declined: according to GATT, in the 1960s the share of developing countries in world trade was about 24 per cent; by 1990 it had fallen to 20 per cent (Hoogvelt, 1997: 73) – a change wholly at odds with globalist expectations.

Meanwhile, industrialized economies have tended to cluster in trade blocs, of which the most significant are the European Union (EU) and the North American Free Trade Association (NAFTA). Of the latter, Judis comments that: "NAFTA is not really about free trade"; rather, he argues:

> [it] is a prudent step towards creating a regional trading bloc that could withstand the devolution of Western Europe and Asia into rival blocs. The treaty's free trade proponents would never admit this, but NAFTA's underlying thrust is towards managed trade and investment. (Kegley and Wittkopf, 1995: 247)

Such alliances ostensibly link national economies for mutual advantage. In fact they usually serve the interests of dominant local states: the United States in the case of NAFTA ; Germany in the case of the EU (Milward, 1992). The vast majority of states, notably those of the Third World, are excluded and as a result their bargaining power vis-à-vis the centres of world commercial activity becomes even weaker. Notions of progressively "globalized" trade, which through the free market serve a universal developmental interest, are implausible.

Extreme unevenness within the world system is even clearer in the area of investment. Foreign Direct Investment (FDI) is often declared a key aspect of globalization, largely because of the very rapid rise in cross-border investment proportional to trade and other measures of world economic activity. During the 1980s, FDI grew five times faster than world trade (Hirst and Thompson, 1996: 55). By the early 1990s, the 300 largest MNCs – the main agents for FDI – mobilized over a quarter of the world total of capital (Waters, 1995: 76). Some MNCs had also moved towards alliances of "networked" companies able to operate from a number of nation-states and which moved capital relatively freely across national economic frontiers. Like developments in finance, such activity has mesmerized many economists and corporate strategists, prompting assertions that capital movements have accomplished globalization. Even the radical journal *New Internationalist* can declare that: "The power of global capital in the form of trans-national organizations and institutions has made a nonsense of national economic decision-making . . . Today this transformation is common wisdom" (277: 9). Robinson, who declares himself strongly opposed to capitalism as a system, nevertheless identifies "the globalization of the process of production itself" as a key element activitating the "juggernaut" of global integration (1996: 14-15). His co-thinker Sivanandan sees capital as so mobile that an enterprise "can take up its plant and walk to any part of the world where labor is cheap and captive and plentiful" (1997).

But capital movements have been much more restrained than these accounts suggest. A series of studies of FDI, notably that by Ruigrok and van Tulder (1995), present very firm evidence that MNCs invest primarily within quite limited territories. Their cross-border activity is overwhelmingly of a *regional* character and often amounts to no more than investment in a country or countries adjacent to the nation-state of origin – as with many of the most prominent European corporations. On the basis that most of world invest-ment takes place within (and to a lesser extent between) the "Triad" of North America, the EU and Japan, Ruigrok and van Tulder argue for a notion of regionalization or "Triadization," rather than of glob-alization. Larger sums have recently been mobilized outside the Triad: by 1996, 37 per cent of total FDI entered developing economies. But of this sum 90 per cent was directed towards just nine countries, the most favored being those already classified as Newly Industrializing Countries (NICs) (World Bank, 1997). These figures suggest that trans-national capital is in general avoiding real-ly low wage economies, contrary to the assumptions of many glob-alists and to the approach of most corporate executives, who have attempted to discipline their workforces with the notion of world wide "portability" of jobs – a very important part of the globaliza-tion myth. As Kiely has pointed out, FDI does not express a world-embracing pattern of investment activity: rather, it testifies to a pat-tern of unevenness in which capital bypasses most states, ignoring most of Africa, Asia and Latin America. The world system is *not* integrating the Third World, it is marginalizing it (Kiely, 1998: 112).

This observation is important. Globalist theory maintains that dualisms such as those which distinguish First and Third Worlds are outdated – relics of an earlier era during which the market was con-strained by the irrationalities of state structures. In fact such global difference is being *exaggerated*: the contemporary world shows more inequality and asymmetry. This is the outcome of contradictory developments, of which the most important is the greater fluidity of finance capital on the one hand, and the limited changes in trade and investment on the other.

Integration of financial markets has facilitated the movement of money worldwide with unprecedented speed. This takes place against a background of increased weakness of most developing economies, which are less engaged in trade than in an earlier era, and which receive a mere fraction of world FDI. Speculative activity weakens already fragile local systems, producing high levels of volatility which further inhibit long-term investment. The combina-tion is lethal: many economies in Africa, Asia and Latin America have recently been very seriously weakened, with the result that the local state may begin to fragment, prompting factional conflict, civil strife and – with sometimes terrifying consequences for the mass of the population – complete collapse. This was the fate of Somalia in the early 1990s and of Liberia and Sierra Leone in the mid-1990s.

Globalist references to a generalized weakening of the nation-state are inadequate to account for these developments, for some states, notably in the West, remain extremely resilient. It is the marginalized states of the Third World – supposedly the beneficiaries of a new global prosperity – which are subject to the destructive energies of forces which had been allocated the role of developmental liberation.

Rational model

Changes in the world system over the past 30 years have intensified global inequality. In 1960 the difference in per capita income between the richest fifth of the world's population (largely in developed countries) and the poorest fifth (largely in developing countries) was in the ratio of 30:1; by 1995 the ratio was 82:1 (UNDP, 1997). By 1997 the richest fifth of humanity received 86 per cent of world income; the poorest fifth received 1.3 per cent (UNDP, 1997). The "global era" has been a period of regression in which, despite great increases in world productivity, vast numbers of people have been thrust further from the mainstream of economic activity towards immiseration and suffering. Increasingly, hundreds of millions of people in what the UN calls "crisis zones" face the prospect of political instability, civil conflict and sudden, traumatic population movements. In most of the Third World – home to over 80 per cent of humanity – the idea of a globalized system which liberates economic energies and delivers new opportunities for mass consumerism is no more than fantasy.

Yet these developments should not be attributed to "globalization." Neither the positive scenario presented by ideologues of globalism, nor that presented by critics who wish to emphasize the "downside" of globalizing change, accurately depict the dynamics of the world system. This has *not* changed fundamentally since the 1970s. Although internationalization of finance has become more pronounced, other patterns of economic activity have confirmed well-established dualities. The outcome has been intensification of *uneven development* within local economies and at a world level. The gap between "developed" and "developing" has grown wider, with emergence of the NICs, hailed in the early 1980s as harbingers of globalist change, now seeming a specific and probably unrepeatable experience. There is scant evidence of candidate "late developers": on the contrary, states which 10 years ago might have hoped to join the "Tiger" economies in a surge to industrialization now face a more unpredictable and unstable future.

Why have theorists of globalism found it so difficult to accept contradiction and failure within the world system? Most have assumed that globalization is possessed of a developmental logic, that it is evolutionary or at least processual. This is suggested by the frequent references to global integration as expressing a higher state of world affairs. It is also inherent in the very general assumption that progress towards a free-market model is an assertion of rationality. Some social theorists drawn towards globalist notions have noted some of the difficulties: Kavolis comments that globalization postulates "a Durkheimian inevitability of moving, sooner or later, towards a universal value hierarchy" (Robertson, 1992: 129) and Turner notes the criticism that globalist theory "is evolutionary and teleological . . . in fact a new version of Westernization" (1994: 108). But such comments are rare: in general globalizers have assumed that recent changes advance the world in some meaningful way.

Capitalism, however, is not possessed of an inner logic, apart from that of the restless drive for profit. Even Marx was forced to recognize contradictions within what he had at first thought was a "progressive" dimension of industrial capitalism. Assuming that its rapid expansion from Europe would sweep aside unproductive non-industrial societies, he was forced to confront the reality of colonialism, with its grossly unequal relations – its *limits* upon world development. He and his co-thinkers were also compelled to address the outcome of such contradictory processes, most importantly the phenomenon of mass resistance in the "colonial world" (Marx: nd). Such resistance has continued unabated for 150 years and its recent manifestations constitute a further challenge to the globalist paradigm.

Human agency

Battles for bread

Globalization theory denies human agency. For management strategists, economic analysts and business people who have embraced the globalist creed, human beings are significant only to the extent that they are abstract investors, managers or consumers. In some accounts, human agency is also minimized or excluded because of the perceived power of systems and machines: as in Gray's observations that "technologies . . . condition us" and that "the flood of inventions which drive the world economy cannot be controlled" (1998: 206-7). Such determinism is especially common in accounts of global culture: Robertson, for example, writes of social phenomena as "products of globality" (1992: 170). Elsewhere I have examined the dangers of this approach in accounting for emergence of social movements, including those described as "globalist" in character (Marfleet, 1998). In the present context it is important to note that some of the sharpest critics of a "globalized" world are also the most pessimistic about the prospect of changing it. Gray (1998: 207-8) sees only "deepening international anarchy . . . which we are powerless to overcome" and Sivanandan (1997: 19) maintains that recent technological changes have "fragmented or ... destroyed" mass organizations worldwide, rendering the international working-class movement "impotent."

Those who assert most readily that human beings are of decreasing importance in a integrated world system do not seem to have noticed a significant synchronization, for as trans-national agencies have more systematically imposed adjustment programs on Third World economies, there have been repeated waves of mass protest. These programs were introduced by the IMF and World Bank initially as a response to problems generated in Third World economies by the world crisis of the early 1970s (Walton and Seddon, 1994: 4). A very striking feature of world politics since this period has been the scale of mobilization *against* such "globalizing" measures. Walton and Seddon (1994: 5) comment:

> recent growth of popular struggles and protest [is] a distinctive political development of the past two decades, involving an exceptionally wide range of social forces, both responding to, and itself shaping, the process of structural adjustment that has accompanied a global crisis.

They note almost 150 events between 1976 and 1992, since when there have been many further protests (Walton and Seddon, 1994: 39-40). Some of these struggles have moved beyond the specific focus of austerity to pose a serious challenge to local regimes and even to regional power arrangements. They are not a product of "globality," nor a novel development, there being other periods of mass activity corresponding to crisis within the world system, as during the First World War and in the 1930s. These movements are striking, however. Almost no part of the world has been untouched: a testimony to the systematic character of the neo-liberal offensive and to both the desperation and vigor of hundreds of millions of people.

By the 1980s mass protests against "adjustment" or "stabilization" programs had become so general that they were routinely
referred to as "IMF riots." The first such protests were in Peru and
Egypt in the mid-1970s. The Egyptian case is especially important,
representing an "ideal type," aspects of which have been manifested
in many subsequent events. Egypt was the first of the developing
states to opt for a policy of radical liberalization: Sadat's *infitah*
("opening"). The turn from statist development to an embrace of the
open market had already been a factor in stimulating a host of
strikes and demonstrations when, in 1976, the Sadat regime reached
what it called "full understanding with the IMF and the World
Bank" (Hirst and Beeson, 1981: 237). In January 1977, in line with an
IMF plan for reducing state expenditure (setting a "realistic"
exchange rate and tightening control of credit and consumption) the
government cut overnight the subsidies on bread and other staple
foods. The outcome was the biggest national movement for 60 years,
an uprising which required both army intervention and reinstate-
ment of subsidies to save the regime (Hirst and Beeson, 1981). The
movement was notable for its speed of development, its scale, for the
energies of the participants, and the wide range of parties, currents
and communities involved. There has been a host of similar protests
across the Middle East – in Morocco, Tunisia, Sudan, Turkey,
Algeria, Jordan and Lebanon. In Tunis in January 1984, I witnessed
vast demonstrations by protesters described locally as *les insurges de
la faim*. In strikes and street mobilizations against reduced subsidies,
protesters made the *baguette* a symbol of their hostility to the government and to the IMF. As in Egypt, price increases and reductions
in subsidies were rescinded. A few days later a mass protest against
the IMF in Morocco (apparently stimulated in part by the Tunisian
events) achieved a similar outcome. In March the following year,
demonstrators in Sudan protested against increases in prices with
the slogans: "We will not be ruled by the World Bank, we will not be
ruled by the IMF." The following month women marched to declare:
"Down, down with the IMF" and vast crowds attacked the Nimeiri
regime, the United States and international agencies, shouting: "We
say no to World Bank policies" (Seddon, 1989: 120 -123). This pattern
of events was later repeated in Algeria, Lebanon and Jordan (twice).

Seddon has examined the response of free-market ideologues to
these protests. Of the Tunisian events he notes that the *Financial
Times* – "which reflects an economic philosophy close to that of the
IMF" – blamed the government for mismanaging cuts in subsidies:

*"In its view, it was not the removal of subsidies that was at fault, but
the suddenness and size of the increases in prices of basic goods, and
failure to consider seriously the social and political implications. It
argued that "neither the IMF nor the World Bank advocated, or would
have advocated, the approach to subsidies adopted by the Tunisian
government . . ." (Seddon, 1989: 130)*

In fact, suggests Seddon, the IMF and the World Bank put pressure on numerous Third World countries to adopt austerity measures immediately "and with little heed for the social, and even political implications" (1989: 130). They had full knowledge of the likely
consequences, but insisted on implementation without delay. The
popular reaction was simply dismissed, the human factor having
long been written out of neo-liberal calculations.

The destabilizing impact of mass protests has not changed the
agenda for the IMF or the World Bank. During the 1990s there has
been a series of similar demonstrations in sub-Saharan Africa, where
living standards have declined precipitously to levels well below
those in the Middle East. The threat to hundreds of millions of people from adjustment programs has increased throughout the decade
as the continent has slipped towards systemic crisis, what the UN
Secretary-General has called "an unrelenting crisis of tragic proportions" (Sandbrook, 1995: 5). In the most recent episode, in Zimbabwe
in May 1998, pressure from the World Bank and the IMF led the
Mugabe government to increase costs of the main staple, maize, by
24 per cent (*The Guardian*, 6 May 1998). Zimbabwe had already witnessed several years of turmoil, largely as a result of a collapse in
prices of its main export commodities, the deficit in productive
investment, and the eagerness of speculators to profit from
increased weakness of the local currency. Trans-national agencies
nonetheless pursued the liberalization dogma in efforts to bring
Zimbabwe "into line," for, as George and Sabelli comment, global
discipline must be affirmed "in the teeth of all the evidence" and
notwithstanding life-threatening consequences for millions of people (1994: 72). As if to a script, troops and police confronted demonstrators for whom the increases meant a new threat to survival.

Discourse of globalism

There is no positive outcome for the mass of local populations
from IMF/World Bank imposition of "market discipline" upon such
states. For many years the sole beneficiaries have been among the
local ruling class – a fraction of society – together with some Western

investors, and banks and creditor governments seeking interest on old debts which have themselves crippled such economies and will continue to inhibit recovery. "IMF riots" have been an amber light for trans-national institutions, a warning of the cost of neo-liberal policies, but one entirely ignored by such bodies, for which they are merely a spasm, an irrational response to world developments that have their own logic. As one observer of World Bank policies in Zimbabwe has commented, the institution's policies only make sense in terms of its overall intention to promote the construction of "a single world market, substantially on the basis of the present world division of labor." He adds that this project is justified "through an ideology that is claimed to be a value-free science" (George and Sabelli, 1994: 62).

The comment is entirely appropriate: in the 1980s and 1990s the "science" of the marketplace has gone by the name of "globalization." As an ideology of change it has instructed the mass of the world's population that all must adhere to universal principles – a world-embracing vision promoted with such zeal that George and Sabelli (1994: 72) describe it as "a religious Utopia." They observe:

> The salvation of the people and the nations shall come about through binding them ever more tightly to the international market, equated with the world community. There the poor shall partake of the same substance as the rich. Like any universal truth, adjustment is a purely abstract notion even if its application causes concrete pain. The available choices are reduced to one. There Is No Alternative; we are all bound by a single, compulsory truth which shall be recognized. Then shall the wayward nations be freed from their errors. (1994: 72)

Among all manner of popular struggles worldwide, mobilizations against adjustment programs are particularly important, for they spell out that vast numbers of people find themselves constrained to intervene against such policies. Acting in a collective interest, they *do* challenge the market – but architects of the neo-liberal program cannot accept that the market-led vision of change is false, that developments associated with "globalization" do not deliver even modest economic and social advance for the majority of people. Instead, the vision of globalism continues to shape strategies which stimulate economic failure, immiseration, crisis and collapse. Meanwhile, the consequences of neo-liberal intervention become ever more serious. In May 1998, the IMF insisted that the Indonesian government remove subsidies on electricity and fuel, stimulating huge protests and strikes that soon spread across the archipelago.

Fermont (1998: 17) comments that, "It was the beginning of the end for Suharto" – the start of a movement which has profoundly affected one of the world's most populous states and which may have implications for the whole of South-East Asia.

The Indonesian case points up the significance of counter-austerity movements, which often take on much wider political agendas. One analyst of international economic affairs recently commented that "a telling symbol" of world change was the sight of unemployed workers reclaiming one of former President Suharto's golf courses – "in order to grow food for survival" (William Keegan, *The Observer*, 15 November 1998). Are such people – and the protesters of Egypt, Tunisia, Zimbabwe and scores of other states – perverse, or, as in some globalist accounts, are they engaging merely in "anti-global gestures," encapsulated within a discourse shaped by forces above and beyond their influence? Neither interpretation is appropriate. It is ideologues of globalism who remain within a "discourse" which inhibits apprehension of world affairs and which has influenced even some critics of the world system to accept its terms of reference. It is very likely that further mass movements will emerge, challenging the agenda of trans-national institutions and dominant states, together with the notion that the "juggernaut" of capital flows renders them helpless. To paraphrase Shaw, it is not the whole body of contemporary social theory that needs to be reassessed, but the notion of a globalized entity in which our fate is to be shaped by logics of the market.

References

Axford, B. 1995. *The Global System*, Cambridge: Polity.

Beeson, I. & Hirst, B. 1981. *Sadat*, London: Faber.

Caulfield. C. 1998. *Masters of Illusion: The World Bank and the Poverty of Nations*, London: Pan.

Cerny, P. 1993. *The Politics of International Finance*, Oxford: Oxford UP.

Economist, *The World in 1998*.

Fermont, C. 1998. "Indonesia: The Inferno of Revolution," *International Socialism* NS, No. 80.

FitzGerald, N. 1997 "Harnessing the Potential of Globalization for the Consumer and Citizen," *International Affairs*, Vol. 73, No. 4.

George, S. & Sabelli, F. 1994. *Faith and Credit*, London: Penguin.

Gray, J. 1998. *False Dawn*, London: Granta.

Held, D., with D. Goldblatt, A. McGrew, J. Jerraton, 1997. "The Globalization of Economic Activity," *New Political Economy*, Vol. 2, No. 2.

Hirst, P. & Thompson, G. 1996. *Globalization in Question*, Cambridge: Polity.

Hoogvelt, A. 1997. *Globalisation and the Post-Colonial World*, Basingstoke: Macmillan.

Kegley, C. & Wittkopf, E. 1995. *World Politics*, New York: St Martins.

Kiely, R. 1998. "Globalization, Post-Fordism and the Contemporary Context of Development," *International Sociology*, Vol. 13, No. 1.

Marfleet, P. 1998. "Globalisation and Religious Activism," in Kiely, R. and Marfleet, P. (eds.), *Globalisation and the Third World*, London: Routledge.

Marx, K. no date. "The Future Results of the British Rule in India," in K. Marx, *On Colonialism*. Moscow: Foreign Languages Publishing House.

Milward, A. 1992. *The European Rescue of the Nation State*, London: Routledge.

Ohmae, K. 1990. *Borderless World*, London: Collins.

Ohmae, K. 1993. "The Rise of the Region-state," *Foreign Affairs*, Vol. 72, No. 3

Robertson, R. 1992. *Global Culture*, London: Sage.

Robinson, W. I. 1996. "Globalisation: Nine Theses for our Epoch," *Race and Class*, Vol. 38, No. 2.

Ruigrok, W. & Van Tulder, R. 1995. *The Logic of International Restructuring*, London: Routledge.

Sandbrook, R. 1993. *The Politics of Africa's Economic Recovery*, Cambridge: Cambridge UP.

Seddon, D. 1989. "Riot and Rebellion in North Africa: Political Responses to Economic Crisis in Tunisia, Morocco and Sudan," in Berberoglu, B. (ed.), *Power and Stability in the Middle East*, London: Zed.

Shaw, M. 1994. *Global Society and International Relations*, Cambridge: Polity.

Sivanadan, A. 1997. "Capitalism, Globalization, and Epochal Shifts: An Exchange," *Monthly Review*, February 1997.

Spybey. T. 1996. *Globalization and World Society*, Cambridge: Polity.

Stopford, S. & Strange, S. 1991. *Rival States, Rival Firms*, Oxford: Oxford UP.

Turner, B. 1994. *Orientalism, Postmodernism and Globalism*, London: Routledge.

UNDP. 1997. *Human Development Report 1997*, New York: Oxford UP.

UNDP. 1998. *Human Development Report 1998*, New York: Oxford UP.

Walton, J. & Seddon, D. 1994. *Free Markets and Food Riots*, Oxford: Blackwell.

Waters, M. 1995. *Globalization*, London: Routledge.

World Bank, 1990. *World Development Report 1990*, New York: Oxford UP.

World Bank, 1997. *Global Economic Prospects and the Developing Countries,* Washington: Oxford UP.

Regional Responses

Developmental Stalemate in the Eastern Mediterranean: Some Conceptual Tools for the Understanding of Contemporary Problems

Ivan Ivekovic

Conventional social sciences of both Weberian and Marxian inspiration assumed that the processes of modernization, urbanization, mass education and intensified social communication would gradually standardize the world population, leading to the lessening of social and cultural differences. Contrary to such expectations, it seems that on the eve of the 21st century ethnic and religious conflicts multiplied. Recent wars in the space of former Yugoslavia, in the Caucasus, communal violence in the Indian sub-continent, internal troubles in Turkey, Algeria, etc., seem to confirm such a diagnosis. Could it be that there are some common causes that actually generate them?

Trying to answer this question, the assumption of this chapter is that development is a disruptive process and that it affects in various ways even the most isolated and remote communities. Old social institutions, habits and ways of life related to traditional agrarian communities are being undermined or change beyond recognition, while new institutions and norms of conduct are being shaped under the impact of hectic and uneven modernization, but are still not consolidated and generally accepted. Disruption, whether it comes from outside or from within the community, exercises pressure and pressure provokes resistance. Pressure and resistance lead to tension, which may escalate into political violence.

Without pretending to give a comprehensive answer, this chapter offers some conceptual tools which, in my belief, could be used for the explanation of contemporary problems. The chapter is divided into three sections: (I) it briefly discusses the long-term historical trajectory of human society; (II) it introduces the geopolitical concept of regional laboratory, describing in the same time the role of regional client-states and pivots; (III) it explains the process of transition to mass industrial society as a three-stage process.

I. The long-term historical trajectory

Braudel's (1980) *long term trajectory of humankind* may be reduced to the process of growth, geographic expansion and maturing of stationary agrarian or pastoral communities, and of their subsequent transition to mass and mobile industrial society. This overlaps the process of transition from use-value to commodity production. The transition to mass industrial society is in fact the latest sequence of this long-term historical trajectory.

The process itself was initiated with the Agricultural Revolution some 10 000 years ago when foraging (food-gathering, hunting and fishing) began to be replaced with systematic plant cultivation and animal breeding. Archeological evidence confirms that this revolution originated in the Middle East and then spread to the Mediterranean basin, to the regions north of the Black Sea and finally rolled over Europe. Systematic planting allowed an increase in population density and it was hypothesized that demographic growth stimulated in its turn the "wave-of-advance" or the geographic expansion and consolidation of peasant communities, which at that time used a primitive slash-and-burn technique. Humans discovered that with their labor, they could improve their condition. Prior to this discovery, the creature which was to become a human being only through labor found in nature goods of a *use-value* for his survival, like the rest of the animal world. Labor itself arose from the scarcity of the means necessary for human survival. Yet the value of a good produced did not arise out of this scarcity, but out of labor. Labor molded man's consciousness and made out of him a human being. Labor also created all the goods needed by humankind for its existence. As explained by one researcher:

> With his labor, man started taking from nature even those goods which previously had been inaccessible to him. Thus he began taking control of the laws of his own reproduction, making his survival dependent on the quantity of foodstuffs that he could produce with his own labor. Man had no need to create those goods which were available in nature; he worked only to acquire those which he lacked, which he needed for his survival and which were scarce. In this respect nothing has changed to the present day.

> Millennia had to [pass] before production began, before the existing world system of commodity production came into being. Yet all the goods in nature have retained unchanged their form of <u>use-value</u>. They remain so until such time as man with his labor transforms them into a <u>commodity value</u>, i.e. until he takes them to the market for the

purpose of trading, when they become commodities. (Dakovic, 1994: 5)

The man in question was, of course, a peasant and he lived in scattered and mutually isolated agrarian communities. The subsequent development, expansion and maturing of these communities, their political organization, their continuous transformation and interaction represents the long-term historical trajectory of humankind. This strikingly simple statement requires a re-reading of history. This chapter is, however, focused on the last sequence of this trajectory, when industrialization linked to the capitalist mode of appropriation/production was initiated, leading to the emergence and consolidation of the modern nation-state.

The switch to merchant agriculture, producing food for the increased urban population in Europe and raw materials for European nascent industries, announced the beginning of this uneven and hectic sequence of transition to mass commodity production, as well as the beginning of the capitalist integration of the world economy. Capitalist relations gradually spread from Europe into peripheral and less developed zones through direct colonization or, as was the case of the Ottoman Empire, Persia, China or Latin America, through the imposition of free trade. By the end of the 19th century most of the globe was already drawn into the orbit of this whirlpool.

This process is today called globalization, or, to be more accurate, globalization seems to be the highest stage of the capitalist integration of the world economy linked to trans-national capital. Globalization has recently speeded up the process of regional and local political fragmentation, including the fragmentation of the Middle East, which for the last 40 years was masked with Cold War confrontations. It seems that economic integration on one side and political volatility on the other are integral parts of the same dialectical process of modernization. Of course, such a hypothesis has to be documented or refuted in each specific *regional laboratory*. The Eastern Mediterranean is only one of them.

Each step forward in the capitalist integration of the world economy required the readjustment of the domestic *productive forces* (PF), of the related *social structure of accumulation* (SSA) to both internal and international change. The above concepts will be elaborated in the next section. This process of transition is proceeded by *stages or sequences of socio-economic, political and technological development*. The transition from one stage to another invariably leads to destruction in order that a new SSA at the domestic level could be constructed and a new articulation established between the national and international levels.

Destruction of social institutions and relationships that had up to that moment governed the life of social communities may lead to their fragmentation, i.e., to their internal social polarization and break up. Pressured from within and outside, the threatened communities usually crack along their internal fault lines (ethnic, religious or class), which may be reinforced if some of these fault lines overlap. If institutional channels for peaceful conflict resolution do not exist or can not be found, or if the confronted parties and their political elites are unable or unwilling to compromise, then the clash of mutually confronted exclusive interests becomes inevitable. It will take a particularly violent form if the community in question or confronted groups still have one foot in their agrarian past and another in an uncertain future already affected by modernization.

At this stage the perceived scarcity of resources, especially a worsened land-to-labor ratio, may aggravate the clash of interests and the competition for the appropriation of these resources both between rival political elites and between the communities they represent and/or manipulate (especially in countries with a sizeable rural population). A short survey of conflict-zones will indeed show that contemporary political conflicts are the most acute in regions of peasant overpopulation and of surplus manpower which was not absorbed by the modern sector of the economy. The related and unresolved Peasant Question generates in turn violent *patriarchal reactions or neo-patriarchal convulsions* (Ivekovic, 1996) which are characteristic of threatened agrarian communities. For this reason perhaps current conflicts and political violence took such a violent and bloody turn in some countries and not in others. That is the second hypothesis of this chapter.

Although presenting themselves and seen by many analysts as ethnic, racial, communal or religious conflicts, all of them have underlying material causes. The clash of material interests may result in developmental violence, whose aim is the control of natural and human resources linked to specific territories, and the appropriation of the products of other people's labor. In some countries such conflicts erupted over the appropriation of foreign aid. Developmental violence is then justified/explained by political elites with different ideologies, or with contradictory national interests (Morgenthau, 1952: 961), with allegedly opposed political cultures (Almond and Powell, 1988: 40-46), with the clash of civilizations (Huntington, 1993) or with mutually exclusive ethnic, racial, communal or religious identities. Such explanations most of the time ignore the fact that these collective identities are not God-given or genetically reproduced, but are politically constructed and reconstructed as *imagined political communities* (Anderson, 1983) out of pre-existing human material. The modern nation state is such a historically-derived political artifact. Rejecting the idea that such communities are static and immutable, and adopting a constructivist approach, this chapter, nevertheless, could not avoid such terms as ethnic conflict and Islamist neo-populism because they entered political jargon and are succinct. However, I argue in this chapter that the phenomena in question have nothing to do with ethnicity or religion *per se*, that both are produced and manipulated by elites in order to serve their exclusive political projects.

In the following pages some of the above ideas will be elaborated in more detail in order to demonstrate that most contemporary conflicts – internal, regional or international, whatever descriptive prefix may be attached to them – can be reduced to their developmental dimension.

II. The regional laboratory of the Middle East & North Africa

Interconnected vessels

The concept of regional laboratories is essentially a geopolitical model, wrapping together a moving configuration of forces, both internal and external, with certain enduring constraints and/or comparative advantages of physical space, with its natural and human resources. It is a spatial framework for the analysis of specific clusters of countries which share certain common characteristics. The Middle East, together with North Africa, may be considered such a regional laboratory. The Balkans, next door, is another one. The Soviet successor states of Transcaucasia and Central Asia constitute today a new laboratory, which for the first time in modern history separates Russia from the Middle East. The Vishegrad Group (Poland, the Czech Republic, Hungary and Slovakia) is still another cluster of countries from which most of the candidates for membership in the European Union and NATO had been selected. The three Baltic states, Lithuania, Latvia and Estonia, represent a similar cluster. Russia itself, with all the uncertainties it is facing, is yet another huge laboratory stretched over 11 time zones.

These overlapping regional laboratories are in fact links of one chain, whose pulsating and overlapping boundaries are set by changing configurations of forces and political conventions. These conventions usually take into account some distinctive sets of the physical space, which are then supplanted with human geography and economic considerations. The laboratories themselves seem to operate as interconnected vessels, because internal developments in one often spill over imagined boundaries, directly influencing developments in the more or less distant neighborhood. Sometimes, as is the case with ethnic and regional conflicts in the former Yugoslavia and in the Caucasus region, these developments take strikingly similar forms, which Rosenau (1995) described as distant proximities.

However, these laboratories are not politically, economically or culturally homogenized entities. Even the laboratory of Western Europe, with its unfolding agenda of economic and political integration, is far from being a homogeneous whole. Besides the Ulster, Basque, Corsican and Padanian problems, the very term of "Europe of regions" suggests that the project of European unification is not seeking to eliminate internal diversity. Diversity in itself, whether cultural, social or political, is not necessarily disruptive if a basic consensus holding together a community or a group is maintained.

In the countries of the Eastern Mediterranean, such a consensus never existed in modern times. Not only did different states pursue different, often mutually opposed, political agendas associated with different external powers, but the internal consensus was usually missing in spite of all the efforts of the modernizing state to standardize its population. The Cold War masked these regional and domestic fault-lines until recently, but now it has become evident that they were not generated by exogenous forces only.

Asymmetrical clients and regional pivots

The post-Cold War system of states is hierarchical and may be represented as a step-pyramid in whose structure different states occupy different moving positions. The relative position of each state depends primarily on the level of development of its productive forces, of its technological potentials and of its place in the global division of labor. Military force, unrelated to industrial power, is of secondary importance. The bottom of the pyramid is crowded with weak and small client-states, the modernization process of which has been retarded, but which aspire to improve their precarious position. They will be upgraded only when their productive forces have been re-arranged in the manner that suits the requirements of the global liberal system. Only then they may be co-opted into the EU, but even then non-economic criteria (geopolitical or ideological considerations) may prevail and postpone their co-optation.

Theories of interdependence, as elaborated by Keohane and Nye (1977), even when they point to the unequal cost of inter-state transactions and elaborate the shifts of power in the international system of nation-states, are perhaps able to explain the complex relationships which are established between Western liberal economies, but are hopelessly useless when they have to deal with peripheral or semi-peripheral countries whose national economies are not yet fully integrated into the global system. To put it differently, they may eventually explain the actual international position and the dominant role of the US and describe the nature of its relationship with major Western partners and allies, and even with such small countries as Luxembourg or Singapore, but the voices become elusive and conspicuously silent the moment they have to define the new role of Second and Third World countries in the emerging international liberal order (or disorder). They are written from the perspective of American hegemony and directly or indirectly justify this hegemony, ignoring the other side of the same international equation. What is the position and role of countries such as the FR of Yugoslavia (Serbia/Montenegro), Croatia or Bosnia and Herzegovina? Is the latter an independent country or a mandated territory of the UN/NATO and how much is the Milosevic government really an independent international actor? All three of them are clearly dependent on the wills and whims of the international community and, as we have seen in Dayton and later in Paris, they behaved, at least in this phase of the conflict resolution process, like classical client-states. Even Russia itself, which was given a decorative role in the international Contact Group for former Yugoslavia, had ultimately no other alternative than to acquiesce to what others had decided.

The same description may be applied to the Soviet successor states in Transcaucasia and Central Asia, as well as to the states included in the laboratory of the Middle East and North Africa. What is, for instance, the maneuvering space left to rogue states such as Iraq or Libya?

Trying to answer such questions and not finding more adequate concepts, I re-introduced the old term of client-states, meaning that the international autonomy of most of these countries is objectively limited and that they are forced to behave in the international arena, at least when it comes to options which have a wider geopolitical significance, as clients to powerful patrons. Nevertheless, Milosevic's Yugoslavia, Saddam Hussein's Iraq and Gaddafi's Libya, to mention only these three, are at the same time asymmetrical (Cohen, 1984). Indeed, they do not abide by norms of civilized behavior both internationally and internally. They have two dimensions: externally – they are weak and vulnerable; internally and towards their own subjects – they are repressive and "strong" in spite of the weak level of social legitimacy of their respective governments. Nevertheless, such typical asymmetrical and rogue states are often compelled to play international roles which fit into regional grand scenarios written by more powerful external actors. Indeed, the wars waged by rump-Yugoslavia (Serbia and Montenegro) in Croatia, Bosnia and Herzegovina, and recently in Kosovo, permitted the American administration to reassert its leading position in post-Cold War European affairs, to redefine the role of NATO and proceed with its eastward expansion. The co-optation of new members into the European Union has additionally postponed the project of European unification well into the next century.

Similarly, Iraq's invasion of Kuwait provided the United States with the opportunity to impose itself as the only power-broker in the Middle East and to unilaterally decide which one of the local states will be contained or promoted into pivots. According to Robert Chase and collaborators (1996: 33-51), besides Israel, Turkey and Egypt play such pivotal roles in Washington's Post-Cold War Middle Eastern strategy. Such states are allowed a larger maneuvering space within the region in which they are situated because of their unique geopolitical location and specific weight. To differentiate them from ordinary clients, they are not compelled to support fully all the moves of US foreign policy. If I understood correctly the above cited article, they are given (or won) a certain degree of tactical autonomy in the overall interest of US regional strategy. They are asymmetrical pivots, enjoying a special relationship with Washington, which tolerates their occasional escapades. In that sense, they are in a much better position than the asymmetrical client-states described previously.

III. The transition to mass industrial society

Two inter-linked levels of conceptualization of this scaffold are particularly important: the first is primarily related to internal economic and technological developments, shortly to modernization; the second belongs more properly to the political economy of contemporary international relations.

Some navigational tools

Although other variables play important roles, the level of modernization of each country is essentially the outcome of the maturing of its *productive forces* (PF). These are composed of two elements: (1) the subjective one, consisting of human labor, skills, knowledge, innovation, working habits and organization; (2) the material component, consisting of available tools, machinery, physical and chemical ingredients, and processed raw materials. The performances of the hardware, tools and machinery depend, of course, on the subjective factor, while scientific and technological know-how, which is also the product of human labor, is a basic indicator of the *technological age* achieved by a given community/society. To simplify, I divided the last time-sequence of modernization – which corresponds to the capitalist stage of development on the world scale, to the transition from manufacture to industry and to the emergence of the modern nation-state – into three tiers. Each one of the *consecutive stages of modernization* is characterized by a specific level of development of domestic PF, the related *social structure of accumulation* (SSA) and a specific articulation of modes of production established both at the domestic level, and in-between the domestic and international levels.

Important for the framework adopted in this analysis is the concept of SSA as elaborated by Gordon (1978 and 1980), and Gordon, Edwards and Reich (1982), which insists on the crucial role of institutions which hold together a system. A system, as Maurice Godelier (1978: 56) underlined back in the 1960s, is a group of structures inter-linked by certain rules both at the domestic and international levels. Rules are explicit principles whereby all elements of a system are combined and related, the norms intentionally created and applied in order to organize social life. My addition to Gordon and his collaborators is that structures are made up of institutions and that these institutions are not only economic, but also political, social and cultural. Furthermore, they must be adapted or they have to adapt themselves constantly to changes and innovations. In spite of cyclical and other crises, capitalism has up to now certainly demonstrated a high level of adaptability to new circumstances. State-command economies have not.

Overlapping the transition from agrarian communities to mass industrial society is the transition from natural (use-value) to market (commodity) economy. True, different agrarian communities have exchanged commodities since they were able to produce a surplus above the minimum necessary for their simple reproduction. Since that time marketplaces have existed. Initially occasional and very modest, they gradually expanded, gaining in importance, including in their orbit more and more people, social groups and communities. In spite of this gradual generalization of commodity production, agrarian communities continued to produce use-values not only for their simple but also for their expanded reproduction. They were, nevertheless, adversely affected. In many developing countries, the massive switch to cash crop production resulted in acute shortages of food stuffs and had/has dramatic, even tragic, social effects. It destroyed many previously self-sufficient communities, as illustrated by the example of some hunting communities in Africa, which are presently directly threatened by commercial poaching. Although not completely eliminated as a survival strategy, natural economy was increasingly displaced by commodity production and it seems that it is an irreversible process. However, each time peasant communities were threatened in their very existence because of wars and general disruption of the commodity market, they had the tendency to retreat into subsistence agriculture and informal economy.

Thwarted modernization

The stage of modernization 1 was introduced in Europe by the formally independent nation state and in most of the underdeveloped periphery by the colonial state. It had to solve a number of specific problems linked to the initial accumulation of capital such as: the establishment of a modern bureaucracy and state; the consolidation of individual property; the introduction of standard laws and institutions which can correspond with the exterior world; the standardization of the population; the monetization of the economy. In many independent countries land reform was introduced during this stage of development. This stage was not usually associated with civil liberties or labor protection; on the contrary.

A number of problems continue to burden most of today's underdeveloped countries which entered the stage of modernization 1: the inefficiency of the state and non-consolidated institutions of the legal system; a non-standardized population; a non-integrated domestic market (while their export sector is well integrated into the international division of labor); the constant reproduction of natural economy (self-consumption) and the important share of petty-commodity (non-industrial) production; initial industrial development which cannot cope with the current demographic explosion; the worsening of conditions in the traditional sector of agriculture in which the majority of the population is involved (the land to labor ratio); importance of the informal economy.

All this reproduces distorted development whose main characteristics are: uneven development of different production sectors; a perverted class pyramid with extreme social polarization; non-consolidated institutions of the modern nation-state; a resisting civil society opposing the modernizing state. Distorted development itself became the main obstacle for the smooth transition from modernization 1 to 2.

Modernization 2 is a higher stage of development through which passed practically all the countries which are presently highly industrialized. This stage was initially associated with the protectionist state and was the direct outcome of state-promoted mercantilist policies, the main goal of which was to assure the growth of domestic PF and to lay down the basis for accelerated industrialization. Mercantilism was the dominant economic doctrine of 19th century continental Europe. During the Depression of the 1930s, it took the form of import-substitution industrialization. The state-command economy that was introduced in the USSR in 1929 was one of the variations of this model of development from above which was copied after the Second World War by all Communist-controlled states. Another variation was the Kemalist model of development from above which was introduced in Turkey at the same time and which was later copied by nationalist/populist governments issued from the process of decolonization. Both of them were authoritarian, directly suppressed civil society, and curtailed civic and political rights. In their essence, whatever their ideological rationalization, they were economically autarchic, guided by the idea that economic self-sufficiency and self-reliance were the pre-condition for true national independence and prosperity. They used state power in order to promote accelerated modernization, or what is called self-centered development, based on industrialization. Nevertheless, not a single one of these models of development from above succeeded in de-linking from the emerging global (capitalist) system. The so-called world socialist system promoted in the USSR, southeast Europe or China never became a feasible alternative; rather, it remained an underdeveloped appendix to the existing global system.

Paradoxically perhaps, Leninism-Stalinism and similar models had laid down the basis for capitalist development, not for socialism. Indeed, it seems that there is no such thing as a socialist path to socialism (Leftwitch, 1995).

There is also no way to promote the quantitative and qualitative growth of productive forces of any contemporary society by circumventing industrialization. Industrialization is inseparable from technological innovation (see the second part of this section). Each innovation in its turn creates problems of adaptation of the SSA.

Meanwhile, core countries of the existing world system had reached the stage of modernization 3, which corresponds to the age of electronics/information technologies/biotechnology (see later) and is associated with trans-national capital. In fact, national markets, even of large industrial countries, including the United States, became too narrow for their productive forces, which have now reached such a level of technological development and such outputs that new investments require global market outlets. Business strategist Kenichi Ohmae (1985) argued that the accelerating tempo of technological change meant that the largest corporations now needed to have access to markets of 600 million or more people in order to survive. Thus, they had to break the fences of closed national markets and begin to operate at the global scale, going trans-national. They found out, however, that the protectionist policies of a number of states, still embattled with modernization 2, were blocking their globalization. Nevertheless, they were to a large extent successful and now the ongoing globalization is affecting all countries, irrespective of their level of modernization.

I am aware of the academic debate surrounding such vague concepts elaborated originally as complex interdependence (Keohane and Nye, 1977: 24-29) and translated more recently as globalization (for a comprehensive review of the debate, see Jones, 1995). The first elaboration, obviously written from the point of view of US economic and military supremacy, is little concerned with the fact that most weaker economies and countries are clearly in a position, not only of dependence but of outright submission (remember the dependency theories?). The more neutral term of globalization, which originated from the same perspective, seems more acceptable because it does not *a priori* exclude negative implications. Rejecting for my part the holistic interpretation of the term, I had, nevertheless, no alternative but to use it, defining it as the multiplicity of linkages and interconnections between states, economies, polities, societies and cultures which make up the modern world framework, but it is a historically-evolved, permanently constructed/reconstructed and dialectical process which gained a new momentum only more recently in association with modernization 3.

Globalization proceeds unevenly, productive sector by sector, and not country by country. Different geographical zones, clusters of countries, individual countries and regions are drawn into the orbit of modernization 2 and 3 in different ways, at different times and paces. Each one of them occupies a specific moving position on the imaginary overall scale of modernization. Or, to say the same thing differently – the articulation which is established between the dominant mode of production (capitalist matrix related to modernization 3) and the subservient ones (related to modernization 1 and 2) is in constant evolution and may vary, both regionally, from country to country, and across economic sectors. The inclusion of a specific country into the orbit of modernization 1 (colonial conquest, for example) has usually been a dramatic political and social process for the native population (resistance to pacification and the related destruction or subjugation of the traditional economy and way of life). Similarly, the advent of modernization 2 world-wide, as well as the related re-adjustment of the relationships between the core and periphery, has been marked by major social disturbances and political upheavals (world wars, anti-colonial revolutions, civil wars, *putsches*).

In Eastern European countries and in the Soviet Union, where the modernization process was always one or two steps behind the industrialized West, the internal transition from modernization 1 to 2, which is always painful, was more recently affected by global trends linked to modernization 3. We know the result: the state-command system, which internally more or less efficiently managed the process of modernization 1, proved incapable of adapting itself further due to the lack of dynamism, general rigidity and impotence of its *ruling nomenklatura*. It proved unable to build up a new and adequate SSA which would contain qualitatively buttressed productive forces that already corresponded to modernization 3. It collapsed, opening the way to anti- and post-Communist counter-elites who promised a utopian capitalist future, which they are for the time being unable to deliver.

Dealing in such a way with the transition from agrarian to industrial society, I intended to avoid world system simplification, which represents another abstraction because the world capitalist system is not a comprehensive and homogeneous whole as these theories purport. As the recent economic crisis in Asia and Russia has shown, mechanisms of unequal exchange between core, semi-periphery and periphery do not operate as automatically through self-regulating markets as was often presented. The actual global system is subdivided into imperfectly connected sub-systems and into productive sub-sectors whose mutual relations evolve with the development of new productive forces. Some sub-systems, also called international regimes, function better than others and are maintained by international treaties and institutions, supported, of course, with the economic leverage of industrially-advanced countries and by trans-national capital.

The "to be or not to be" question for peripheral countries today is no more how to break the bonds with the world capitalist system or to de-link, which proved to be an inoperative strategy, but rather how to insert themselves as advantageously as possible into the existing international division of labor. However, the countries which had not succeeded in absorbing modernization 1 successfully and in creating a favorable environment for the growth of their domestic productive forces (including a technological basis) have no chance. They will be subjected to the process of globalization, but on discriminatory terms which are likely to reproduce the "development of underdevelopment" (Frank, 1960). In short, I argue that most of the Third World countries are today either unable to solve the problems of modernization 1 or trapped in the process of transition from modernization 1 to 2. That is for the time being also the case of ex-Communist countries.

Technological ages and innovation

The stage of modernization 1 was announced by the introduction of machines. Their subsequent rapid proliferation soon began to undermine not only the mode of production of traditional agrarian communities, but also to erode their social tissue and pre-existing relationships. The machine is more than a complex tool invented by man, because it carries out certain tasks that living labor cannot perform. Besides, the machine can produce other machines. Their introduction marked the beginning of mass production displacing petty commodity production, as well as unskilled and artisan's labor. It had, however, less success in displacing the subsistence and informal economies which both found their niches as survival strategies of the poor. Once human know-how/labor invested into the machine has been paid back (constant capital) the machine continues to produce gratuitously new values, although, quite paradoxically, the prices of its products are not always decreasing. This surplus output of the machine has not only presented its owner with opportunities for earning additional profit, but has depreciated human labor, exerting a continuous pressure on wages. The owner of the machine thus gained an unprecedented leverage over the whole process of production and over manpower. On the other hand, the owner of the technological know-how that has produced the machine, and almost all technological innovations originating from and still monopolized by the corporations of highly industrialized countries, gained a powerful pressure tool against those who import and use such a machine, i.e., against technologically less-developed countries.

Physical and skilled workers alike became appendices of the machine, some kind of extension that could be replaced as any other spare part. With the spread of industrialization, there gradually emerged a mass and anonymous industrial society in which standardized workers/individuals, previously personalities in their own right, with their own social statuses and roles, became part of the amorphous mass, a phenomenon which was magisterially described by Ortega y Gasset. As remarked already by Marx, this anonymous and replaceable individual became alienated from his work and from such a society. Alienation creates social frustration, but that is a theme to which I will return in more detail later.

At the same time, technology gained its own momentum, directly dictating the organization of work and tempo of production, the size of the market, as well as shaping social relations. This is important when speaking of "technological ages" (Chirot, 1991), because each one of the levels of technological development requires a re-arrangement of the pre-existing SSA.

Shifts in the composition of the labor force, usually concomitant with technological progress, may become major sources of new social tensions. If these shifts correspond more or less to the ethnic stratification of society, i.e., if certain ethnic groups are over-represented in one category or another, then such disparities may generate conflict. The emphasis on rationality and productivity inevitably leads to the introduction of wage-incentives, rewarding skilled workers (managers, engineers, specialists and technicians), provoking on the other side an "egalitarian" reaction of less-favored labor groups, which with their philosophy of equal "bellies" attempted to block technological modernization and economic reforms. All over the Soviet Union and Eastern Europe, the share of manual labor in the final product has dramatically dwindled in the 1980s, creating new disparities within the working class itself, sharpening cleavages between blue and white collar workers.

Chirot's periodogram of technological ages may offer an idea concerning the quality and the level of technological development reached by individual countries. He distinguished: (1) the initial age of cotton-textile industries of the Manchester type that ran roughly between the 1780s and 1830s, opening the way to (2) the age of rail and iron somewhere between 1840 and 1870; then came (3) the age of steel exemplified by the Pittsburgh type of industrialization running between the 1870s and the First World War, opening in its turn the way to (4) the age of automobile and petrochemicals, roughly between 1910 and the 1970s, which no import-substitution model of development or "planned economy" succeeded in mastering fully; (5) finally, while the West and Japan were already well into the age of electronics/information technologies/biotechnology, which was initiated somewhere in the 1970s, state-command and import-substitution economies were still struggling with social and political problems created by the social structure of accumulation related to the Pittsburgh type of industrialization that Chirot described as the most impressive rust belt in the world (Chirot, 1991: 6).

Scientific activities and technological research in less developed countries tend to be a form of consumption rather than investment and the reasons for this lie in their dependence on external sources of know-how and technology, as well as in the structure of underdevelopment itself. Many less developed countries only recently acquired through transfer the technology corresponding to the age of cotton-textile, and are unable for the time-being to produce iron and steel or are making only the first steps in that direction.

Second World countries successfully attained the technological age of steel. By various indices of economic production, human capital or social welfare, several East European countries narrowed the gap or even overtook some Western European countries. Some of them even made significant steps into the age of petrochemicals (but not automobile) but that was the threshold they could not trespass without adapting their SSA both domestically and internationally. Trying to explain "what went wrong" in the economies of these countries, Eric Hobsbawm (1991: 19-20) asserted that they could have survived if these economies were insulated from the rest of the world, which was not the case, and added that they were complete-ly incapable of developing the equivalent of the information society.

Chirot's periodogram is, however, only an abstract model. Certain highly developed countries were practically able to avoid building the technological infrastructure for the production of cer-tain industrial commodities. Switzerland's corporations, for exam-ple, never bothered to build up a relevant automobile industry, but they had the know-how for such a technology. Similarly, there is today an exclusive club of countries which mastered nuclear tech-nology, yet some of them have no intention of building a nuclear bomb. Possessing the nuclear or even cosmic technology, as the Soviet case clearly indicates, is not in itself a sufficient condition for the access to modernization 3. Rather, *general technological maturity*, more evenly distributed among different domestic industrial sec-tors, seems to be one of the crucial pre-conditions for such a promo-tion.

Political fragmentation and the agenda for economic integration

The shaping of segregated ethnic communities, i.e., the emer-gence of ethno-states in the Yugoslav and Caucasian space, was cer-tainly a redefining response to internal and external economic pres-sures of modernization 2. It also represented a response to the pres-sures of productive forces that were bolstered up by the moderniz-ing state. The modest absorption capacity of internal administrative markets limited in the same time industrial output (quantity), while the rigidity of state-regulations did not permit technological innova-tion and the shift to new products (quality). It is quite natural then that the horizontally increased output of the same range of products puts the opening up of previously closed economies to trans-border trade on the political agenda. In other words, as in any modern econ-omy, over-production without innovation became a fetter. However, the products offered to external purchasers had to satisfy required quality-standards at competitive prices, which was not the case with most manufactured goods produced in the European East or in the USSR (except for the Soviet or Czechoslovak military hardware). As the market principle eroded state-command economies, both from inside and outside, and the old system of state-redistribution was collapsing, generating new social differentiation and new conflict of interests in the process, it became important to redefine the role both of the state and of its SSA. The systemic blockade quite naturally put on the political agenda the formation of smaller state-entities which would allow the reorganization of the society's productive forces and of its SSA, and of the re-distributive function of the state, satisfying in the same time the power-ambitions and material appetites of new nationalist elites. Expansionist global markets associated with modernization 3 at the world scale speeded up the process of internal disintegration.

Global economic processes proceed gradually, sector by sector and country by country. Because their capacity for absorption is still relatively limited, they are predisposed to handle smaller and weaker productive units (state entities). Thus political fragmentation on one side became the precondition for the integration of markets on the other side. Both are parts of the same contemporary global mosaic. Or, to put it simply, the political fragmentation of the European East and of the Middle East is only the other facet of the uneven and convulsed process of (West) European integration. Or, to put it still differently, the "resurgence" of ethno-national identities on one side is correlated with the construction of a European supra-national identity on the other side. However, Western Europe itself is not immune to a special kind of fragmentation. The very term "Europe of regions" is self-explanatory: as the process of "supra-national" European integration is gaining momentum – different regional, "sub-national" identities assert themselves, perhaps with more vigor than previously. At the same time, it seems that today's Second and Third World states are reduced to flexible productive units which may be decomposed and recomposed according to the economic necessities of global markets. The decomposition of the Soviet Union, Yugoslavia and Czecho-Slovakia seem to confirm this thesis.

It also seems that there are time-sequences when global economic processes require the establishment of larger territorial states (for example, the constitution of the Ottoman or of the Habsburg states, or the unification of Germany and Italy in the 19th century), followed by periods of political fragmentation (the emergence of nation-states all over Eastern Europe between 1830 and 1918-23), followed by political and economic standardization of larger clusters of countries (the Cold-War division of Europe into two antagonistic power-blocs), replaced again with political fragmentation (Eastern Europe and the Soviet space after the collapse of Communism). The idea is that these remodeled state-entities will fit better into the readjusted international division of labor, which is of course characterized by inequalities. The present inequalities are not only the consequence of self-regulating market mechanisms of "unequal exchange" or of the "accumulation of capital at the world scale," but also of the post-Cold War configuration of forces dominated by the United States.

Globalizing processes which are intentional, and therefore more or less rational human projects, prefer to handle clusters of countries and not single free-lance state-units, although a few "asymmetrical" states are tolerated for special geopolitical reasons (Ivekovic, 1998). The integration of the former German Democratic Republic into the *Bundesrepublik* was unique and so extravagantly costly that it is not likely to be repeated in the foreseeable future. Fragmentation also should be organized, because it is impossible to invent a specific, separate model of integration for each country. Therefore the economic systems of these countries should be standardized first, which is done through international financial institutions and their "structural adjustment programs," and through regional economic-cooperation projects. One such regional project in the fragmented Eastern European space is the Vishegrad Group, which evolved into the Central European Free-Trade Association (CEFTA). These countries form today the *"cordon sanitaire"* bordering the European Union, from which the first candidates for integration into the EU and NATO were selected.

In January 1997 the Clinton administration launched the Southern Eastern Cooperation Initiative (SECI), which covers the Balkan region, the aim of which is to promote economic cooperation among 12 countries: Hungary, Slovenia, Croatia, the FR of Yugoslavia, Bosnia and Herzegovina, Macedonia, Greece, Turkey, Albania, Bulgaria, Romania and Moldova. All these countries, except Croatia, whose authorities fear the "renewal of Yugoslavia," accepted the initiative. Perhaps more important, the Americans succeeded in convincing the West Europeans that Washington's initiative in fact complements future EU projects in the European East. The idea is to facilitate, within this cluster of countries, trade exchange and human communication, the build up of common infrastructure (roads, railways connections, pipe-lines), and standardized custom tariffs and trade legislation, which could lead in the future to the establishment of another free trade zone in southeastern Europe and neutralize potential sources of conflict. The fact that Turkey is included in the SECI illustrates American concerns with the pivotal geopolitical position of this country as a continental link between Europe and the Middle East.

The idea behind the future Middle Eastern and North African Market (MENA), also promoted by the US and EU, is the same. The economies of the countries located in the Eastern Mediterranean have to be gradually standardized, which for the time being seems an impossible task. However, if the ruling elites of the countries situated in this regional laboratory want to promote domestic development, they will, sooner or later, in spite of present political animosities, have to find a common ground for regional cooperation linked to global economic processes.

The agenda in front of Transcaucasia and Central Asia is similar. This regional laboratory is part of the new Russian "Near Abroad" which is presently fragmented into a number of vulnerable small state-entities, nominally independent nation-states, in dispute with each other and torn by internal contradictions or break-away movements. The Russian-dominated Commonwealth of Independent States (CIS), ultimately joined not only by Armenia but by Azerbaijan and Georgia as well, did not succeed to become the structure that would integrate economically, politically or militarily the former Soviet political space. It serves for the time-being only to mask Russian hegemonic projects in the "Near Abroad." The problem is that the Russian Federation itself is economically shattered and politically fragmented. Although Russia remains a regional power, it has been downgraded to the rank of a Third World country (Petras and Vieux, 1995). Its productive forces will need quite a time to regenerate on a new basis and to reach once again the level of modernization 2. If this happens in the future, it can be only in association with global capital markets, not in opposition to them. The Chinese 20-year-long "experiment" with capitalism seems to confirm such a scenario. A radically restructured and re-invigorated economy of Russia along market principles may indeed become a formidable force of regional economic, and then political, integration, but in an uncertain future.

It seems that the above described "balkanization" of the European periphery is an integral part of the dialectical process of global integration/fragmentation, or, to put it simply, that the fragmentation of the European periphery is the other face of the process of Western European integration. If that is the case, then even the apparently irrational destruction of the economic infrastructure and human capital both in the Yugoslav and Transcaucasian spaces has a kind of external rationale. Smaller and weaker state-units, all of them on the waiting list for integration (into EU, WEU and NATO), are likely to be swallowed and digested more easily by the global system than larger and more complex states. If that is so, then the ethno-national exclusiveness (economic nationalism) and the bazaar mentality of peripheral elites (whose members are recruited from the bureaucratic petty bourgeoisie or the former communist *nomenklatura*) may prove to be major obstacles for the integration of these peripheral countries into the mass industrial society of the 21st century. The logic of segregated ethnic development directly contradicts globalization processes.

References

Almond, G.A. & Powell, G.B. 1988. *Comparative Politics Today. A World View.* Glenview, Boston and London: Scott, Foresman and Co.

Anderson, B. 1983. *Imagined Communities: Reflections on the Origin and Spread of Nationalism.* London: Verso Press.

Braudel, F. 1980. *On History.* Chicago: The University of Chicago Press.

Chirot, D. 1991 (ed.). *The Crisis of Leninism and the Decline of the Left.* Seattle: University of Washington Press.

Chase, R., et al. 1996. "Pivotal States and Global Political Equilibrium." *Foreign Affairs* (January-February 1996): 33-51.

Cohen, S.B. 1984. "Asymmetrical States and Global Political Equilibrium." *SAIS Review,* Vol. 4, No. 2 (1984): 193-212.

Dakovic, V. 1994. *Anticapital.* Harare: SAPES Books.

Frank, A.G. 1960. "The Development of the Underdevelopment." *Monthly Review 18,* 14 (September 1960).

Godelier, M. 1978. "The Object and Method of Economic Anthropology." In D. Seddon (ed.). *Relations of Production. Marxists Approaches to Economic Anthropology.* Trans. by H. Lackner. London and Totowa: Macmillan.

Gordon, D. 1978. "Up and Down the Long Coaster." In *US Capitalism in Crisis,* ed. by the Union of Radical Economics. New York: Union of Radical Economics.

Gordon, D. 1980. "Stages of Accumulation and Long Economic Cycles." In T. Hopkins & I. Wallerstein (eds.). *Processes of the World System*. Beverly Hills: Sage Publications.

Gordon D., Edwards, R. & Reich, M. 1982. (eds.). *Segmented Work, Divided Workers*. Cambridge and New York: Cambridge University Press.

Hobsbawm, E. 1991. "What Went Wrong?" *Contention*, No. 1 (Fall 1991).

Huntington, S. 1993. "The Clash of Civilizations." *Foreign Affairs* (Summer 1993).

Ivekovic, I. 1996. *Neo-patriarchy and Political Violence: Understanding Ethnic Conflict in the Balkans and Transcaucasia*. Bologna: Bologna University, Europe and the Balkans International Network, Occasional Paper No. 6. Ravenna: Longo Editore.

Ivekovic, I. 1998. "State, Development and the Political Economy of International Relations: the Asymmetrical Client-State in the Balkans and Transcaucasia." In S. Bianchini & R.C. Nation (eds.). *The Yugoslav Conflict and its Implications for International Relations*. Bologna: Bologna University. Ravenna: Longo editore.

Jones, R.J.B. 1995. *Globalisation and Interdependence in the International Political Economy*. London and New York: Pinter Publishers.

Keohane, R.O. & Nye, Jr., J.S. 1977. "Power and Interdependence: World Politics," in Keohane, R.O. & J.S. Nye, Jr. *Power and Interdependence: World Politics in Transition*. Boston: Little Brown.

Leftwich, A. 1995. "Is There a Socialist Path to Socialism?" In B. Gills & S. Qadir (eds.). *Regimes in Crisis. The Post-Soviet Era and its Implications*. London: Zed Books Ltd.

Morgenthau, H.J. 1952. "Another Great Debate: the National Interest of the United States." *American Political Science Review, LXVI* (December 1952).

Ohmae, K. 1985. *Triad Power: The Coming Shape of Global Competition*. New York and London: Macmillan Press.

Petras, J. & Vieux, S. 1995. "Russia: the Transition to Underdevelopment." *Journal of Contemporary Asia*. Vol. 25, No. 1 (1995).

Rosenau, J. 1995. "Distant Proximities: The Dynamics and Dialectics of Globalization." In B. Hettne (ed.). *International Political Economy: Understanding Global Disorder*. London and New Jersey: Zed Books.

The Dynamics of Trade Liberalization and Poverty in Africa

Danbala Danju

Introduction

Since the mid-1970s developing countries, especially in Africa, have been experiencing profound economic crisis characterized by chronic balance of payment deficits, huge external indebtedness, public sector deficits, high rates of inflation and unemployment. Initially, in response to the crisis, most governments embarked on short-term stabilization measures. However, from the early 1980s, this proved increasingly inadequate in overcoming the deepening crisis. Therefore, several African countries, more out of external pressure than conviction, embarked on structural adjustment programs (World Bank, 1989).

A key component of the adjustment programs involves the reform or liberalization of a country's trade regime. This has generally entailed reduction in controls on trade through the removal or conversion to tariffs of import quotas, import licensing and other quantitative restrictions, the reduction of the level and variability of taxes on trade, adjustment of the real exchange rate, export promotion incentives and other complementary macro-economic policies (Dollar, 1994; World Bank, 1989 and 1994).

This chapter discusses the dynamics of trade liberalization and poverty in Africa. The discussion is developed in sections. The links between liberalization and poverty are explored in section I. The extent of trade liberalization in Africa is reviewed in section II. Macro-economic evidence of the extent of poverty in Africa since the liberalization efforts of the 1980s is surveyed in section III. Finally, section IV concludes the discussion.

I. The trade liberalization-poverty nexus

The centrality of trade liberalization in adjustment programs derives from the consideration that the trade regime has a crucial impact on economic performance. A major presumption is that protectionist, inward-looking trade regimes, pursued by most African countries in the past, have sheltered domestic producers from foreign competition and introduced distortions in both factor and product markets. These were said to have resulted in inefficiencies, rent-seeking and wastage, all of which, in turn, impaired growth and development. Typically, inward-looking trade regimes are said to have benefited mostly the minority, powerful and organized interest groups, at the expense of the majority, unorganized groups. For example, it is argued that African governments tax agricultural exporters exorbitantly in order to transfer wealth from politically unorganized rural groups to vocal urban groups. Protectionist import-substitution policies favor powerful urban-based producers, government officials and modern sector workers.

Trade liberalization, emphasising a shift to a neutral or outward-looking regime, is expected to integrate an economy further into the world system by reducing the distortions in the structure of relative prices, fostering, among other things, greater competition, more efficient resource allocation and use, access to better inputs and technologies, greater technological dynamism and higher rates of growth and development based on the reforming country's comparative advantage.

Trade reforms, while generating both static and dynamic efficiency gains, have also distributional consequences in the reforming country. The Stolper-Samuelson theorem suggests that trade reform will generate losers and winners depending on the pre-reform relative characteristics of income distribution, poverty, factor mobility and price flexibility. Trade reform alters the relative price between tradeable and non-tradeable goods and therefore their relative profitability. For instance, if prices in the non-tradeable sector are inflexible downwards, some factors will become unemployed, causing the distribution of factor income to worsen. As factor prices in the non-tradeable sector begin to decline with the pressure of excess supply of factors, overall factor incomes will fall relative to those in the tradeable sector, and this will impact on the overall income distribution. As factors migrate across sectors in search of higher returns, output in the tradeable sector will expand and that in the non-tradeable sector will contract. However, if the conditions of the Stolper-Samuelson theorem hold, the relative return to the factor, which is used more intensively in the tradeable goods sector, will rise with trade liberalization.

Trade reform is therefore expected to foster greater equity and growth by increasing the return to the factor (mostly labor in Africa) used more intensively in the tradeable goods sector (exports and import competing production). This, it is argued, was the mechanism behind the greater equity in the labor-intensive export processing booms in the East Asian economies (Kanbur, 1997). The distribution of physical and human capital emerges in the theoretical and empirical literature as the key distributional consequences of growth, and as a determinant of growth itself. For example, several studies have found that equality and growth benefit from universal basic education and from widespread secondary education (Kanbur, 1997). Trade reform will affect wage inequality between skilled/unskilled wage differentials both within and between countries. Trade reform leading to increased imports of labor intensive production into developed countries could also increase wage inequality in developed countries and decrease it in developing countries. In a model in which labor has no, or limited, education, trade reform by expanding exports that require basic education in developing countries can increase the return to those with basic education, which while narrowing the gap between them and those with higher education, increases the gap with those with no education.

While theoretically producers in the tradeable goods sector will benefit from trade reform and those in the non-traded sector will lose, questions are raised as to who are the entrepreneurs in the tradeable good. The tradeable good sector covers a wide range of situations in Africa. For example, it includes small holder primary export sector, the mineral exporting sector and the newly emerging non-traditional sectors. The main beneficiaries of a sudden improvement in the profitability of non-traditional exports are likely to be those who have the capital, the skills and the contacts to take advantage of the opportunities opened up by reform. Thus, in the tradeable sector, some already rich people will benefit, although many poor farmers may also do so. In the non-tradeable sector, not all nontradeable production is concentrated in large, inefficient, state-protected enterprises. Women often carry out domestic services and the production of food crops, thus trade reform will act on inequality to the extent that it depresses the relative price of the non-traded sector (Kanbur, 1997).

In several African countries, land, education, political contacts and other physical assets are unevenly distributed among the different regions and ethnic groups. Hence, a growth pattern based on, for example, higher labor skills will lead to greater inequality and even impoverishment of those without education. Those with higher levels of education will benefit while those with lower or no levels of education may lose out and this may cause social tensions. Targeting of public expenditures and transfers to compensate losers may also prove difficult under authoritarian regimes where patronage and intimidation are the key to the regime's hold on state power. Besides, taxing the better-off at higher rates to support the less well-off is hardly possible in the context of increased competitiveness fostered by trade liberalization. Even if the administrative weaknesses in African bureaucracies could be excused, transfers based on socio-demographic characteristics rather than efficiency considerations are frowned on as capable of generating other distortions.

Thus, the role of trade liberalization, in both developed and developing countries, has remained a subject of intense controversy. While for the more fervent advocates the relevance, and indeed necessity, of re-orienting trade regimes towards a more open, outward-oriented strategy is unquestionable (Dornbusch, 1992; Havrylyshn, 1990), critics have continued to question both its theoretical and empirical relevance to developing countries (Rodrik, 1992; Taylor, 1993; Lall, 1994; Lall and Stewart, 1995; Stein, 1992; Mosley and Weeks, 1994). They argue that the advocacy of trade liberalization is based on the assumptions of perfect competition, which do not accord with the realities of imperfections and distortions in most developing countries.

Several constraints, both internal and external, are seen as limiting the capability of African countries to exploit their comparative advantage. At the internal level, these may involve factor immobility, factor price rigidity, low levels of productivity and technology, shortages of skill and entrepreneurial ability, absence of key inputs and infrastructural inadequacies. At the external level, the constraints involve high and rising levels of protection in developed countries, rising external debt burden, monopolistic structures and uneven technological development.

Moreover, trade reforms have focused mostly on relative price changes with little, if any, attention paid to some of the structural barriers to production such as improving the technological base, supply of raw materials and intermediate inputs, as well infrastructural facilities. The reforms have also ignored the domestic as well as external socio-political forces and processes that may hinder or corner the gains from trade reforms. Under these conditions, exposing weak economic agents to international competition, especially in Africa with its fragile economic-cum-political base, may result in significant loss of output, employment and investment (de-industrialization) as well as political instability (Stein, 1992; Lall and Stewart, 1995).

Proponents of trade reform have counter-argued that some of these constraints need not prevent a country from realizing the gains from trade liberalization (World Bank, 1994). For example, it is argued that although trade reform may lead to a contraction or closing down of some inefficient economic activities, which may be harmful to welfare in the short run, in the long-run more efficient and dynamic activities will emerge or expand to replace existing ones (Dornbusch, 1992). Proponents have also argued for a variety of approaches in the sequencing, timing and speed of liberalization, especially within the context of macro-economic crises, and are divided on whether political liberalization is a prerequisite for durable reforms.

It is argued further that carefully phased liberalization tailored to manage integration into the world economy can be put to good effect in reconciling rapid growth and distributional objectives. Liberalization in the developing world is only one part of the equation, another part is an enabling global environment (UNCTAD, 1997). Neo-structuralist scholars have also suggested a more proactive and selective interventionist policy stance involving increased government expenditure on infrastructure, human capital and efforts to build supporting institutions and sound macro-economic policies as some of the complementary measures required if trade policy reforms are to have any chance of success in Africa (Lall and Stewart, 1995: 2)

II. Trade liberalization in Africa

Studies in other regions of the world have highlighted the harmful effects of protectionist polices on growth and distribution. Hence the growing consensus in the literature on the need to de-monopolize trade: streamline the import regime, reduce bureaucratic red tape, replace quantitative restrictions with tariffs, avoid extreme variations in tariff rates and excessively high tariff rates, allow exporters access to duty-free imported inputs and refrain from large doses of anti-export bias and reduce taxation of export crops. However, African countries have continued to be characterized by high and varied levels of protection and overvalued exchange rates. Table One below shows the extent of tariff reform in some African countries.

Table One: Tariff Reform in Africa

| | Average Tariff | | |
	(1)	(2)	(3)
Country	Pre-reform	Current	Tariff ratio (TR)1
Cameroon (PR, CR) 2	59.0	59.0	1.00
Côte d'Ivoire (1985, 1989)	26.0	33.0	1.27
Ghana (1983, 1991)	30.0	17.0	0.57
Kenya (1987/88, 1991/92)	40.0	34.0	0.85
Malawi (1990)	25.5	--	--
Madagascar (1988, 1990)	46.0	36.0	0.78
Mali (1990)	25.0	--	--
Nigeria (1984, 1990)	35.0	32.7	0.93
Senegal (1986, 1991)3	98.0	90.0	0.92
South Africa (1993)	--	29.0	--
Tanzania (1986, 1992)	30.0	33.0	1.10
Uganda (1986)	30.0	--	--
Zaire (1984, 1990)	23.8	24.7	1.04
Average Nominal Tariff 4	(a) 37.2	36.6	--
Average Tariff Ratio	(b) 41.1	37.6	0.94

Notes:
1 (TR) = column 2: column 1
2 Data is import weighted. PR: pre-reform; CR: current regime. Exact dates are unavailable.
3 Includes surcharges.
4 (a) Average over all countries for which nominal data is available.
   (b) Average all countries for which both pre-reform and current nominal data is available.
Source: Dean, J.M. et al. (1994). p. 53.

The average tariff level for Africa both before and after the 1980s reform stood at about 37 percent. This is considerably higher compared to other regions like South Asia and Latin America. In fact, Table One shows that the post reform tariffs are at roughly 94 per cent of their pre-reform level. Some countries like Côte d'Ivoire, Tanzania and Zaire have actually raised their tariff levels above the pre-reform levels. Relatively few countries, such as Kenya, Ghana and Madagascar, have made significant cuts in their tariff levels. And even these were counteracted by increases in other taxes (Dean et al., 1994).

Another significant indicator of the extent of trade liberalization
is the proportion of import taxes to tax revenues. Table Two below
indicates that more than half of the countries in the sample had a
dependency ratio of between 20 per cent to 40 per cent. Senegal,
Madagascar, Côte d'Ivoire, Kenya and Nigeria have particularly
high dependency ratios even by African standards. There is also a
very high positive correlation between the height of the dependency
ratio and the height of tariffs both pre-reform (0.60) and post-reform
(0.73).This indicates that although countries with high dependency
ratios did make some cuts in their tariff levels, in order to avoid loss
of revenue from tax they still maintained high tariff levels in the
post-reform period (Dean, et al., 1994).

Table Two: Dependence on Imports for Tax Revenues and
Tariff Levels

	Average Tariff		
	(1) Import Rev./ Tax Rev.	(2) Pre-reform	(3) Current
Senegal	0.43	98.0	90.0
Madagascar	0.32	46.0	36.0
Cote d'Ivoire	0.31	26.0	33.0
Kenya	0.23	40.0	34.0
Nigeria	0.23	35.0	32.7
Malawi	0.22	25.5	--
Cameroon	0.19	59.0	59.0
Ghana	0.18	30.0	170.
Zaire	0.17	23.8	24.7
Mali	0.14	25.0	--
Uganda	0.11	30.0	--
Tanzania	0.07	30.0	33.0
South Africa	0.03	--	29.0

Notes:
Rank correlation coefficient (computed excluding Cameroon) between
columns 1 and 2 = 0.60
Rank correlation coefficient between columns 1 and 3 = 0.73
Column 1 refers to revenue from import duties ash share of total tax revenue
in 1984.
Column 2 refers to average tariff in the pre-reform period.
Column 3 refers to average tariff in the current (post-reform) period.
Source: Government Finance Statistics, IMF. Quoted by Dean, J.M. et al.
(1994). p. 54.

The parallel market premium is also another indicator of the extent of an economy's liberalization. Although all the countries in the sample have reduced the parallel market premium in the post-reform period, there are still substantial distortions in African exchange rate regimes. Table Three shows that the most distorted regimes are to be found in Ghana, Nigeria, Tanzania, Uganda and Zaire in the pre-reform period. The distortion continued in Tanzania and Uganda even in the post-reform period. In the countries where some substantial reduction was recorded in the parallel market premium, there has also been the inauguration of multiple exchange rates, which while reducing the restrictiveness of the exchange rate regime also generates other distortions in the economies concerned. Ghana, Nigeria and Uganda in particular introduced a secondary auction market for foreign exchange as part of the liberalization process. Alongside the devaluation of many African currencies, explicit export taxes were also lowered in most countries so as to reduce the degree of anti-export bias in African countries. Export monopolies of major crops were eliminated and in a number of countries the extent and severity of export licensing systems were reduced (Dean, et al., 1994).

Table Three: Changes in the Average Parallel Market Premium (1) (Non-CFA Africa)

	Pre-reform (2)	Post-reform (3)
Ghana (1986)*	984.6	16.5
Kenya (1988)	16.3	8.8
Madagascar (1987)	37.4	13.0
Malawi (1988)	50.7	12.1
Nigeria (1986)	209.7	27.4
South Africa (1989)	-0.4	3.0
Tanzania (1984)	241.8	118.7
Uganda (1987)	302.9	78.6
Zaire (1986)	711.1	9.4

Notes:
1. The premium is calculated as (parallel market rate-official rate)/official rate *100
2. Pre-reform averages are calculated from 1980 up to and including the reform year.
3. Post-reform averages are calculated from the first year after reform up to and including 1992.
4. Year of reform in parenthesis.
Source: Dean et al. (1994). p. 55.

III. Liberalization and poverty in Africa

Some empirical studies in Africa have found a positive association between macro-economic adjustments and decline in poverty, although they also noted that relative inequality did increase with policy reform. However, these studies suffer from some methodological problems. As Kanbur (1997) observes, macro-economic evidence on poverty and inequality based on the aggregation of a myriad of income changes, combining the fortunes of winners and losers, while useful, loses the fact that if the losing groups are sizeable, but the winning groups are larger, there will be some among the winners who are very rich (the relatively well-off civil servants), and some among the losers who are very poor (non-unionized urban workers).

Although there are significant differences between countries, overall African economic performance has been dismal since the enforcement of liberalization. The available evidence suggests, contrary to what the proponents had expected, that trade liberalization does not automatically bring faster growth and development, nor do growth and development automatically bring about reduction in inequality. On the basis of the most common income poverty measure, the headcount index, which measures the percentage of the population falling below the poverty line, there has been little to celebrate after the first wave of liberalization in Africa. It can be read from Table Four below that the number of people below the poverty line actually increased from about 38.5 per cent to over 39 per cent in Africa. Similar increases were recorded in Latin America and Eastern Europe. Even in the Middle East and South Asia, not much progress was recorded in the period under review despite the relatively higher growth rates recorded in these regions. On the other hand, the number of poor people rose in all the regions other than East Asia. Even in this region, the number of poor people must have risen dramatically following the East Asian crisis of 1997.

Table Four: Population Living on Less than a Dollar a Day

	Headcount			Number of Poor		
	1987	1990	1993	1987	1990	1993
Sub-Saharan Africa	38.5	39.3	39.1	179.6	201.2	218.6
East Asia and Pacific	28.2	28.5	26.0	464.0	468.2	445.8
Eastern Europe & Central Asia	0.6	n.a.	3.5	2.2	n.a.	14.5
Latin America & Caribbean	22.0	23.0	23.5	91.2	101.1	109.6
Middle East & North Africa	4.7	4.3	4.1	10.3	10.4	10.7
South Asia	45.4	43.0	43.1	479.9	480.4	514.7

Note: Headcount refers to the percentage of people living below the poverty line. Number of Poor refers to the absolute number of people (in millions) living in poverty.
Source: World Bank (1996: 4)

Although on the basis of social indicators of development some progress has been recorded, as White (1998) observes, the gains have come about more as part of the development process than results of policy reform. In fact the figures in Table Five below suggest that in absolute terms, the numbers of infant deaths, malnourished children and illiterate females are rising. In particular the figures for Africa are worse than those for other developing countries.

Table Five: Social Indicators, 1970-95

Infant mortality rate (per 1000 live births)	1970-79	1980-85	1986-92	1993-95	Change
Sub-Saharan Africa (n=44)					
Mean	134	116	102	94	-30
Median	131	111	99	90	-31
Other LDC (n=100)					
Mean	68	53	40	34	-50
Median	51	40	26	23	-55
Developed (n=25)					
Mean	19	12	9	7	-63
Median	15	10	8	6	-60
Malnutrition (per cent of children under five)					
Sub-Saharan Africa					

Mean	-	28	29	28	0
Median	-	28	29	28	0
Other LDC (n=10)					
Mean	-	33	31	28	-15
Median	-	30	30	26	-13
Developed (n=0)					
Mean	-	-	-	-	-
Median	-	-	-	-	-
Female illiteracy (per cent)					
Sub-Saharan Africa (n=30)		Change			
Mean	68	60	-12		
Median	71	64	-10		
Other LDC (n=51)					
Mean	34	30	-12		
Median	29	22	-24		
Developed (n=0)					
Mean	-	-	-		
Median	-	-	-		
Note: n = sample size Source: *World Development Indicators*, 1997					

Far from trade liberalization leading to the convergence of countries, the gaps between developed and developing countries, as well as within the latter, are widening. Opening up of African economies does not make these economies and living standards converge automatically towards those in the developed countries. If anything, trade liberalization is widening the social and economic divisions among, and within, countries. According to UNCTAD, in 1965, average GNP per capita for the top 20 percent of the world's population was 30 times higher than that of the poorest 20 percent; 25 years later, in 1990, the gap had doubled to 60 times.

> *The rich have gained everywhere, and not just in comparison to the poorest sections of society; "hollowing out" of the middle class has become a prominent feature of income distribution in many developing and developed countries. Also, the share of income accruing to capital has gained over that assigned to labor. Profits shares have risen in developed and developing countries. Increased job and income security is spreading. Rising interest charges have eaten into business revenues, corporate restructuring, labor shedding and wage repression have become the order of the day in both the North and the South.* (UNCTAD, 1997)

It can be read from Table Six below that the degree of inequality as measured by the Gini coefficient has worsened following the liberalization measures of the 1980s in Africa and in the developed countries. Even in those areas with some remarkable growth rates, such as East Asia, the degree of inequality has remained higher than was the case in the 1960s. As White (1998) observes, growth in recent years has been anti-poor.

Table Six: Inequality (Gini coefficient) by region, 1960-1990s

	1960s	1970s	1980s	1990s
Latin America & the Caribbean	53.2	49.1	49.8	49.0
Sub-Saharan Africa	49.9	48.2	43.5	47.0
Middle East & North Africa	41.4	41.9	40.5	38.0
East Asia & the Pacific	37.4	39.9	38.7	38.1
South Asia	36.2	34.0	35.0	31.2
High Income Countries	35.0	34.8	33.2	33.8
Eastern Europe	25.1	24.6	25.0	28.9
Source: Deininger and Squire (1996: 565)				

V. Conclusion

Trade liberalization has not stemmed the crisis of growth and poverty in Africa. Although the process is still unfolding, available evidence suggests that African economies have responded rather slowly to reform. While the pattern of response has been uneven with no firm links between liberalizers and growth, there are concerns that the initial reform measures did not seek to address poverty directly. Poverty might have been aggravated by reform.

The distributional or self-interest group perspective, within which the liberalization-poverty nexus has been discussed, while shedding light on the problems of reform, does not explain why the prevailing, economically-dysfunctional policies are the endogenous outcome of interest group pressures. The extreme fiscal distress, macro-economic instability and reduced incomes do not create obvious winners who benefit from contradictory protectionist policies. For example, why should governments seek to kill the goose that lays the golden eggs by imposing crushing taxes that exceed what is required to maximize revenue? Why do governments discriminate against their cash crops so badly that the sector is devastated over time, depriving government of revenues in the long run? It is argued that there is need to go beyond the conventional urban-bias perspective with its emphasis on losers and gainers.

Accordingly, some critics have called for a new perspective that comes to grips with the interplay of power relations both within and outside specific societies. Rising inequalities pose serious threats to the existing order that reforms seek to stabilize. Conventional literature has focussed largely on the distribution of income between households or individuals, but more recently concerns have been raised over distribution across racial, ethnic, religious, regional and gender groupings. The recent ethnic strife in Africa and a host of other places has been traced to partly distributive struggles. Questions are being raised on the links between distribution and ethnic conflicts, and in particular, growing rural poverty and ethnic conflicts. Thus, management of inter-ethnic distributional issues could be considered as an important policy goal in its own right. In other words, social equilibrium fashioned through redistribution may also foster growth, particularly in ethnically-fragmented African societies. Thus, liberalization, though necessary, is not a sufficient condition for the elimination of poverty in Africa.

References

Agosin, M.R. & Frenchdavis, R. 1995. "Trade Liberalization and Growth – Recent Experiences in Latin-America." *Journal of Inter-American Studies and World Affairs*, Vol. 37, No. 3, pp. 9-58.

Bienen, H. 1990. "The Politics of Trade Liberalization in Africa." *Economic Development and Cultural Change*, Vol. 38, No. 4, pp. 713-732.

Bouton, L., Jones, C. & Kiguel, M. 1994. "Macroeconomic Reform and Growth in Africa: Adjustment in Africa Revisited." *Policy Research Working Paper*. 1394. The World Bank; Washington DC.

Brett, E.A. 1988. "Adjustment and the State: The Problem of Administrative Reform." *IDS Bulletin*, Vol. 19, No. 4, October.

Corden, W.M. 1971. *The Theory of Protection*. Oxford: Claredon Press.

Dean. J.M., Desai, S. & Riedal, J. 1994. "Trade Policy Reform in Developing Countries Since 1985. A Review of the Evidence." *World Bank Discussion Papers*. No. 267, The World Bank: Washington D.C.

Demery, L. & Squire, L. 1996. "Macroeconomic Adjustment and Poverty in Africa: An Emerging Picture" *World Bank Research Observer*, Vol. 7 (3), pp. 263-292.

Dollar, D. 1992. "Outward-Oriented Developing Economies Really Do Grow More Rapidly: Evidence from 95 LDCs, 1976-1985." *Economic Development and Cultural Change*, Vol. 40, April, pp. 523-44.

Dornbusch, R. 1992. "The Case for Trade Liberalization in Developing Countries." *Journal of Economic Perspectives*, Vol. 6, No. 1, pp. 69-85.

El-Badawi, I.A., Ghura, D. & Uwajaren, G. 1992. "Why Structural Adjustment has not Succeeded in Sub-Saharan Africa." *World Bank, Policy Research Working Papers*, WPS 1000.

Foroutan, F. 1993. "Trade Reform in Ten Sub-Saharan African Countries: Achievements and Failures." *Policy Research Working Paper*, No. WPS 1222. The World Bank, Washington, D.C.

Havenik, K. (ed.) 1987. *The IMF and the World Bank in Africa*. SAS. Uppsala.

Havrylyshn, O. 1990. "Trade Policy and Productivity Gains in Developing Countries: A Survey of the Literature." *The World Bank Research Observer*, Vol. 5, No.1, pp. 1-24.

Husain, I. & Faruqee, R. (eds.) 1994. *Adjustment in Africa: Lessons From Country Case Studies. A Regional and Sectoral Case Study*. Washington, D.C.

Kanbur, R. 1997. Income Distribution and Development, mimeo., World Bank.

Kirkpatrick, C. & Weiss, J. 1994. "Trade Policy Reform and Performance in Sub-Saharan Africa in the 1980s." *New Series Discussion Papers*. Development and Project Planning Centre, University of Bradford. No. February

Krueger, A.O. 1978. *Liberalization Attempts and Consequences*. Published for the National Bureau of Economic Research. Cambridge, MA: Ballinger.

Lall, S. & Frances, S. 1995. *Trade and Industrial Policy in Africa*. Mimeo. Institute of Economics and Statistics, University of Oxford.

Lall, S. 1993. "Trade Policies for Development: A Policy Prescription for Africa." *Development Policy Review*, Vol. 11, No. 1, pp. 47-65.

Lall, S. 1994. "Industrial Policy: The Role of Government in Promoting Industrial and Technological Development." *UNCTAD Review*. pp. 65-89.

Little, I., Scitovsky, T. & Scott, M. 1970. *Industry and Trade in Some Developing Countries*. London: Oxford University Press.

Milner, C. & Rayner, A.J. 1992. *Policy Adjustment in Africa*. Basingstoke: Macmillan.

Mosley, P. & Weeks, J. 1994. "Adjustment in Africa." *Development Policy Review*, Vol. 12, No. 3, pp. 319-327.

Rodrik, D. 1992. "The Limits of Trade Policy Reform in Developing Countries." *Journal of Economic Perspectives*, Vol. 6, No. 1, Winter, pp. 87-105.

Stein, H. 1992. "Deindustrialisation, Adjustment, the World Bank and the IMF in Africa." *World Development*, Vol. 20, No. 1, pp. 83-95.

Taylor, L. 1993. *The Rocky Road to Reform: Adjustment, Income Distribution and Growth in the Developing World*. Cambridge, MA: MIT Press.

UNCTAD, 1997. *Trade and Development Report, 1997*. Geneva.

White, H. 1998. *Global Poverty Reduction: Are We Heading in the Right Direction?* ISS, The Hague, Netherlands.

World Bank. 1993. *The East Asian Miracle: Economic Growth and Public Policy*. New York : Oxford University Press.

World Bank. 1987. *World Development Report, 1987*. New York: Oxford University Press, June.

World Bank. 1996. *World Development Report, 1996*. New York: Oxford University Press, June.

World Bank. 1996. *Poverty Reduction and the World Bank: Progress and Challenges in the 1990's*. Washington, DC: World Bank.

World Bank. 1989. *Sub-Saharan Africa: From Crisis to Sustainable Growth*. Washington, D.C.

World Bank. 1994. *Adjustment in Africa : Reforms, Results, and the Road Ahead*. Washington, D.C.: The World Bank.

Globalization and Traditional Authority in Africa: Investment, Security and Land in Ghana

Donald I. Ray

I. Introduction

By late 1982, the government of Ghana had begun to adopt a variety of measures that increased the opening up of its economy to the processes of globalization.[1] These measures ranged from foreign currency exchange deregulation through to the selling-off of state corporations to domestic and foreign private investors, as well as other inducements to domestic and foreign capital. These policies were encouraged by the World Bank, the International Monetary Fund (IMF) and the market-driven governments and corporations of the West and Japan (Ray, 1986). During the 1980s and 1990s, many sectors of the Ghanaian economy were drawn into the dynamics of globalization, but land remained a noticeable exception as it remained on the whole under customary tenure.

This land, with certain exceptions, remained under the control of traditional authorities,[2] be they chiefs or extended family leaders. This land could not be alienated completely from the traditional authorities in the form of absolute fee simple sales that rendered for- ever the land from the controlling families and offices (which involved their ancestors, present generation and those yet to come) and which would turn such land into a commodity that could be bought and sold in the global market. Such communal land was for the use of those belonging to the relevant traditional authority. Land under customary tenure could be leased under a variety of condi- tions to those outside the family or chieftaincy. Such leases were usually oral in nature or, even if they were written, were sometimes subject to disputes based on whether the person granting the lease actually had the authority to control the land, because several branches of the family might be themselves in dispute as to who had this authority, based on who was the proper occupant of the relevant traditional authority office – such offices being contested potentially by several members of the relevant family or families.

In a number of prominent cases, such succession disputes resulted in foreign investors and organizations suddenly and unexpectedly finding that their leases to land were also in dispute. Two prominent Western embassies discovered that they were embroiled in such contested leases that involved, at the least, time-consuming negotiations with the different claimants to traditional office (Interviews, Ghana, 1992). In another case during the 1990s, foreign investors decided to establish a plantation that would grow fruit for export to Europe. The foreign investors duly negotiated a long term lease for land on which to carry out the cultivation of the export crop. The lease was signed between the foreign investors and the relevant traditional authority who was believed to control the land. The foreign investors had nearly completed the building of the necessary production infrastructure and the preparation of the fields when a rival group of claimants to the traditional office which controlled the land appeared and demanded that the foreign investors cease all use of the land until the foreign investors had signed a new lease with the "true owners" of the land, i.e., the rival family group. The original lease granters refused their rivals' demands, who in turn took the matter to conflict-resolution mechanisms. Since traditional conflict-resolution mechanisms can also involve recourse to the courts of the Ghanaian state, the foreign investors faced the prospect of their capital and initiative being tied up for years in legal disputes without producing any profit, profit being the key expectation for foreign investors. Such cases are unlikely to encourage other foreign corporations and individuals to invest in Ghana, yet this foreign investment has been a key component for those who have advocated since the early 1980s what is in effect a strategy based on globalization. While the governments of Ghana under J.J. Rawlings have actively followed this strategy since late 1982 by attempting, *inter alia*, to remove, or at least lessen, obstacles to foreign investment in Ghana and to increase the security of such private investments once the capital, expertise and technology have arrived in the country, as these cases illustrate, customary land tenure has emerged as a question that needs to be addressed.

Yet control over customary land tenure has not been easily exercised by the contemporary Ghanaian state (or its colonial predecessor). Indeed, from the 1890s to the 1980s, those chiefs and family heads who controlled land under customary tenure had rebuffed the attempts of the colonial and post-colonial states to end customary land tenure and replace it with systems of land tenure that would commodify land and offer greater security to foreign and domestic investors whose activities constitute part of the process of globalization. Consequently, the 1996 request from the Ghana government's Ministry of Lands and Forests to the National House of Chiefs for assistance in achieving these goals of globalization was to be expected since the systems of traditional authority and customary land tenure have been so intricately inter-connected. Traditional authority in Ghana has been of interest to the processes of globalization, not only for the administration of customary land tenure itself, but also for the general security context that traditional authority can involve for foreign investment and the profitable, secure use of land as well as other aspects of "development." These questions of land and security are indicative of the needs of globalization for the assistance of traditional authority in those aspects of life that globalization has not yet permeated. In order to better understand these particular questions, it is first necessary to examine a number of conceptual and contextual questions.

II. Conceptual and contextual questions

The state that is now Ghana has gone through three main periods. This particular dynamic has had effects on the manifestations of sovereignty and legitimacy in Ghana with regard to state-chief relations. These appear to have resulted in the creation of particular constitutional-legal mechanisms which reflect the articulation of different modes. The manifestation of these processes within the permeation of globalization in Ghana will lead to new insights with regard to the land and land-related security questions associated with traditional authority.

State, government and chiefs

The term "state" is used to denote a set of political structures and processes directed ultimately by one political authority (be that an individual such as a king/sovereign or a body such as parliament) that exercises control over all the people within its territorial boundaries. For example, the *International Encyclopedia of the Social Sciences* defines the state as constituting "a geographically delimited segment of human society united by common obedience to a sovereign" (Watkins, 1968, p. 150). Watkins emphasizes the Western notion that an undivided supreme political authority or sovereign is key to understanding the "state" or "government" (in its broadest sense): "The state is a territory in which a single authority exercises sovereign powers both *de jure* [in law] and *de facto* [in life]."[3] This assumption needs to be revised with regard to the state in Ghana because of the continued presence of traditional authority there.[4] It is useful to first consider these points within the three main historic periods of the state in Ghana, i.e., pre-colonial, colonial and post-colonial, as well as briefly outline the main governments or regimes of the post-colonial state.

The state manifested in three different forms that accord with three different historical periods during the 19th and 20th centuries. While these state forms share many of the same characteristics as those of the classic conceptualization of the state, they differ in several respects, most notably in terms of the effects of the imposition of colonialism on the factors of legitimacy and sovereignty. In turn these effects have ramifications for the operation of both the colonial state and the post-colonial state.

By the beginning of the 19th century, a constellation of African states and other more decentralized political entities had emerged, and in some cases they could trace existence and/or roots back several more centuries.[5] Until the 1830s or 1840s, these African states and other political entities in what is now Ghana existed virtually free from European colonial control. European states had little control beyond their West African coastal castles, forts and trading posts, which represented outposts of the emerging global market or capitalism. These pre-colonial states experienced growth, ascendancy, hegemony, decline and incorporation into other states in rather similar ways to that experienced by the European states. They had their own structures and processes for exercising authority and carrying out various functions. These and other political entities had economies that were organized on pre-capitalist bases, which did not preclude trading at their peripheries with the European-dominated global market. Land tenure was organized on a non-capitalist basis.

Britain had begun the process of imposing its claim to control, administer and exercise sovereignty by the mid-1800s. This process was carried out tentatively at first, as in the Bond of 1844, which extended limited British judicial jurisdiction to some of the coastal states. After Britain's defeat of the Asante state in 1874, Britain moved decisively by means of conquest or treaty to impose its colonial state and certain aspects of capitalism over the political authorities who, in large measure, had run the pre-colonial states in what is now Ghana. In the main, the British colonial state did not extinguish these political authorities, but rather transformed them from kings into "chiefs," otherwise called traditional authorities or traditional leaders.

The leaders of the former pre-colonial states and other political entities lost some key aspects of their states, such as their own armies and foreign policies, much of their control over their legislative, administrative, executive and judicial powers, but they retained a significant if variable amount of their authority, legitimacy, power and even elements of sovereignty into the colonial and post-colonial periods.[6] These chiefs or traditional leaders may have lost power at the "national" or state level, but in many cases they have remained influential at the local and regional level, especially in the rural areas, and especially over the land held under customary tenure, such land accounting for nearly all the land contained within the boundaries of the colonial state. For whatever reasons, Britain was content to let this situation continue despite the occasional urge to commodify land. So too in the social/cultural sphere, Britain did not attempt to extinguish the pre-colonial, non-capitalist values and social practice that did not directly conflict with British interests. In fact, the overwhelming majority of these pre-colonial, pre-capitalist values and practices were not attacked by the British colonial state, thus further reinforcing customary land tenure and traditional authority.

The British colonial state in Ghana was fundamentally transformed after 1951 when nationalist forces led by Kwame Nkrumah's Convention People's Party (CPP) shared power within the colonial state after their electoral victory. This sharing was ended in 1957 when the British state transferred total control over what had been the colonial state to Ghanaians, who in turn transformed this after independence into the Ghanaian post-colonial state. The post-colonial state has had elected, civilian governments as well as military and revolutionary governments. Prime Minister and later President Kwame Nkrumah's CPP rule started during the diarchy of the colonial period (1951-1957), but also included his post-colonial governments (including the First Republic, 1960-1966). He was overthrown in 1966 by the military-based National Liberation Council (NLC), which handed over power in 1969 to the Second Republic, which in turn lasted until it was overthrown by the military in 1972. A series of military-led governments, including the National Redemption Council (NRC, 1972-1975) and the Supreme Military Council (SMC, 1975-1979) and the Armed Forces Revolutionary Council (AFRC,

June-September, 1979) then ruled Ghana before handing over to the Third Republic (1979-1981). It was overthrown by the Provisional National Defence Council (PNDC, 1982-1993), which in turn handed over to the Fourth Republic (1993 to present).[7]

The market or capitalist mode has continued to expand from its colonial beachhead throughout much of Ghana's economic life during the period of the post-colonial state, but has not been able to make much headway in the sector of land. Here customary land tenure, with its accompanying values, relationships and the political and social structures of traditional authority, has continued to survive.

Despite the opposition of certain key traditional leaders to Nkrumah, he (and subsequent regimes) did not abolish chieftaincy. Rather, the governments of the post-colonial state, following the predecessors of the colonial state, have sought to find the optimum relationship with traditional authority, often by adjusting formally the governmental powers and authority that the post-colonial state believed it was granting to the traditional leaders. Indeed, both the colonial and post-colonial states expended considerable efforts in drafting and implementing constitutional and legislative arrangements, e.g., ordinances, laws, parts of constitutions, designed to govern the state's relationships with traditional authority (Ray, 1996, 1998).

This concern of the post-colonial state has even extended to attempts to include traditional authority into state structures ranging from the presidential advisory "Council of State" of the Fourth Republic to the creation of the Houses of Chiefs system (Ray, 1996, 1998). The constitution of the Fourth Republic defined a chief as a political leader who derived his/her legitimacy from custom or tradition that was rooted in the pre-colonial period:

> *"chief" means a person, who, hailing from the appropriate family and lineage, has been validly nominated, elected or selected and enstooled, enskinned or installed as a chief or queen mother in accordance with the relevant customary law and usage (Article 277).*

While this constitution of the post-colonial state was able to construct a general definition as to what were the proper methods that would enable the state to recognize what types of political offices and office holders were legitimate chiefs or traditional authorities, this constitution (Article 270) also forbade the executive and the lawmaking bodies of the state (i.e., Parliament) from determining the recognition of individuals as chiefs, and other chieftaincy recognition questions. In fact, this question of the post-colonial state's ability to control traditional authority by recognizing or withdrawing recognition of chiefly status has been quite contentious (Arhin, 1985, 1991). The state has changed its policy a number of times since independence in response to the varying political strength of those in Ghana who feel that the post-colonial state should not control chieftaincy. Indeed, it could be argued that this contention between these political forces within the Ghanaian state reveals a deeper-rooted debate over the degree to which traditional authorities have claims not only to their own bases of legitimacy, but even to remnants of their pre-colonial sovereignty (Ray, 1996). This, in turn, has further implications for the continued survival of the customary land tenure in Ghana.

The Ghanaian state has attempted to incorporate chiefs not only by reserving seats for chiefs in various administrative structures, such as regional committees supervising the police or prisons, or by addressing the question of chiefly recognition, but also by establishing what may be termed a "Houses of Chiefs" system. Nkrumah started a major reorganization of chieftaincy institutions within what became the Ghanaian state. During his time in power (1951-1966), Nkrumah removed control of local government from chiefs and instead restricted their legislative, administrative and judicial functions to customary matters as defined by the state's parliament, which were largely to be carried out through what was initially a two-tiered structure of Traditional Councils and Regional Houses of Chiefs.

At the local level, each paramount chief is to be president of his[8] Traditional Council, which considers local traditional matters. The paramount chief is at the top of the traditional authority political hierarchy for a given area of land and the people who live on that land: in this sense one can immediately see parallels between Watkin's definition of a state and a paramountcy. Below the paramount chief there are several levels of subordinate traditional office holders as well as the subjects, all of whom owe allegiance to the paramount chief. Most paramount chiefs do not have a traditional overlord: in this sense there is at least a resemblance of sovereignty. Indeed, in the pre-colonial period, and even early colonial period, Europeans often referred to them as kings. The Asante kingdom is a most widely known exception: here the paramount chiefs regularly and publicly swear allegiance to their king (whom the state deems to be a paramount chief in his own right but also occupying a special position of permanent constitutional overlordship).[9]

Each of the ten Regional Houses of Chiefs is composed of all the paramount chiefs in the region as well as other lesser chiefs according to regional circumstances. These regional houses of chiefs deal with customary judicial and other appeals from the traditional council level as well as matters referred to them for advice. Each regional house of chiefs elects five of its members to the National House of Chiefs.

The National House of Chiefs was established in 1971 by the Chieftaincy Act of 1971, thus adding a third tier of traditional authority structures within the Ghanaian state. The National House of Chiefs acts as (a) an advisory body to the government, especially for all matters regarding chieftaincy, (b) a judicial body on customary matters appealed from the Regional Houses of Chiefs or for certain other customary cases and (c) a body in which chiefs can raise and debate a variety of chieftaincy and state issues. In 1996, the government referred the question of changing the basis of land tenure from custom to one driven by market forces.

Divided sovereignty and divided legitimacy: An underlying dynamic of state-chief relations

Underlying the hundreds of pieces of legislation and articles of constitutions enacted by the colonial and post-colonial states in Ghana that seek to regulate traditional authority are two interrelated concepts: divided sovereignty and divided legitimacy. Chiefs constitute a parallel power to the state because they have, inter alia, different sources of sovereignty and legitimacy to those of the colonial and post-colonial states. The claims of chiefs to legitimacy and authority are rooted most distinctively in the pre-colonial states whose sovereignty was subordinated but never completely and totally eliminated by the British colonial state in Ghana, which introduced its own claims to legitimacy, state forms and conception of sovereignty. The post-colonial state of Ghana inherited much of the colonial state's structures and claims to legitimacy and sovereignty, but it had little claim to those available to traditional authorities: the links between the pre-colonial states and the post-colonial state were ruptured by the imposition of colonialism by British imperialism (Ray, 1996). That the post-colonial state and chiefs are rooted in two different, if very unequal, sovereignties may go some way in explaining the relative lack of overlap of the legitimacy bases of the chiefs and state, as well as accounting for their ambiguous relationship and also the continued survival of traditional authorities and their continued control over land under customary tenure, i.e., most of Ghana's land.

Political legitimacy can be based on different arguments as to why people should obey those in political authority. These bases can vary over time, between and within cultural and historical contexts (Baynes, 1993; Connolly, 1987). The legitimacy of the African postcolonial state is based mainly within three sources, all of which are secular: nationalism (anti-colonialism), democracy and constitutional legality.[10] Constitutional legality may be rooted in the colonial period to varying degrees according to the state's history. Thus, the contemporary African states may be seen as the successors to the colonial states created by the European imperialist powers, just as the United States and Canada can be seen as post-colonial states to Great Britain's colonies in North America. The post-colonial state inherited and has to deal in one way or another with a considerable number of constitutional and legislative instruments from the colonial state period.[11] In this sense, at least in the initial period of independence, the post-colonial state is usually the successor to the colonial state, and much of that legislative and constitutional framework continues to influence that of the post-colonial state in either positive or negative ways. Thus the post-colonial state demands obedience to those aspects of the colonial laws and constitutional framework that it deems acceptable because these are seen to be acceptable or legitimate in legal and/or constitutional terms. In short, whatever evaluation of the colonial state the post-colonial state might have, it may continue to accept a particular law or constitutional measure or principle on its own legal merit. Legality thus may be the legitimacy basis of the continued usage of a colonial measure, even if the colonial state period as a whole has reduced or no legitimacy in the eyes of the post-colonial state and its citizens because of the lack of democracy that imperial or colonial rule means.

The post-colonial state could also appeal to "nationalism" derived from the anti-colonial struggle as well as "democracy" as important bases of its legitimation. This assumes that the post-colonial state represents itself as the democratic result of the nationalist struggle for independence. This could be seen as a mechanism by which the post-colonial state distances itself from the essentially undemocratic past of the colonial state. Sometimes military coups and governments have shrunk the "democratic" legitimacy of the post-colonial state to only that of the achievement of independence. However, where the democratic content of the post-colonial state has been preserved or re-invented, the state is able to base its claims to legitimacy on having its government "duly" elected by their people. All of these democratic claims by the post-colonial states are ultimately rooted in the concept and practice that the citizens really do have the ability to select and to change their governmental leaders through elections held at specified intervals.

Traditional leaders have two distinct claims to political legitimacy in the contemporary era. First, traditional leaders can claim to be the carriers of political authority and legitimacy that is derived from the pre-colonial period. Traditional leaders occupy structures supported by official and unofficial constitutions and laws that, while they may have been changed in varying degrees by the colonial and post-colonial states, still retain a core of customary legitimacy that predates the imposition of colonialism. In other words, traditional leaders have a special historical claim to pre-colonial roots – i.e., the first period of African independence before it was lost to colonialism (primarily during the 1800s). Traditional leaders can point to the antiquity of their particular office and make the argument that since it was founded (either directly or indirectly through an office that was pre-colonial) in the pre-colonial period, their particular traditional authority represents those indigenous, truly African values and authority that existed before the changes imposed by the colonial system began to take effect.[12]

Another distinct claim to legitimacy by traditional leaders in the post-colonial democratic state is that based on religion. To be a traditional leader is to have one's authority, one's power, legitimated by links to the divine, whether the sacred be a god, a spirit or the ancestors. For a traditional leader to function that office must maintain and demonstrate its link to the divine. In Africa, the divine basis of traditional legitimacy pre-dates the imposition of colonialism. This timing thereby reinforces the other distinct basis of legitimacy for traditional leaders. In much of Africa, these religious beliefs were established before the introduction of Islam and Christianity, but in some cases these later religions have been added to, or superseded, the earlier religious beliefs. If one distinguishes between states in which a religion is present as a system of belief and one in which the state has formally adopted the religion as part of its legitimacy, then there are few states in Africa which have state religions and thus the differences in the bases of legitimacy which were argued above hold. It should be added that the absence or presence of any religion does not detract from the ability of a state to be democratic.

The historical and religious legitimacy claims can be interpreted as contributing to the view that traditional authority and leadership have deep roots in indigenous culture. Traditional leaders thus may be seen as the "fathers" and "mothers" of the people. Traditional leaders may be recognized, as they are in Ghana, as very significant transmitters of culture by their peoples, themselves and by the state. There are thus, it is argued, two different roots of legitimacy present within a contemporary post-colonial state such as Ghana. The legitimacy roots of the traditional authorities pre-date those of the colonial and post-colonial states and were not incorporated to any significant degree into the sovereignty claims of the colonial and post-colonial states.

III. Security, globalization and traditional authority

Those directing and implementing globalization (i.e., foreign and domestic investors, the World Bank, the IMF, etc.) expect that they will be able to carry out their established market-driven business and also be able to expand into new economic activities and geographic areas in a secure context. In short, globalization activities best exist in situations in which violent conflict is not actually happening around those attempting to do business. Globalization, once established, demands security. The carriers of globalization expect the state to implement the needed levels of "peace, order and good government," to use a Canadian phrase, and that in the state there will be clearly defined lines of authority for decisions to be pursued, culminating in one final, sovereign decision-maker. In short, globalization expects to deal with a state in the conventional, Western mold with undivided sovereignty and undivided legitimacy.[13] While those responsible in the main usually view the Ghanaian state as being in this conventional mold,[14] it is argued here that the Ghanaian state is different from the conventional view of the state precisely because it is a post-colonial state in which sovereignty and legitimacy are divided in the sense of being fundamentally differently-rooted for the post-colonial state and the traditional authorities. This, then, has implications for the Ghanaian state's ability to guarantee security for the carriers of globalization.

Traditional authority presents two major, inter-related questions of security for the post-colonial state: a) disputes related to succession and other questions of who should be the chief and (b) chieftaincy disputes involving land. These disputes can take many forms, but for the time being, pending the results of a larger analysis presently under way,[15] two different scales of violence will be discussed.

Content analysis of Ghanaian newspapers reveals a fairly constant but occasional, indeed episodic, series of largely unrelated events of violence linked to chieftaincy disputes of one sort or another. These can range from violence initiated by the faction of a losing candidate for the paramount chieftaincy in Winneba (*People's Daily Graphic*, December 13, 1993), to the beheading of a chief by some of his subjects over accusations of improper behavior (*Daily Graphic*, May 4, 1994), to a land dispute between two traditional authorities which resulted in two people being killed before the Ghana police arrived and prevented further bloodshed (*Ghanaian Voice*, January 31-February 2, 1994; interviews in Ghana, August-September 1994). Such incidents are recorded as having occurred in many different parts of Ghana. The cost to people in terms of lives lost and injuries likely amounted to several hundreds over several years. Houses, farms, vehicles, crops and other property are usually burnt or otherwise destroyed or damaged. Much of the economic and social activities in the affected area come to a stop for varying periods of time.

Far more serious are the northern chieftaincy wars that have started over traditional authority disputes. Over the last two decades, at least 5000 people have been killed – many more were wounded – in these chieftaincy wars. Many tens of thousands of people became refugees in their own country, losing their crops, livestock and houses. The economic and social infrastructure over significant areas of the north was destroyed. Development projects, the production of food crops for the urban areas in the south as well as for local subsistence, investment, transportation and other economic activities all came to a standstill for varying periods of time.[16] The 1994 war pitted the Konkomba against their Dagomba, Nanumba and Gonja overlords and resulted in over 3000 dead. President Rawlings and Parliament were forced to declare an emergency, postpone the district assembly elections and send in hundreds of Ghanaian soldiers in order to re-establish order. The affected countryside and towns remained devastated for many months. President Rawlings drew the link between the fighting, chieftaincy and land:

Certain imperatives fall on the chiefs of this country because it is becoming increasingly true that at the root of this rapid profusion of strife lies some kind of stool or skin [i.e., chieftaincy] palaver, and at the deeper root cause in land litigation. (Daily Graphic, February 4, 1994)

In short, those leading the Ghanaian state clearly saw that chieftaincy disputes which were rooted in land questions had the potential to erupt into bloody chieftaincy wars which threatened the lives, property and security of the Ghanaian people and the state. Clearly the state had to act. Besides restoring order, it also was able, using chiefs from other areas, to get the various sides to agree on peace. These events may also have influenced the state to initiate, two years after this outbreak, a process designed to transform customary land tenure.

IV. Globalization, traditional authority and land

In early 1996, the Ghanaian state in the form of the Ministry of Lands and Forestry returned to the question of changing land tenure policy, a question that it had last visited in 1987. In March, the Ministry circulated a draft land policy that was designed to promote the Ghanaian government's development strategy. The major objective of the land policy was "to facilitate the present investment drive." The draft policy was to establish a set of guidelines that would direct public sector institutions that administered land, especially its use, and which would open up the use of land for private sector investment initiatives, among other goals.

The need to protect private sector investment in land presently held under customary land tenure was a theme that was frequently emphasized. The Ministry stated that:

Land administration in Ghana has been guided both by customary practices and by enacted legislation. Since most of the land is owned by the stools and skins [i.e., traditional authorities], customary practices have played a dominant role in providing access to land. While these varied customs have served a vital role traditionally, they have also hampered development and, because of the lack of formal documentation, have contributed to protracted disputes between owners, which have been difficult to resolve, even with legal intervention.

In sum, the Ministry argued both here and elsewhere in the document that the customary, i.e., non-capitalist/market, form of land tenure that currently was in practice over "most of the land" presented a series of problems to the operation of "free market forces," especially with regard to the commercial use of land for agriculture, forestry, mining, industrial development and housing. Non-capitalist land tenure, which was and is administered, on the whole, by traditional authorities, was seen as a major blockage to globalization. One of the highlighted "major continuing problems" from this perspective was:

> *inadequate security of land tenure due to conflicts of interest within and between the land owning groups and the state, land racketeering, inadequate legislation, slow disposal of land cases by the courts, weak land administration systems which have deprived landowners and investors of the means for facilitating investment and development;*

This problem was accentuated by conflicts and lawsuits between traditional authorities over the boundaries between them, a problem in part caused by the use of unreliable and unapproved maps. As this last point demonstrates, the Ministry did recognize that not all of the perceived problems were caused by the pre-capitalist land tenure system. Amongst other measures there was a need to overcome the lack of accurate survey information, and reforms to the seven major government bodies that administered land in one way or another were needed. Overall, though, the Ministry believed that investors faced serious difficulties in getting access to land for commercial purposes, that even when this was nominally achieved, such access was subject to challenge from competing interests within traditional authorities. It hinted that these disputes could go beyond legal measures to the use of violent measures by contending parties within the traditional sphere – perhaps this was a reflection of the security issues, such as the northern chieftaincy wars that were raised in the previous section.

The Ministry proposed several major strategies to solve existing land problems that undermined the movement to the globalization of land in Ghana. Besides such technical matters as implementing more effective systems of surveying and registering land, or a lengthy statement of the government's commitment to equitable access for all Ghanaians to land as a social safety net, most of these measures referred to mechanisms that would make land more easily available for commercial, rather than subsistence and other non-capitalist use. Traditional sharecropping systems, which had been perceived as being rife with abuses, were to be transformed into commercial leaseholds with clearly defined conditions with a proposed Leasehold Law. Land value was to be determined by the free market, and undeveloped land was to be taxed at that new value in order to "allow land to be available on the market." The National and Regional Houses of chiefs were to be brought into these reforms by having them "[u]ndertake reform studies towards streamlining customary practices and adapting them to updated land use and management principles." On analysis a major policy paradox emerged: how was the state going to get the cooperation of the traditional "owners" of the land, i.e., the traditional authorities, when a number of the proposals of the draft policy paper on land involved a shift of administrative, political and economic control from them? The response from the traditional authorities on this and other points was not long in coming.

The Chairman of the Lands Committee of the National House of Chiefs, Osagyefo[17] Kuntunkununku II (Okyenhene[18] and President of the Eastern Regional House of Chiefs) responded with an extensive memo, which included his 1987 comments that had been made in response to the proposal of the previous Rawlings government's PNDC Secretary for Lands and National Resources for a transformation of customary land tenure into a system more responsive to the needs of globalization. The 1996 National House of Chiefs (NHC) memo argued that the customary system of land tenure was highly appreciated by Ghanaians because it reflected their history and guaranteed that all Ghanaians (i.e., those who were linked to the system of customary land tenure administered by chiefs and family heads) had access to land for farming and housing. Customary land tenure was a social safety net:

> Not least among the merits [of customary land tenure], is what could be described as the system's "in-built insurance policy," by making land the recourse of last resort available to every citizen. This fact was demonstrated, during the lean period of recent past (1983), when most city workers were able to repair quickly to family and other acquired lands, for cultivation to supplement their meager city earnings – a contingency which substantially mitigated an otherwise intolerable situation. That this could happen so easily was due to our indigenous system.

He went on to defend the essence of the traditional share-cropping systems, to approve of some of the technical measures and to suggest others. He challenged especially those measures that would convert land into a commodity that would respond quickly to globalization (i.e., market) needs and which would to varying degrees remove land from the control of traditional authorities. He noted that attempts to do this in the past by the colonial and Ghanaian governments, e.g., 1894, 1897, 1912, the 1940s and 1950s and most recently in 1987, had failed and that the 1996 attempt was likely to provoke strong opposition against any government that tried to do so: "History teaches that in Ghana, there is a psychological attachment to ancestral lands and stools of such potency that it is ignored or under-estimated, at great social risk." Indeed, he raised the spectre of violent uprisings by invoking "the recent land disputes involving certain ethnic groups in the northern parts of the country." Without going into the rest of this debate, the point can clearly be seen that there are two major differing views of land tenure in Ghana. The state sees the need to reform land policy in order to meet the needs of market globalization, in this case investors, as well as maintaining equitable access for Ghanaians to land. The traditional authorities, in the form of the national House of Chiefs, had a non-capitalist view of land and were firmly determined not to undermine customary land tenure.

V. Conclusions

From a political scientist's point of view, the dynamics of the global expansion of the market economy, or globalization, have often been examined from the perspectives of the contemporary state or supra-state structures. However, in many sub-Saharan African countries, these post-colonial states and international structures co-exist in the presence of traditional authorities (otherwise called chiefs or traditional leaders or traditional rulers) who are, or claim to be, rooted in the pre-colonial period and its non-capitalist values. These traditional authorities, as demonstrated by the Ghanaian case with regard to land and security, thus represent a political factor which still had the ability to contest, politically, socially and even economically, the expansion, penetration and diffusion of globalization throughout many of the countries of sub-Saharan Africa. Thus the analysis of globalization needs to take into account traditional authority wherever it exists in Africa, or indeed elsewhere. The case of Ghana has been used to address this gap in the globalization debates.

Acknowledgments

This research was made possible with the permission, encouragement, cooperation and sharing of insights by the chiefs, government and people of Ghana. I especially wish to thank the Office of the President and the Chieftaincy Division in Accra, the National House of Chiefs and the Ashanti Regional House of Chiefs in Kumasi, the Northern Regional House of Chiefs in Tamale, members of the civil service, the National Commission on Culture, the political parties, the University of Ghana and the University of Science and Technology. The research was funded by the Social Sciences and Humanities Research Council of Canada, the International Development Research Centre and the University of Calgary. I wish to thank Rosemary Brown, Tareq and Jacqueline Ismael, and Peter and Ama Shinnie for their encouragement and discussions over the years. I would like to thank Laura Dunham and Andrew Grant for their research assistance. Research included fieldwork in Ghana during 1983, 1984, 1987, 1990, 1992, 1994 and 1996.

Endnotes

[1] Globalization is seen as the latest phase of the expansion of capitalism. Colonialism is seen as part of an earlier phase.

[2] The terms "chief" and "traditional authority" are used interchangeably in this work. Other English language terms such as traditional leader or traditional ruler are also used in Africa. A chief refers to an office and its holder that exists independently of the contemporary state, and which exercises some sort of authority, usually over customary matters, and the legitimacy and activity of which date back to the various pre-colonial states and other political entities rather than the colonial state and its successor, the post-colonial state.

[3] Watkins' view of the state in this regard is not an isolated one; indeed it could be argued that virtually all the authors and approaches to the study of the state who are included in Chilcote's 1994 survey of comparative politics share this assumption about the state, even if they disagree on other aspects of state analysis.

[4] Chiefs in Ghana are based in villages, towns and cities as well as rural areas. Chiefs are organized into hierarchies, most of them based on the pre-colonial situation.

[5] The history, structure and nature of these pre-colonial states is increasingly well documented. See for example the following: Amenumey, 1986; Asamoa, 1986; Boahen, 1987; Boahen, Ajayi and Tidy, 1986; Fynn, 1971; Kwamena-Poh, 1972; McCaskie, 1995; Shinnie and Shinnie, 1995; Ward, 1948; Wilks, 1989. For a useful overview using maps, see Catchpole and Akinjogbin, 1983.

[6] For a summary of this process, see Ray, 1998, pp. 49-50.

[7] For a variety of analyses of these governments, see Apter, 1968; Austin, 1964; Austin and Luckham, 1975; Chazan, 1983; Ninsin, 1985; Ninsin and Drah, 1981; Nugent, 1995; Oquaye, 1980; and Ray, 1986.

[8] Only under the most extraordinary of circumstances could a woman become a paramount chief in Ghana. A woman from the relevant royal family could become the queen mother (i.e., the senior female royal officeholder, not necessarily being literally, physically the mother of the chief), if the institution existed in that particular paramountcy, or possibly serve as regent until a male candidate could be found or achieved the necessary age.

[9] In all but one of the regional houses of chiefs, the president is elected at the start of each three year period, usually from amongst the paramounts present. The constitutional exception is that of the Asantehene (i.e., Asante king) who is always the President of the Ashanti Regional House of Chiefs.

[10] There are religious and monarchical state exceptions.

[11] See Ray, 1996, for an elaboration of this argument. The degree to which the post-colonial state accepts this inheritance is another question.

[12] The historic cultural and religious claims to legitimacy by traditional leaders in the era of democratic, post-colonial states are subject to the overriding principle of consent of the people to these claims. If people do not agree to be bound by these claims, there seems little that traditional leaders (or the state) can or should do to demand that they be honored in special ways.

[13] In federal states, sovereignty may be diffused but still undivided. See King, 1987, p. 492, for a discussion of federalism and "diffuse sovereignty." For a preliminary discussion of the applicability of this to traditional authority and divided sovereignty, see Ray, 1996, pp. 182-183ff.

[14] See Ray, 1996, for a preliminary analysis of Ghanaian constitutional and legal instruments, which suggests that there is some unresolved debate within Ghana over this question.

[15] See Ray, 1996, for preliminary results.

[16] For accounts of the various wars, see for example, Skalnik, 1986; Drucker-Brown, 1988-89; Ray, 1986, 1996.

[17] Traditional authority title.

[18] Traditional authority title.

"Internationalization" and "Localization" in the Chinese Search for Human Justice[1]

Ronald Keith

This chapter identifies and assesses the local understanding of "internationalization," *guojihua*, and "localization," *bentuhua*, as it relates to law and the self-conscious search for "human justice" in China's contemporary context of domestic economic and social adaptation to "globalization" and the transition to a "socialist market." "Localization" self-consciously conveys the positive connotations of the law's sensitive adaptation to the underlying values and understandings of distinctive society and political culture, but its assertion has sometimes come under external criticism as "cultural relativism." "Internationalization," within the context of contemporary Chinese theoretical debate, connotes "the international developmental process in law in which the particular legal systems of each country in the world, approximate more closely and come together and converge in order to take shape in mutual interdependence and linkage."[2]

In the 1990s, Chinese legal circles, even while self-consciously aware of the rational necessity of "localization," increasingly adapted to what is really the European natural law tradition as it underlies the contemporary notion of "human rights." Also related, domestic legislation highlighted problems of both substantive and formal justice, as such justice specifies rules regarding economic, political, social and cultural rights, and recommends procedural fairness so as to insure the enjoyment of rights on the familiar basis of the "like application of [such] rules to like persons."[3]

The changing human rights content of Chinese law has been recently spotlighted as a result of major changes in 1996 and 1997 to China's Criminal Law and Law of Criminal Procedure, and China's October 1996 signing of the International Covenant on Economic, Social and Cultural Rights, and the signing of the International Covenant on Civil and Political Rights in October 1998. Since 1978, whole new legal codes have appeared and China's legal circles have been involved in the elaboration of a new jurisprudence and underlying theory of justice which they hope will effectively respond to Chinese culture and the changing relationship between China's contemporary state and society. At the same time they have often used comparative international experience and international criticism to push forward a newly conceived agenda for "human rights" and the "rule of law."

In the West, analysis by and large has been inspired by the censorship of the nature of the PRC's "authoritarian" regime, and human rights monitoring has been concerned with allegedly sweeping human rights violations. By comparison, analysis has only episodically tracked and analyzed the contradictions and related human rights costs of the socially complex transition to the socialist market economy. Most importantly, the contemporary substantive changes in the Chinese political and legal treatment of human justice are in urgent need of analysis given the unprecedented domestic trend towards "internationalization."

"Globalization" in east and west

The developing conceptual connotations of "globalization" are important to any discussion of the response of contemporary Chinese law and jurisprudence to prospective "internationalization" in law. In the West and in the PRC, "globalization" is a politically sensitive and highly symbolic term which often aspires to tell the whole story of contemporary social, cultural and economic life.

In the Cold War, "globalism" once connoted the baldly "realist" foreign policy of "hegemonial states" as it related to global North-South political alignments.[4] The latter were also important to the "New International Economic Order" of the mid- to late-1970s challenge to "power politics" and "neo-colonialism." Chinese analysis eagerly highlighted superpower hegemony and neo-colonialism in its correlation of the NIEO with a "New International Political Order." In the West, however, international relations study began to correlate issues of order and justice, and the study of "world order" offered new perspective on the creation of regimes so as to mitigate inter-state anarchy and reduce the resort to violence. Order was deliberately placed in synthesis with justice as analysis focused on a new mix of international actors so as to provide a politically cooperative and hopefully rational legal basis for the resolution of conflict, the advancement of human justice and the protection of the "global commons."

All of this implied a political activism on the part of proliferating actors as suggested in the popular slogan, "think globally, act locally." "Complex" or "global governance," if not world government, could conceivably evolve out of such an admittedly ideal development. In basic structural terms, the non-governmental actor became a widely recognized participant in inter-governmental fora as well as social critic or popular advocate pressuring state actors from outside such fora so as to conform with universal standards of human justice.[5]

The Princeton series of World Order Model Projects perhaps best articulated this kind of trend when it linked "global constitutionalism" to a nascent "global civil society" in an analysis of "the countervailing trends of global integration and ethno-nationalist fragmentation." Richard Falk provided us with a working definition of "global civil society" as "globally constituted attitudes, social connections, information networks, trans-national collaboration and citizens' associations – an ensemble of diverse cumulative forces and tendencies that has many innovative potentialities."[6]

In response to the possible emergence of a "global civil society," G. Dale Thomas recently warned of the persisting realities of "cultural pluralism" with respect to the prevailing liberal understanding of a global civil society predicated upon a new global *ius civile*:

> *Continuing cultural differences undermine feelings of unity and consensus on rules and institutions even though discussion at the global level may be couched in liberal terminology. The same words often have radically different applied meanings. Furthermore, if such a global civil society exists, one cannot assume that it is benevolent and benign. It may instead reflect an evolving discourse, liberalism, that was once anchored in the decaying European state system, but must now seek a new foundation to maintain dominance. Might made liberalism right in the Twentieth Century with the overall dominance of liberal Western states, but cultural pluralism and alternate identities may leave behind only a liberal facade in the Twenty-First Century.[7]*

John Baylis and Steve Smith, in their text on world politics, highlighted the apparently innocuous connotation of "increasing interconnectedness between societies such that events in one part of the world more and more have effects on peoples and societies far away."[8] Similarly, Charles Kegley and Eugene Wittkopf defined "globalization" as "the growth and intensification of political, economic, social, and cultural relations across borders."[9] Such perspective steadily advanced the formal distinction between "world politics" and formerly state-centric "international politics."[10]

François Chesnais pointedly claimed that the early notion of "globalization" as "totalizing economic, political and ideological processes" which foster a borderless, stateless world, originated from within the ideological agendas of the US "business management schools" of Harvard, Columbia and Stanford.[11] Whether the "globalization" process constitutes a benign linear homogenization which fosters cross-border integration and intellectually enlightened convergence of what Hedley Bull once referred to as a *civitas maxima*, or whether it is more likely to promote simultaneous local and international societal polarization, is increasingly a matter of great contention.

Indeed, Post-Cold War "globalization" has often been correlated specifically with liberalized trade, investment and finance. Those who work in this area often do assume that regardless of some hiccups, liberalized trade and investment ultimately contribute to a harmony of interests which is fostered from within a supposedly transparent international rule of law.[12] There are other ways of looking at this. A recent Canadian world politics text referred, for example, to the "globalization thesis" as "the argument that sovereign nation-states are losing their relevance because they have lost the capacity to protect the nation state against influences from 'outside' because of the increasingly *globalized economy*."[13]

The critics of "globalization" have focused on a presumably pathological economic opportunism which attacks state sovereignty, is inconsistent with democracy and civil society and forecloses any real prospects for national economic development. In light of these assertions, the proponents of a "neo-liberal" economic globalization are growing concerned over possible "globalization backlash" or "global-phobia."[14] In response to such backlash, Canada's Minister for International Trade, Sergio Marchi, recently noted that, as governments become smaller, professional and business associations would have to increase their support for "growing locally, thinking globally." The Minister sought to educate Canadians on the correlation of international trade and local prosperity. His notion is to "localize" trade by "demonstrating the benefits of our trade abroad to our neighbors down the street."[15]

Chinese interpretations of "globalization"

Given the Chinese reputation for a no-nonsense political critique of the vicissitudes of "imperialism" and "neo-colonialism," "globalization"/"globalism" is obviously more than a passing interest in Beijing. However, the basic connotations of these terms are now more subject to scholarly controversy. There is open disagreement as to what constitutes the principal contradiction in world politics.[16] In the history of the Chinese revolution, reference to "international-ism" immediately invoked the international communist movement in its struggle to resist imperialism, especially as it was entwined with the struggle against "feudalism" in China. In the post-Cold War context, international contradictions appear to have become less systemic and more discrete in nature, and the related loss of sys-temic coherence is reflected in open debate over the conceptual rel-evance of Post-Cold War "hegemonism."

"Globalization"/"globalism," *quanqiuhua*, or "internationaliza-tion," *guojihua*, are Chinese usages of the 1990s. "Globalization" still invokes a critical Marxist view of the exploitative trans-national dimensions of internationally and regionally expanding market economies; however, "globalization" and "regionalism" have both positive and negative connotations as Post-Cold War Chinese schol-arly analysis highlights the domestic purposes of contemporary eco-nomic reform and open door policies and China's need to partici-pate in wider patterns of regional and international economic coop-eration.

According to one recent analysis, there are at least two current-ly important lines of interpreted "globalization," *quanqiuhua*. First it may imply a more or less innocuous multi-dimensional historical process which inevitably cuts across state territory and involves greater economic, cultural, political and military exchange as well as flows of news, people, culture and capital. Perhaps this approxi-mates what Baylis and Smith benignly referred to as "interconnect-edness."

However, there is the more familiar Chinese view that equates "globalism"/"globalization" with Western-led modernization. The latter is often depicted as an economically and politically self-serv-ing "Westernization."[17] Chinese critical analysis does not automati-cally accept a progressive characterization of "globalization." Such criticism will, for example, point to the selective impact of "global-ism": "Does [such globalism] happen to entail a reduction of the sovereignty of the US and other rich countries?"[18] Notwithstanding benign neo-liberal "globalization" and the related prospect of "blind" or "complete Westernization," Chinese policy has accepted the importance of international economic cooperation and the applicability of what are essentially Western human rights understandings to China.

At least since the late 19th century, Chinese policy and historiography have self-consciously grappled with the problematic relation of "inner" (*nei*) and "outer" (*wai*). There have been a variety of self-consciously nationalist views through time as to what is reasonable adaptation to the outside as compared to unacceptable assimilation and cultural self-negation. For example, China's adaptation to foreign learning and technology was discussed across different periods in terms of the appropriate interpretation of "Chinese learning for essence and foreign learning for use," *zhongxue wei ti, xixue wei yong*. This strategy allowed for the import of science and technology while insisting on the purity of Chinese values and civilization. It involved an optimal adaptation to domestic conditions and a deliberately minimalist position regarding cultural concession to outside values and institutional experience.

A direct relation with the history of modern imperialism and the struggle for national self-determination certainly informed Chinese Communist Party perspective on how to deal with the "outside," but CCP ideology assumed the modern relevance of an international division of labor and state policy never did formally endorse autarchy as a reasonable alternative. Deng Xiaoping's notion of the "open door policy" grew out of previous policy perspective, but it was less qualified than Mao's original mid-1950s policy of "making foreign things serve China."

Deng's famous "open door policy" was rationalized in Mao Zedong's 1956 rejection of "national nihilism" and "left-wing closed doorism,"[19] Deng highlighted Mao's principle of "learning the strong points of all nations;" Deng's "open door" was, however, distinguished from "complete Westernization," *quanpan xihua*, which he believed was not only an affront to Chinese nationalism, but also objectively irrational in its neglect of local reality.[20] Deng steadily expanded the field of learning from the outside to include areas of economic management and legal development.

Chinese international relations analysis continues to presume that "globalization" is just as much about politics as economics,[21] and that despite claims for the ultimate harmony and inevitable and progressive harmonization of "globalization" as a linear process, "globalization" has to be understood as a politically complex process which evolves dialectically in stages of contradiction and synthesis and which may have either negative or positive results for local state sovereignty and development. With this in mind, one can drop the analysis down to the mundane level of the Chinese adaptation to foreign legal experience and the pursuit of domestic justice in a time of transition from the planned to a market economy. Arguably, the current adaptation to "internationalization" is unprecedented.

"Internationalization" and "localization" in China

It is questionable as to whether the Chinese are ready to embrace "global constitutionalism." While "complete Westernization" is often disavowed, they disagree with Huntington's "clash of civilizations." Perhaps because Chinese analysis is instinctively suspicious of the liberal origins of "global civil society," this particular notion has not received widespread support. On the other hand, the Chinese have not allowed their anxieties over Westernization to distract them from an extensive discussion of the legal dimensions of "internationalization." The fundamental issue of rational cultural adaptation and synthesis versus assimilation on the basis of "complete Westernization" has been directly addressed in key areas of contemporary legal and institutional development as China undergoes fundamental economic changes and related value change.

The dialectical balance of "internationalization" and "localization" has become a critical matter of formally construed dialectical adaptation to foreign legal thinking and standards. Even as extraordinary internationalization has taken place, various Chinese reformers have claimed a balanced approach which effectively responds to outside international standards while preserving a positive domestic adaptation to the realities of Chinese culture and society. This project has indeed fostered formal conceptual opportunities to pursue human justice, but at the same time the balancing of "internationalization" and "localization" has engendered practical misunderstanding and contradiction which inform the Chinese pursuit of human justice.

Furthermore, in my "revisionist" view, American critics of China's human rights stance have not always appreciated the complexity and the inherent potential of this balancing, particularly as they have stressed that a) the Chinese believe that all human rights are exclusively domestic and b) the Chinese focus exclusively on economic, social and cultural rights at the expense of civil and political rights. This is not to deny that there has always been a very strong Chinese advocacy of state sovereignty and positive law. The Chinese, however, are not entirely wrong in their conclusion that the latter are integral rather than antithetical to international law.

The Cold War context of East-West "convergence" did not allow for a real Sino-Western discourse on matters relating to human justice and the rule of law. Western focus on "convergence" was automatically understood in China as a non-reciprocal process of concession to Western values. Convergence was apparently a thinly disguised form of ideological and cultural aggression against the integrity of socialist states and societies. In the immediate aftermath of the Tiananmen Square event, the Chinese government saw in the heightened Western reference to human rights a familiar agenda for the "peaceful evolution" of China away from socialism towards capitalism and liberal democracy.

Given such a guarded reaction to allegedly specious "human rights diplomacy" and contemporary "engagement," as distinguished from the historically forthright US policy of "containment," Western analysis focused on human rights infraction and was not especially interested in finding a compelling explanation of how and why Chinese formally adapted to human rights categories in the years immediately following Tiananmen Square.

In the context of international censure and domestic political backlash against Tiananmen Square dissent, the Chinese moved in November 1991 to endorse human rights categories as applicable to the measure of contemporary Chinese society. This ended previous claims that citizen's rights were all-inclusive and more substantive than "human rights." Then, beginning in 1993, the Chinese started to establish human rights institutes and societies, and they began to insist on their own involvement in the negotiated development of international categories of human rights.

Over the last several years the Chinese have offered specific rebuttals to the annual State Department report on Chinese human rights performance. Indeed, such rebuttal asks why the US is excluded from international monitoring of human rights infractions. However, this new engagement is still qualified with reiterations on the importance of equality and reciprocity as conveyed in the "five principles of peaceful coexistence," "seeking common ground while reserving differences." Paradoxically or not, these are Cold War principles which have been brought forward into the Post-Cold War Chinese adaptation to "internationalization."[22]

The November 1991 white paper gave the earliest and quite possibly the most extensive formal rendition of the Chinese view on the domestic and international dimensions of human rights. This statement opposed "any country making use of the issue of human rights to sell its own values, ideology, political standards and mode of development." This was a particular reference to the US, which has been suspected of the "hegemonic" manipulation of a double standard in human rights diplomacy.

The same statement set out a dialectical understanding of *nei/wai* whereby the Chinese endorsed state sovereignty while at the same time indicating reserved support for the selective international creation and protection of human rights. The 1991 statement indicated: "A human rights system must be ratified and protected by each sovereign state through its domestic legislation." While generally subscribing to the systemic principle of non-interference, this position also acknowledged:

> . . . *the international community should interfere with and stop acts that endanger world peace and security, such as gross human rights violations caused by colonialism, racism, foreign aggression and occupation, as well as apartheid, racial discrimination, genocide, slave trade and serious violation of human rights by international terrorist organizations.*[23]

The theme of internationally appropriate interference was not repeated in quite the same way as in the subsequent 1995 white paper, "The Progress of Human Rights in China." This report highlighted the need to "strengthen international cooperation in the sphere of human rights." It featured China's positive contributions to international exchange on human rights matters:

> *[Within international organization] China always conscientiously performs its duty, actively participates in the examination and discussion of subjects on human rights, and elaborates its views, making its contributions to constantly enriching the connotation of human rights and promoting universal respect for human rights.*[24]

Even the US State Department has begun to recognize that Chinese officials no longer "dismiss all discussion of human rights as interference in China's internal affairs." However, in relation to Chinese subscription to the universality of human rights at the Beijing Fourth World Conference on Women, the US State Department alleged:

> *Despite this public acknowledgment of universal human rights principles, Chinese officials accept only in theory the universality of*

human rights. They argue instead that a nation's political, economic, and social system, and its unique historical, religious, and cultural background determine its concept of human rights.

While the Chinese argument may not be that exclusive, recent US reports have dismissively referred to specific Chinese Human Rights Society rebuttals to US claims, and these rebuttals have not been systematically addressed in US annual country reporting.

Since the early 1990s there has been a very explicit internal adaptation to human rights terminology in Chinese legislation. The inside/outside dimensions of human rights have become a matter of softened, if not benign "convergence" rather than absolute antithesis. The Chinese may emphasize the evolution of international categories of human rights out of domestic experience and legislation, but they are not automatically opposed to creation of international categories of human rights.[25]

Moreover, the deliberately self-conscious balancing of "internationalization" and "localization" was informed by important conceptual breakthroughs such as the liberation of "human rights," *renquan*, from the hitherto orthodox category of "citizen's rights," *gongminquan*. This justified new national debates and research in the 1990s on human rights and the comparative scholarly study of human rights.

With growing realization in the US of the extent of related Chinese legislation, there is a noticeable shift in the American emphasis from the question of universality towards emphasis on the apparent disjuncture between Chinese form and practice.[26] In this context, there is still an unwillingness to factor in China's circumstances of development, and yet there is an interesting forgiveness in the view of the new market consequences for Chinese human rights performance.[27]

US State Department monitoring has not undertaken to review and assess domestic complaint about market-induced infractions of human rights as these are presumably "unintended." On the contrary, active discrimination against women in foreign enterprise may well be intended. With respect to Chinese women's rights and interests, Beida Professor, Ma Yinan, has, for example, argued that the administrative disciplinary measures, entrenched in the April 1992 women's law, need to be extended more widely into foreign and joint enterprise, which have thus far failed to adapt to existing state disciplinary procedures regarding gender discrimination.[28]

Chinese policy does stress the importance of state sovereignty and remains suspicious of the political implications of complex interdependence,[29] as a Western-inspired non-reciprocal and seemingly politically neutral form of economic globalization. Huntington's "clash of civilizations," was rejected as a double standard. While Europe is free to think in terms of its common house and cultural heritage, Western bias casts "Asian" regional cultural or economic cooperation as necessarily anti-Western and anti-modern. Certainly, Huntington's "clash" cannot possibly explain wider Chinese involvement in trans-regional and international organization and the extraordinary extent of China's adaptation to Western legal experience and concepts, particularly as these directly relate to Chinese endorsement of "rule of law" and "human rights" concepts.

The "rule of law" so often dovetails with "human rights" in the discussion of "human justice," and it is important to recognize the developing Chinese correlation of these concepts.[30] In the author's 4 June 1998 interview with the Director of the Center of Human Rights, at the CASS Institute of Law, Beijing, Li Buyun claimed that now there is a progressive convergence of Western and Chinese thinking about the substantive content of the "rule of law," particularly as this terminology stresses the importance of principles such as the supremacy of law, due process and equality before the law. Li claimed that the latter, as essentially Aristotelian in nature, have been approximated in recent Chinese debate regarding the rule of law as an increasingly international phenomenon. Li placed the "rule of law" within the sphere of "internationalization."

Like so many of China's most senior jurists, Li understood "localization" and "internationalization" in the familiar dialectical terms of *nei* and *wai*. Li believed that China needed a "rule of law" in order to consolidate domestic economic reform, democracy and to facilitate international exchange, and he was gratified by recent Party recognition of the importance of legally protecting human rights. While subscribing to "internationalization," Li's notion of rational legal culture assumed that it would **not** be correct for China to adopt other countries' laws in an uncritical fashion without a respectful and practical understanding of local conditions. Li's "internationalization" looked forward to a relatively benign *nei-wai* dialectic. Other scholars, however, have expressed deep concern over the inherent contradiction between justice or fairness (*gongping*) and benefit (*xiaoyi*) which, they note, operates at both the local and international levels.[31]

Moreover, most of the new generation of Chinese texts on jurisprudence still maintain conventional chapters on the development and nature of law in the different social contexts of Western capitalism and Chinese socialism. Li's more Conservative colleagues warn of an overzealous "internationalization" as the unqualified "transplantation" of Western law to the soil of Chinese culture and society. In other words, beware of the lurking agenda for "blind Westernization" in "internationalization"!

Li Buyun has, nonetheless, argued forcefully that, in contemporary China, the "rule of law" requires a social basis resting on the three related foundations of the market economy, democratic politics and "rational culture," *lixing wenhua*. The last required a universal understanding among officials and people as to the importance of law in society and their acceptance of law as applying to their own conduct.

This does beg the question which the Chinese have been debating since the early 1980s and that is the role of the state and how fast to go in developing a legal system which moves beyond the consciousness of the mass of the population in Chinese society. Some Party conservatives had attempted to delay legal reform by emphasizing the "legal blindness" of the general population. In the 1980s, Li himself had argued for a fast track in legal development on the grounds that this was needed to preempt any political tendency towards "feudalism" and "personality cult."

Li, in my 1998 interview, emphasized Jiang Zemin's personal endorsement of the "rule of law," and he went on to enumerate ten related principles which formed part of the content of scholarly lectures given to the top Party leadership at Zhongnanhai. In order for China to become a "rule of law country," Li cited ten preconditions, namely, the perfection and establishment of a complete legal system, recognition of the people's sovereignty, the protection of human rights, established checks and balances in politics, equality before the law, supremacy of law, government according to law, due process, judicial independence and the ruling Party to conduct itself according to law.

Jiang Zemin, at a Party Congress on 12 September 1997, endorsed "use law to rule the country and create a socialist 'rule of law' state," *yi fa zhi guo, jianshe shehuizhuyi fazhi guo*. The political implications of this terminology were certainly not lost on domestic legal reformers, but one should expect continuing serious reservation about this formulation in the West.

Jiang Zemin chose a deliberate phraseology which rejected the alternative notion of "building a socialist legal system." Some earlier sinological speculation in the West had presumed that Jiang was part of a "core faction" which was resistant to the demands of a "rule of law" faction within the top leadership.[32] However, Jiang's "socialist rule of law country" liberated the "rule of law" from its earlier theoretical subordination as a constituent element of a wider conception of "socialist spiritual civilization." And for the first time, the senior Party leader explicitly presumed a necessary relationship between the rule of law and the protection of human rights. The renewed focus on the supremacy of law and equality before the law militated expressly against conservative formulation, which merely accepted the organizational and policy need for the development of law and regulation. In short, Jiang personally took a big step in endorsing "rule of law," *fazhi*, as opposed to the conservative preference for "building the socialist legal system."[33] His endorsement culminated in the April 1999 revision of the State Constitution to include explicit reference to the "rule of law."

On the outside, there will be skepticism among those who believe that you must have a fully operative liberal democracy, based on some form of separation of power as well as a reinforcing and confident and autonomous civil society, before you begin to talk of the rule of law in any meaningful fashion. Hopefully the "rule of law" is more than a "predicate" or due process which facilitates the conveyance of property in a "capitalist" marketplace. This kind of criticism does, however, raise interesting points of East-West comparative analysis.

One may, for example, recall the view of the great British Constitutionalist, Ivor Jennings, when he said: "Those governed by a true rule of law are so governed because in a very real sense they govern themselves."[34] How is it then that Hong Kong, without the benefit of its own parliamentary system, could achieve a rule of law under British colonialism? Was Hong Kong not dependent upon an offshore Parliamentary system, and yet its commerce enjoyed the fruits of an imported British "rule of law"?

To cite another Asian example, Lee Kuan Yew claimed that Singapore had preserved traditional Confucian values and the related decorum of the five relationships, while at the same time it had dealt effectively with corruption and the problems of domestic and international economic relationships on the basis of a well recognized rule of law. Lee claimed to respect indigenous Chinese "feelings" while promoting the impersonal equality associated with the "rule of law." How is it that despite the authoritarian features of politics in Singapore, that there has been so much progress to the "rule of law?"[35] To what degree is it institutionally possible to advance human rights on the basis of a "rule of law" in China's current transitional circumstances?

Also when we consider the complexities of *nei/wai*, we have to take into account Chinese analysis which presumes that "human rights" were only recently brought forward in the modern revolutionary context of East/West interaction, and that there was very little indigenous conceptual support or formal equivalence for "human rights" as entitlements which accrue to individual rights-bearing personalities, whose enjoyment of rights is predicated not in specific citizenship, but in participation in common humanity. The "rights and interests" which are now, for example, accorded to Chinese women and children have very little grounding in traditional Chinese legal culture. The current issues, such as child abuse, violence in the family and sexual harassment, were not traditionally dealt with on the basis of the state's universal application of legal principle. The current legal trend presumes that the state has, in such cases, a moral responsibility to intervene in family affairs.

One cannot discount the difficulties in achieving an optimal and rational political and legal strategy for the enhancement of human rights protection in China. There is sometimes a pronounced disinclination on the part of some Western feminist analysis to consider the role of an activist state in this regard. In China's case, the revolution never successfully achieved real equality, and the contemporary state as it focuses on economic reform is by definition "patriarchal" in its innermost heart.

Moreover, undue emphasis on the role of the All-China Women's Federation is viewed with suspicion in so far as this massive association is regarded as less of an autonomous advocate for women's rights and interests, and more the controlled arm of the Party-State. On the other hand, domestic legal reformers have often stressed that the state must actively support the "rule of law" in order to implement equality rights, particularly in the absence of a reinforcing tradition of thought and legal development. In the face of persisting "patriarchal" or "feudal" tradition, it has been argued that women's equality rights, as these are anchored in a new evolution of culturally unfamiliar principles of civil law, may need significant reinforcement in an aggressive application of the state's constitutional law regarding equality rights.[36]

Chinese justice and jurisprudence in an era of market "pluralism"

The search for human justice in China has become newly complicated given the advent of the market and its impact on the formation and protection of human rights in law. Also, one may well ask what specifically has happened to the Chinese notion of justice in the context of the elimination of class analysis in Chinese politics? Recent significant controversies over the evolution of a new Chinese jurisprudence really lay bare a profound dilemma of justice and law.

Formerly, "jurisprudence" had to be unified under the requirements of Party leadership and state planning. Now, many reform jurists are arguing that it ought to be "pluralized" so as to reflect the pluralization of new legally-recognized productive social interests which are emerging in market reform and responding to changes in ownership and distribution.[37] This view may need closer scrutiny in so far as it acts to rationalize a prioritized correlation of rights with specifically productive interests. Whether the current focus on social interest in reaction to past emphasis on obligation to the state will support a universality in the enjoyment of human rights is an open question.

Moreover, Chinese jurisprudence is beginning to respond self-consciously to "internationalization" and "localization." The following definition of the "internal" and "external correlations" of jurisprudence, for example, rejects exclusive antithesis between "internationalization" and "localization":

> The law's internal correlations refer to the correlations of legal and social systems. These include those relating to a country's internal environment and they include as well other methods of legal adjustment and control such as correlations of ethics, politics, customs, charters of mass associations, village regulations, people's agreements, etc. The law's external correlations must meet all of the systemic demands of modernization and reaching out to the world, and, at the same time, these correlations must systemically agree with society's laws and regulations, the course of history and a people's rights and ideals. These external correlations are built on the base of internal correlations.[38]

These "external" correlations are still dialectically secondary, but they are now explicitly acknowledged in China's fast evolving jurisprudence.

Moreover, while there appears to be a utilitarian emphasis on the prioritized development of rights in relation to interests which support the objectives of economic reform, participation in international human rights dialogue, response to international criticism of Chinese human rights performance, and political concern over the socially de-stabilizing aspect of economic reform has had a strong influence in 1990s legislation regarding the special grouping, *texu quanti*, of the rights and interests of women, children, the handicapped and the elderly.[39]

This special grouping was politically emphasized as socially necessary given the uneven and unfair impact of economic reform on different sectors of the Chinese population. Moreover, the particular correlation of "rights and interests," *quanyi*, represented a deliberately political attempt to capture favorable popular rather than strictly legal conceptions of equality and justice. This new law on a special grouping of rights was projected on the popular basis of a notion of a just society which was written into law. Moreover, these series of laws were internationally highlighted in Chinese human rights diplomacy with the publication of a series of "white papers," including "The Situation of Chinese Women" (June 1994), "The Progress of Human Rights in China" (December 1995), "The Situation of Children in China" (April 1996).

In response to "internationalization," contemporary jurisprudence and legislation has had to deal with a related "value problem" which is informing the law's response to the new requirements of economic reform. How should law, in its concern for the protection, adjustment and distribution of people's rights and interests, interpret the October 1992 principle of "efficiency is primary, while fairness [or justice] is supplementary"? This principle was given extraordinary policy precedence insofar as it was ideologically rooted in Deng Xiaoping's "three favorable directions," requiring that law facilitate (1) the liberation of productive forces (2) the elimination of exploitation and societal polarization and (3) the achievement of "common prosperity."[40]

The current generation of Chinese texts on jurisprudence do not hesitate to place efficiency in the same formal listing of the fundamental values of law as freedom, equality, justice, public order and security. Will rights be prioritized in relation to the recognized formation of those particular new interests, which are seen to contribute most successfully to the goal of increasing economic productivity? Again, is there a queue in Chinese human rights formation which accepts the short-term paradoxical necessity of compromising universal standards?

The birth of a market economy is often theoretically associated with the development of human rights, but will the focus on market productivity qualify the essential universality of human rights? Li Buyun's June 1998 response to this question was disarmingly blunt. Past emphasis on egalitarianism had resulted in an over-emphasis on fairness, which had resulted in lost motivation to produce. Simply, there was less pie to distribute, and, therefore, less possible expansion of human rights.

In offering his gloss on Deng's "three favorable directions," Li conceded that contemporary efficiency might lead to short-term polarization, and he noted annual increases of nine million in unemployment. On the other hand, he argued that current unemployment levels are not necessarily in contradiction with the universality of human rights. In the short term, there might be less equality, but he also anticipated more freedom and liberty. At the same time, policy would have to create a favorable adjustment of interests so that in the long term more people would enjoy human rights. To the cynical observer, this may appear as a shopworn rationalization for postponed, if not perpetual, inequality, but this is an increasingly accepted point of view within China's legal and jurist community.

The current development of human rights concepts has been increasingly disengaged from conventional socialist argument regarding distributive justice, and this would appear to constitute a serious paradox. Under the planned economy, for example, there was little development of labor law. Curiously, this was justified in the political pre-eminence of the working class. Simply, the focus on distributive justice was presumed to be more important in the life of a socialist society than any specified legal stipulation. Now as the worker contends with the unpredictable marketplace in all of its legal complexity, there is an urgent need for a developed labor law specifically defining the rights and interests of the worker. Apparently, there is herein something of a tradeoff. Economic reform pares back the obligations of the state, requires a clear break from traditions associated with the "big common pot," and the "iron rice bowl" and a qualification of conventional policy on "fairness." In return, the worker is promised new legal status under contractual law. While policies which provided ironclad guarantees of servic- es and benefits are sacrificed to "efficiency," the worker is offered the law's theoretical protection and due process governing mutual contractual relations.

Currently, internal politics would appear to favor imminent legal recognition of the right to strike, particularly as instances of wildcat strikes and workplace disputes are on the rise. At the October 1998 five year Congress of the All-China Federation of Trade Unions, this rise was correlated with the growth in overseas investment and private business. Apparently, only one third of China's 145 000 foreign-owned firms have union representatives in place; labor unrest in this sector was traced to too-long working hours, the lack of safety and physical abuse.[41]

Possibly, such a tradeoff might not satisfy either Western human rights critics or internal critics of Chinese policy, law and jurispru- dence. But we should also drop into our "scales of justice" an acknowledgment of the tremendous strides in Chinese law with respect to formal justice and the establishment of new procedural law which affects the position of the state vis-a-vis the individual cit- izen. "Internationalization," in this particular area, is remarkable in its scope and departure from past experience and formal under- standings.

Even skeptics in the West have grudgingly acknowledged the importance of substantive changes to Chinese criminal law and criminal procedural law. In his special report on revision to China's criminal law of procedure to members of the American Bar, Jonathan Hecht expressed concern as to the inner Chinese under- standing of "presumption of innocence" but he also indicated: "Still the 1996 NPC Decision demonstrates that China has begun to reori- ent its basic approach to criminal justice away from a dominant pre- occupation with social control toward a somewhat greater concern for the protection of defendant's rights."[42] Similarly, the US State Department human rights monitoring for 1997 expressed continued concern over the safeguarding of basic legal safeguards for defen- dants, but also noted: "If fully implemented, the law would bring China's criminal law closer toward compliance with international norms."[43]

The 1997 massive revision to the Criminal Law, itself, continued the trend towards substantive change in the conceptualization of legal safeguards for human rights. This revision highlighted the break from the past focus on class struggle and counter-revolution to emphasize the current adaptation of the law to the purposes of economic reform. The latter re-emphasized the importance of equality before the law particularly as this principle militates against corruption, and it required the identification of new categories of crime in the marketplace.

Of seminal importance was the deliberately rational focus on the specific stipulation of crime and a break with the traditional deployment of criminal law-based social control through the unreserved application of analogy. The latter allowed the state extraordinary leeway in the ad hoc political determination of criminal activity. The new strategy of criminal law application broke with past political justification for the law's "flexibility" and sustained wider and more emphatic reference to the natural justice principles of *nullem crimen, sine lege*; and *nulla poena, sine lege* (no crime without a law; no punishment without a law).[44] In short, such reform eliminated the conventional rationale for state instrumentalism in the application of criminal law.

"Internationalization" and prospective human justice in China.

One really should expect that, in the complicated and unprecedented circumstances of China's contemporary social and economic transition, there are many contradictions in the making. To overindulge in East-West metaphor, the junk of modern Chinese justice is attempting to negotiate the boiling straits between Scylla and Charybdis. Both "localization" and "internationalization" can present difficulties in the attempt to insure high formal and applied standards of human justice.

Despite self-conscious articulation of the dangers of "Westernization," Chinese analysis has opposed the "clash of civilizations." On the other hand, there is no natural predisposition accepting an emerging "global civil society." "Internationalization," in China, has brought about an unprecedented recognition of the key concepts necessary to the pursuit of human justice. Neither the local tradition nor "localization" have offered a substantive intellectual base facilitating the "rule of law" as it relates to essential notions such as supremacy of law, equality before the law, no punishment without law, no crime without law and the priority of human rights vis-a-vis citizen's rights.

Not only has the category of citizen's rights been placed within the larger category of human rights, but the Party has freed the "rule of law" from its subordination to "socialist spiritual civilization" and has also explicitly accepted the "rule of law" as necessary to the protection of human rights. Such principles have received unprecedented priority in the context of market reform. Indeed, the international monitoring of China's situation ought to give full credit to such formal change in that such change facilitates the essential framework within which practical improvements to human rights performance can take place.

However, as significant as these formal advances are, they do not in and of themselves guarantee practical and logically consistent results. There is not necessarily an even societal development towards what Hedley Bull skeptically referred to as "an imagined *civitas maxima*."[45] Indeed, skeptics might defer to ancient Chinese wisdom suggesting that there is no point in "drawing a cake to satisfy one's hunger" (*hua bing chong ji*).

Also, while mainstream Western analysis generally locates Chinese human rights failure in the authoritarian nature of the Party State, Chinese scholarship has pointed to how newly emerging market forces are generating societal challenge to, as well as conceptual opportunity for the creation of new human rights categories in law. International monitoring of Chinese human rights performance has been rather exclusive in its correlation of human rights performance with the "authoritarian" nature of China's political regime, but it also needs to place the domestic consequences of market reform in the scales of a Blindfolded Justice before it can, itself, claim a true "internationalization."

That having been said, and while there is an encouraging new recognition of a "special grouping" of rights, rights, in China, are increasingly correlated with specific subjective "interests." And the new utilitarian politics of the marketplace may yet challenge the practical implementation of this "special grouping of rights" and such politics may even encourage a prioritized pluralism at the expense of the universality of human rights. Human justice is now receiving more formal attention in unprecedented substantive and formal recognition, but such justice may be politically parceled out on the basis of a local policy of economic reform subordinating justice to efficiency.

Endnotes

[1] The Author gratefully acknowledges the supportive funding provided by the Social Sciences and Humanities Research Council of Canada and by the University of Calgary Research Grants Committee.

[2] This definition is provided in Li Lin, "*Quanquihua beijingxide Zhongguo lifa fazhan,*" (China's legislative development in the globalization context), *Falixue, fashixue,* (Jurisprudence and legal history), No. 3, 1998, p. 31. This definition closely resembles the verbatim definition given to Ronald C. Keith by Li Buyun, Director, Center of Human Rights, Institute of Law, Chinese Academy of Social Sciences, on 4 June 1998. Li indicated: "Internationalization includes generating links with the international community which includes increasing participation in international convention and the convergence of the spirit, purpose and form of law between China and the West."

[3] These conventional distinctions concerning human, substantive and formal justice largely follow upon Hedley Bull's analysis of the meaning of justice, in *Anarchical Society: A Study of Order in World Politics.* New York: Columbia University, 1977, pp. 78-84.

[4] This is as noted under "globalism," in Graham Evans & Jeffrey Newnham, eds., *The Dictionary of World Politics.* New York: Simon & Schuster, 1990, p. 138.

[5] This distinction is discussed by Ann Marie Clark, "Non-governmental organizations and their influence on international society," *Journal of International Affairs,* vol. 48, no. 2, (Winter 1995), pp. 505-25.

[6] Richard Falk, Robert C. Johansen & Samuel Kim, eds., *The Constitutional Foundations of World Peace.* Albany: State University of New York Press, 1993, pp. 10 & 14.

[7] G. Dale Thomas, "Civil Society: Historical Uses versus Global Context," *International Politics,* 35, (March 1998), p. 62. Thomas linked *ius civile* with the modern onset of international law, whereas it is possibly more common to stress the relationship between *ius gentium* and international law.

[8] John Baylis & Steve Smith, eds., *The Globalization of World Politics.* Oxford University Press, 1997, p. 7.

[9] As cited in Charles Kegley & Eugene Wittkopf, *World Politics: Trends and Transformation,* 6th edition. New York: St. Martin's Press, 1997, p. 533. This definition originated with Hans-Henrik Holm & Georg Sorensen, eds., *Whose World Order? Uneven Globalization and the End of the Cold War.* Boulder: Westview, 1995, pp. 1-17. Similarly Robert Mansbach defines the "global system" as "the political system embracing actors worldwide among which a pattern of interaction is discernible." Robert Mansbach, *The Global Puzzle: The Issues and Actors in World Politics.* Boston & New York: Houghton Mifflin, 1997, p. 592.

[10] See fn 3 on "globalism" which implies in an identified second sense the definition by non-state actors of the international situation and non-state actor involvement in international organization, which "may be required to establish the ground rules and monitor the subsequent conduct of participants."

[11] Claire Sjolander has pointed out the dialectical properties of Chenais' argument, which raises the question as to whether globalization produces convergence and or local and global societal polarization. See François Chesnais, *La mondialisation du capital* (Paris: Syros, 1994), p. 14, and Claire Sjolander, "The Rhetoric of Globalization: What's in a Wor(l)d?" *International Journal*, vol. li, no. 4, 1996, p. 609.

[12] The related regional and multilateral issues of trade and investment are explored in Donald Barry & Ronald C. Keith, eds., *North America, Europe and the Asia Pacific: Cooperation or Conflict?* Vancouver: University of British Columbia Press, forthcoming.

[13] Kim Nossal, *The Patterns of World Politics*. Scarborough: Prentice Hall, 1998, pp. 457-8, 499.

[14] Recently, in Canada, there was, for example, an unexpectedly vociferous debate and spontaneous literature concerning the draft MAI. NGOs attacked the Canadian government's duplicitous support for a "Charter of Rights for International Corporations." The latter was placed in antithesis to democracy and civil society. Tony Clarke & Maude Barlow, *The Multilateral Agreement on Investment and the Threat to Canadian Sovereignty*. (Toronto: Stoddart Publishing, 1997), pp. 5-6. Also see Andrew Jackson & Mathew Sanger, *Dismantling Democracy*. (Ottawa & Toronto: Canadian Center for Policy Alternatives & James Lorimer & Co., 1998, and Murray Dobbin, *The Myth of the Good Corporate Citizen: Democracy under the Rule of Big Business*. Toronto: Stoddart Publishing, 1998.

[15] "Notes for and Address by the Honorable Sergio Marchi, Minister for International Trade to the Golden Opportunity 1998 Business Development Seminar and Trade Show," Toronto, 21 October 1998.

[16] See, for example, Lu Xinguo, comp., "*Shijie zhuyao baodun wenti yantaohui jiyao*" ("Summary of a Symposium on the World's Principal Contradiction"), *Xiandai guoji guanxi* (*Contemporary international relations*), no. 4, 1995, pp. 2-41.

[17] Wang Yizhou, "*Dangqian woguo guoji zhengzhi yanjiude jige zhengming dian*" ("Points regarding several controversies in China's study of international politics"), *Tianjin shehui kexue*, 1998.1. 14-8 as reproduced in *Guoji zhengji* (*International politics*), 1998, 2, p. 9.

[18] See Gu Dexin, "*Quanqiuzhuyi*," *Renmin luntan* (*People's commentary*) 1996, 10, p. 58-9, as reprinted in *Guoji zhengzhi*, 1996, 12, p. 31.

[19] Ronald C. Keith, "China's Modernization and the Policy of 'Self-Reliance,'" *China Report*, vol. xix, no. 2, March-April, 1983, pp. 19-34. For Mao on national culture in its adaptation to "progressive foreign culture" see R.C. Keith, "Mao Zedong and his Political Thought," in Anthony Parel & R.C. Keith, eds., *Comparative Political Philosophy: Studies under the Upas Tree*. New Delhi, Newbury Park & London: Sage Publications, 1992, pp. 94-6.

[20] In the aftermath of the Tiananmen Square event, Deng used this argument against student dissidents claiming that they wished to overthrow the socialist regime so as to establish a "totally Westernised vassalage bourgeois republic" (*xifang fuyonghuade xichanjie gongheguo*). See Deng Xiaoping, *Deng Xiaoping wenxuan*, vol. iii. (Beijing: Renmin chubanshe, 1993), p. 303.

[21] See, for example, Wang Hexing, "*Quanqiuhua dui shijie zhengzhi, jingjide shi da jingxiang*" ("Ten points on the world political and economic impact of globalization"), *Guoji wenti yanjiu* (*Research on the problems of international relations*), no. 4, 1996, pp. 10-15.

[22] See, for example, Sun Guohua, ed., *Falixue jiaocheng* (*The rules of jurisprudence*). Beijing: Zhongguo renmin daxue chubanshe, 1997, pp. 213-4.

[23] "Human Rights in China," (November 1991), in *Beijing Review*, Nov. 4-10, 1991, pp. 44-5. This important reference to genocide was ignored in Beijing's recent condemnation of NATO's position on the Serbian treatment of the Kosovors.

[24] "The Progress of Human Rights in China," *Beijing Review*, Special Issue, 1996, p. 27.

[25] US State Department, *Country Reports on Human Rights Practices for 1995*, Washington, D.C., 1996, pp. 587-88.

[26] This already started to become clear in the November, 1991 State Council "white paper" on human rights. See "Human Rights in China," *Beijing Review*, No. 44, 4-10 November, 1991, pp. 8-45. The Chinese participation in human rights dialogue and the extensive inclusion of both international and domestic categories of human rights is explicit in the massive organization of the five year project of the Institute of Law, Chinese Academy of Social Sciences, *Zhongguo renquan baike quanshu* (*The human rights encyclopedia of China*). Beijing: Zhongguo dabaike quanshu chubanshe, 1998, passim. For further analysis and background see Ronald C. Keith, "The New Relevance of 'Rights and Interests': China's Changing Human Rights Theory," *China Information*, vol. x, no. 2 (Autumn 1995), pp. 39-41.

[27] For example, Chinese women "are sometimes the unintended victims of economic reforms." Ibid., p. 732.

[28] Ma Yinan,"*Guanyu wanshan funu quanyi boazhangfade ruogansikao*" ("Several thoughts on the perfection of the law on the protection of

women' s rights and interests"), *Zhongguo faxue* (*Chinese legal studies*), no. 5, 1994, p. 102. As cited in Keith, "Legislating Chinese Women's and Children's Rights and Interests in the PRC," *China Quarterly*, no. 149, March 1997, p. 49.

[29] The Chinese search for independence in a world of interdependence has been the subject of controversy. Scholars in the West disagree on the extent of adaptation to such interdependence. Chi-yu Shih has declared that ongoing emphasis on independence has blocked China's full participation in the world economy. See Shih, *China's Just World: The Morality of Chinese Foreign Policy.* Boulder: Lynne Reinner, 1993. Thomas Robinson has argued that while affected by history, the Chinese are moving rapidly towards interdependence. See Robinson, "Interdependence in China's Foreign Relations," in Samuel Kim, ed., *China and the World*, 3rd edition. Boulder: Westview, 1994. This controversy is considered in R.C. Keith, "The Post-Cold War Symmetry of Russo-Chinese Bilateralism," *International Journal*, vol. xlix, no. 4, 1994, pp. 764-5. As this issue touches on controversy over the Chinese view of trade and investment liberalization, see Ronald C. Keith, "Reflections on Sino-Canadian Cooperation in APEC," *Canadian Foreign Policy*, vol. 5, no. 2, Winter, 1998, pp. 196-7.

[30] For sample "western" advice to the Chinese on this point, see Franz Michael, "Law: A Tool of Power," *Human Rights in the People's Republic of China.* (Boulder & London: Westview Press, 1988), p. 33.

[31] See Xie Hui, *Falu xinyangde linian yu jiqu* (*The foundations and reasonings of belief in law*). Jinan: Shangdong renmin chubanshe, pp. 135-7

[32] Richard Baum, *Burying Mao.* (Princeton, NJ: Princeton University Press, 1994), pp. 389-90.

[33] The 1980s debate on this is detailed in Ronald C. Keith, "Chinese Politics and the New Theory of the 'Rule of Law,'" *China Quarterly*, no. 125, March 1991, pp. 109-18 and in *China's Struggle for the Rule of Law.* London & New York: Macmillan Press Ltd. & St. Martin's Press, 1994, passim. The recent Post-Deng debate on this subject is covered in Chapter One of Ronald C. Keith & Lin Zhiqiu, *Law and Justice in China's Marketplace*, London: Macmillan Press Ltd., forthcoming.

[34] Keith, *China's Struggle for the Rule of Law*, p. 5.

[35] Ibid., p. 221.

[36] Ronald C. Keith, "Legislating Women's and Children's 'Rights and Interests' in the PRC," *China Quarterly*, No. 149, March 1997, pp. 51-2.

[37] For discussion of "pluralized jurisprudence" see Ronald C. Keith, "Post-Deng Jurisprudence: Justice and Efficiency in a 'Rule of Law' Economy," *Problems of Post-Communism*, May-June 1998, vol. 45, no. 3, pp. 48-48 and Ronald C. Keith & Lin Zhiqiu, *Law and Justice in China's Marketplace*, Chapter One, forthcoming.

38 Qiao Keyu, ed., *Falixue jiaocheng (Instructional program in jurisprudence).* Beijing: Falu chubanshe, 1997, p. 79. As cited in Keith & Lin, *Law and Justice in China's Marketplace,* forthcoming.

39 The core of this legislation includes, but is not exclusive to, the following four laws: *Zhonghua renmin gongheguo funu quanyi baozhangfa (The PRC Law on the Rights and Interests of Women,* 3 April 1992); *Zhonghua renmin gongheguo canfeiren baozhangfa* (The PRC Law on the Handicapped, 20 December 1990); *Zhonghua renmin gongheguo weichengnianren baohufa* (The PRC Law on the Protection of Minors, 4 September 1991); *Zhonghua renmin gongheguo laonianren quanyi baozhangfa* (The PRC Law on the Protection of the Rights and Interests of the Elderly, 29 August 1996). All of the recent human rights legislation have been recently aggregated in *Zhongguo renquan baike quanshu (The Human Rights Encylopedia of China).* Beijing: Zhongfuo da kequan chubanshe, 1998.

40 See Ronald C. Keith, "Post-Deng Jurisprudence," p. 49.

41 "Authorities Promise to Resolve Workplace Disputes and Develop State-Sector Reform," *CND,* 10, 26, 1998.

42 Johnathan Hecht, *Opening to Reform: An Analysis of China's Revised Criminal Procedure Law.* New York & Washington, D.C., Lawyers Committee for Human Rights, October 1996, p. 79. A similar view was expressed in H.L. Fu, "Criminal Defence in China," *China Quarterly,* no. 153, March 1998, pp. 31-48. For more extended analysis see Zhiqiu Lin & Ronald C. Keith, "The Changing Substantive Principles of Chinese Criminal Law," *China Information,* Summer 1998, forthcoming.

43 US State Department, *Country Reports on Human Rights Practices for 1997,* p. 714.

44 This is to repeat the argument in Zhiqiu Lin & Ronald C. Keith, "The Changing Substantive Principles of Chinese Criminal Law," *China Information,* Summer, 1998, passim.

45 Hedley Bull, p. 84.

Globalization: Aid, Trade and Investment in Egypt, Jordan and Syria Since 1980

Paul Sullivan

Introduction

One of the questions I intend to answer in this chapter is what might globalized aid, trade and investment have to do with development in these three countries? First of all, have these countries been developing? The GDP per capita of Egypt grew from $560 in 1980 to $750 in 1985 and 1986. Thereafter there was a drop in GDP per capita to $600 in 1987. It hovered between $600 and $700 for the next five years. Then there was a steady increase, possibly part of the results of Egypt's economic reform and structural adjustment program and the benefits from Egypt's decision to join the Gulf War multi-national coalition against Iraq, such as debt being cut almost in half, remittances increasing, particularly in 1992, and increased aid from the GCC (Gulf Cooperation Council), the EU, the USA and Japan. GDP per capita may have been close to $950 in 1997.

There were a few years, during the precipitous decline in the price of oil in the 1980s, when the GDP per capita was falling. Then there was an upturn after the Gulf War. This upturn, in real per capita terms, has just barely made up for the losses of the late 1980s.

GNP per capita grew from $570 to $630 in 1980 through 1985. It then dropped below $600 for 1988-1991. After 1991, it increased to over $1000 by 1996. It may be as much as $1100 by now.

In real terms wages in Egypt, on average, were about the same in 1993 as they were in 1973. They have increased somewhat since 1993. This has been enough to increase past the years of losses in the late 1980s. However, it may not be enough yet to make up for the frustrations of the years of stagnating real wages. However, since the economic reforms really started moving in 1994, some real positive changes have happened. The improvements in wages followed the developments of the ERSAP (Economic Region Structural Adjustment Program).

For Jordan GDP per capita increased from $450 in 1980 to about $730 in 1983. It then stagnated at about $800 for the years 1983 to

1993. It has increased slightly since then. Jordan's GNP per capita first increased from $1600 to $2200 from 1980 to 1985. Then it dropped to $1000 by 1992, a precipitous drop that started in 1986-87. That is, it happened more because of the drop in oil prices than the effects of the Gulf War. After the Gulf War we see a slow rise in Jordan's GNP per capita. GNP per capita in 1997 was about $1600.

Even so, real wages in Jordan are now not much more than they were in 1973. Unemployment is still high in Jordan. Much of this is due to the continuing effects of the forced repatriation of about 400 000 Jordanians during and after the Gulf War of 1991, and because of Jordan's historically high birth rate and labor force growth rate.

The peace dividend to Jordan from its 1994 peace treaty with Israel has been minimal. But it seems that even Jordan has bounced back from the shocks of the Gulf War. It has been reforming and improving its economy to a moderate extent with some successes. Even so, poverty had increased from 2% of the population in 1987 to 16% in 1992. It is likely that about 15% of Jordan's population still remains at or below the poverty line.

For Syria, GDP per capita was about $1200 in 1979. By 1983 it was $1800. But there was a steep drop-off from 1983 to the $890 figure for 1988-89. Thereafter, it has increased erratically to around $1200-1400 in recent years. Syria's GNP per capita grew from 1980 to 1983, from $1400 to $1800. Then it dropped massively to $820 by 1989. From 1989 to 1991, partly due to the Gulf War boomlet in Syria, GNP per capita increased to about $1200. It then dropped off again and leveled at about $1050 to $1100 until 1996.

There has also been a real slide in the value of the Syrian dinar since 1985. In conversion rate measures in 1985 there were 5 dinar to the US dollar. Recently the figure has been 42 to the dollar, a slide in the value of the Syrian dinar since the Gulf War. The Syrian dinar has been losing its value much faster than the Jordanian dinar and the Egyptian pound since 1980. The Jordanian dinar seems to have been the most stale currency, excepting the time period just after the Gulf War, when one looks at the historical average value of the currencies over the time period 1980 to 1996. In the last three years the most stable currency has been the Egyptian pound. The Syrian dinar has been shedding its value relative to the dollar quite rapidly in recent years. The stability of a country's currency affects that country's economic stability and economic development in many ways. The more stable the currency, the more likely real development in real terms can happen in the long run. In the short run a country can benefit from devaluations. However, for all three of these countries, devaluations seem to have little to do with export growth and a lot more to do with internal inflation and increased debt payments in terms of the local currency.

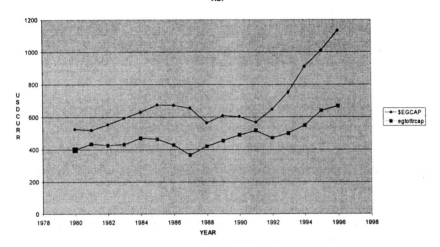

EGYPT: GNP PER CAPITA AND TOTAL TRADE PER CAPITA: SOURCE, WORLD BANK, WDR AND WDI

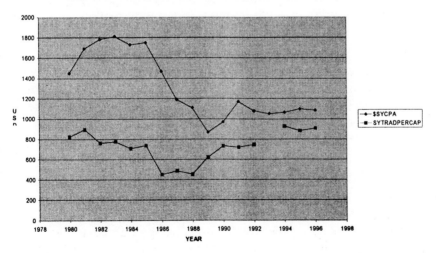

SYRIA: GNP PER CAPITA AND TOTAL TRADE PER CAPITA: SOURCE: WDI, WDR, WDT

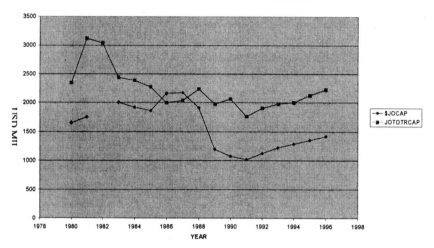

Real wages in Syria in 1993 were just about what they were in 1973. It does not seem likely that real wages have increased significantly since then. The precipitous drop in the dinar along with the relative stagnation of the Syrian economy, combined with Syria's high population growth rate, add up to not much change in the real wages of the average Syrian since 1993.

Furthermore, Syria has had tough times in the last three years. As the oil prices dropped, the post-war aid diminished, the economic reform program showed its weaknesses, and government showed its unwillingness to follow through with real economic and political reform, Syria has faced some significant economic difficulties.

However, according to the *Human Development Report* of 1998, Syria is doing the best of the three with a human development index (HDI in 1995) of .75. Jordan is second with .73 and Egypt is way behind with .62. Jordan's score had remained the same for the previous 15 years. Egypt is the most improved of the three. Its HDI has increased from .5 to .62.

For all three countries there have been improvements in health and education. However, this has been more in quantity than quality in education. Health improvements are undeniable in both quantity and quality measures. The average life span of the average person in these three countries has increased by 2 years in the last 15 years. The under five mortality rates have halved in all three countries in the last 15 years. Well over 90% of the populations of the three have access to health care. Jordan has been in the 90% category since 1980. These are increases in 10-15% of the population having access to health care in Egypt and Syria.

Food production per capita has stayed steady for Jordan and Egypt, but has fallen rapidly for Syria. Food aid has dropped significantly for Egypt, yet has doubled for Syria and nearly quintupled for Jordan.

Telephone lines have increased in all three. Access to safe water has improved. Water systems have improved. Roads have improved, and have increased in miles of paved roads. Rail lines have improved and increased in miles of track, but to a lesser extent than for roads. Syria has increased its length of track but uses it much less than in the past. There have been many infrastructure projects in all three of these countries, mostly paid for by foreign aid and each government. In all three countries there have been very few private sector infrastructure projects. Yet, worldwide infrastructure has been increasingly developed by the private sector.

The manufacturing bases in all three were stronger in 1996 than they were in 1980. Agri-based industries were stronger and more competitive in 1996 than they were in 1980, especially in Egypt. The manufacturing and tourism sectors may have had the best improvements, with construction and trade services running close behind. Again, Egypt seems often to be the most successful at these changes. The petroleum and natural gas industries have also had improvements in Syria and Egypt over the time period. Yes, even as the price of oil has declined in real terms, these industries have improved in their structures and performances relative to their earlier years, especially in Egypt. Syria has shown some moderate improvements, especially in the late 1980s and early 1990s, but there has been some back-stepping lately. Foreign oil companies have been leaving Syria.

Export diversification has been pretty much a failure in all three. Egypt and Syria have depended mostly on petroleum and labor exports. Jordan has depended on phosphates, fertilizers and labor. Yet, since 1980 manufacturing exports have been taking the place of phosphates and fertilizers, slowly, but surely. As the price of phosphates declined, manufacturing exports took part of the phosphate percentage of Jordan's exports. Food exports from Jordan have also increased in their relative importance to the rest of all the exports of Jordan. The real growth in the relative importance of food exports has occurred from the start of the Gulf War and the sanctions against Iraq. Most recently, however, such trade with Iraq has seen some decline.

Exports of manufactures have also been an increasing percentage of all of the exports of Egypt from 1985 to 1995. As fuel exports and many other categories of exports declined in importance, manufactures took their place. Metal exports, particularly exports of aluminum, have also increased in importance since 1980. Food exports have also increased in importance since 1985, obviously with the initiation of serious reforms in Egyptian agriculture and the agricultural trade of Egypt. Non-food primary products, such as cotton, have been in relative decline, but have not shown a rapid decline like that of petroleum.

For Syria, since 1980 textiles showed some improvement – at least until 1991. Since 1985 food exports have also become a more important part of Syria's trade. Non-food primary exports, like cotton, have shown a relative decline in importance. Petroleum exports boomed in the late 1970s to the late 1980s. Then there was a brief drop-off around the time of the Gulf War. Then, unlike with Egypt, oil increased in importance after that. Oil is now about 60-65% of all of Syria's exports. It could be that Syria's non-oil industry could not respond to the changing global marketplace as Egypt's non-oil industry did. Egypt responded slowly compared to the former "tigers," but certainly much faster than Syria. Jordan seems to have the quickest response time to changing circumstance in the international market place. Its size might have something to do with that. However, it has also been the most private-sector oriented of the three. It also has the least number, and weight, of regulations on its industry and its investors. The same might be said about Syria's ability to increase its food exports relative to the ability of Egypt and Jordan to do the same. Jordan is the "most free" economy, Egypt comes second and Syria is the "least free" economy.

All three have been remittance, and, hence, oil price sensitive countries. Egypt and Syria also rely on oil for their internal revenues and as a source of foreign exchange. There have been significant changes since 1980 in the structure of the trade of these countries. However, these changes have not been enough to sufficiently diversify their exports. Also, they could have used these structural changes in trade to help develop industry and employment domestically, but government policies and internal and external political, financial and economic events got in the way often. This was most particularly the case in Syria.

EGYPT: STRUCTURE OF TRADE: WDI, WDR, EIU

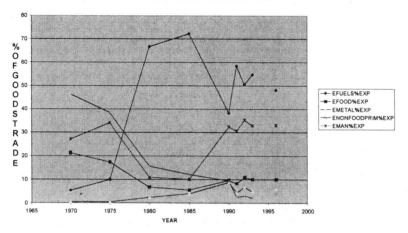

JORDAN: STRUCTURE OF TRADE: WDI, WDR, EIU

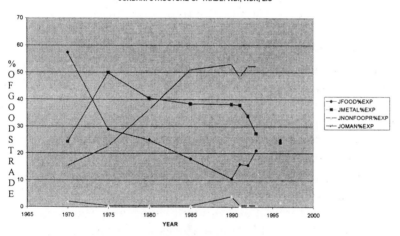

SYRIA: STRUCTURE OF TRADE: WDI. WDR. EIU

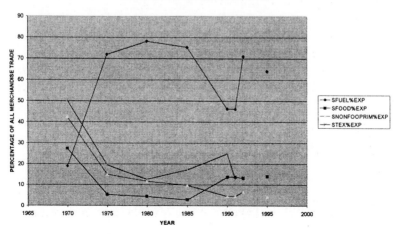

Egypt, Syria and Jordan still rely on volatile sources of income such as oil, remittances, tourism, transport, phosphates and trade in primary commodities. Many other countries have developed away from their reliance on primary commodity trade and toward technology-intensive, human capital (skill) intensive trade and (for labor surplus economies) labor-intensive manufactures exports. These three, especially Egypt and Syria in the 1980s, continued to rely on labor-saving industries and volatile primary products trade, oil in particular. Jordan has been moving in the direction of human capital intensive and technology intensive trade most recently. They have been surprisingly successful in medicines and chemical products. Sometimes these developments in Jordan are tied to some outside investments in the form of foreign direct investment. But more often than not such successes are mostly due to domestic investments. Egypt has also shown some surprising success in chemicals and pharmaceuticals. The recent purchase of Amoun pharmaceuticals by Glaxo-Wellcome may bode well for the development of these very important industries.

All three of these economies have fragile economic connections internationally, because of the structures of their domestic economies, their human and natural resource bases, and the relative non-diversification of their international trade. Once these frailties have been shored up, these countries will be more likely to reap the benefits from the globalization whirlwind.

Of the three, Jordan's economy has been the most private-sector oriented. Jordan was also the first of the three to leap into economic reform and structural adjustment with some zeal. This occurred in part due to the fall in phosphate prices in the early 1980s and its untenable debt and unemployment situations in the late 1980s and early 1990s. Egypt got its ERSAP program running with some zeal only within the last couple of years, after a switch in Prime Ministers and cabinet officials in early 1994. Syria is still unwilling, it seems, even with Law 10 and other so-called liberalization measures, to privatize, restructure and let the economy free itself from the heavy hand of the government that has controlled it for the last three-plus decades.

There have been many improvements in these countries, but hardly the improvements one would have expected if the policy environments of these three countries were more developmentally oriented. To be fair, however, these countries have also been subject to the whipsaw political cycles of the Middle East during the 1980s and 1990s. They have had to face embargoes, peace negotiations, fundamentalism, the fallout from the Iranian revolution, the Iran-Iraq war, Israel's invasion of Lebanon, Syria's virtual takeover of Lebanon, the phony peace process between the Israelis and the devastated Palestinians, and the collapse of the façades of Arab unity and the so-called Arab nation with the Gulf War of 1991. The financial and economic shocks of the Gulf War were in the short to medium run also significant. The Gulf War, however, had very different effects on each of these countries (Sullivan, "Iraq: the Pivot?"). The stunning decline in the real price of oil since the very brief oil boomlet of 1973-1983 has been by far the largest shock to these economies. Some of the results of the collapse of the oil price are political as well as economic.

Debts and the economic polio of the public sector, *inter alia*, drove Egypt to the peace table in 1978. These economic problems continued through the 1980s. As the oil price dropped, the debt of Egypt and the structural weaknesses of its economy drove it to economic reform and structural adjustment. It had no other reasonable choice.

Debts, the Gulf War, consistent over-reliance on volatile sources of income, and so on drove Jordan to the peace table in the 1990s. Economic stagnancy and debt that grew to twice its GNP drove Jordan to a structural adjustment reality check even before Egypt faced its inevitable economic reality check.

The fall of the USSR drove Syria toward at least thinking about liberalization. Liberalization in Syria has been a rough road. Oil companies and other foreign investors have been leaving Syria for the last four years due to foreign exchange rules that have since changed; corruption; a moribund and obsolete banking system; and the sometimes frustrating negotiation practices of certain persons in the government. Syria has been the least willing to change. It has been the most closed polity and economy. It may also be the most backward politically and economically, the HDI aside.

The Gulf War aid booty to Syria and its relatively tiny oil reserves have allowed it to postpone the really tough decisions for a while. The decisions include whether to finally talk peace with Israel, whether to cut back on its massive expenditures on the military and whether it will finally liberalize its politics and economics. A country that postpones such decisions almost always makes them more expensive. Syria has already paid a very high price for its economic and political defiance. It is now a $16 billion dollar economy on a slow slide to, possibly, less than marginality.

Even so, we have also seen another form of development in these three countries: the relative decline of the military. Defense expenditures as a percentage of GDP have dropped significantly in all three since 1980. The greatest drop has been in Jordan, from 16% of GDP in 1980 to 4% of GDP in 1995. Even Syria has seen significant drops, from 16% in 1980 to 5% in 1995. Egypt saw a drop from 7% of GDP in 1980 to 4% in 1995. Syria and Jordan have gone from being two of the most military-dominated economies toward some form of relative normality, or at least "averageness."

A large proportion of the military expenditures of these three countries went to importing weapons. Egypt over the last few years has still remained among the top ten weapons importers in the Third World. Syria, Jordan and Egypt have been some of the best markets for weapons exporters for many years – even though their economies are fairly small in world terms. The GNPs of these three countries combined would not add up to the Gross State product of Kentucky in the USA.

Globalization as a new phenomenon

When we consider the many strong international effects on Egypt, Jordan and Syria, isn't it clear that in many ways they are part of the globalization trend even when they sometimes seem unwillingly so? Furthermore, globalization has hardly been a new phenomena for these three states, which were part of the Ottoman Empire. The Ottoman empire's bankruptcy can be easily traced to globalized supra-national capital. Syria and Jordan were mandate territories after World War I. Egypt was effectively run by the by the British and British investors for years. Many of the 19th and 20th century foreign economic policies of the French and British were governed and controlled by the lobbying of the great industrialists in these countries. Egypt's early mechanized textile industry was in part based on British trans-national capital and technology. The Suez Canal is a globalization phenomenon which was finished in 1869. The making of Israel out of the Yishuv was from a globalized migration of people, ideas and capital. Mohammed Ali would fit right in with Bill Gates, George Soros and Richard Branson at the globalization meetings in Davos. His monopolies were a form of

19th century globalization. Jerusalem, Cairo, Damascus and Alexandria have been global villages for centuries.

Globalization is hardly a new thing for these three countries. For the sake of this chapter the term globalization will be defined as those technological, economic and political changes that have occurred since the new definition of globalization was arbitrarily fixed sometime in the last few years. The time period of our focus is 1980-1997. The variables to be focused on are aid, trade and investment.

The trade and aid environments of Egypt, Jordan and Syria have been globalized for many years – even in the face of high tariff and non-tariff barriers at the borders of these countries. The globalization of trade also occurred even in the face of often anti-export and anti-import laws and regulations, especially in Syria until today, and Egypt until 1991 and the EREIA (Executive Regulations for the Administration of Imports and Exports) (Kheir El-Din, 1992; Handoussa, 1997). Egypt's membership in the WTO, Jordan's observer status and application for full membership, and some signs of opening up of internal and external markets for Syria are indications that such globalization may be expected to increase. The recent ministerial decrees on limiting imports of cars in Egypt may indicate a stepping back, but compared to all that has been going on there moving the country toward globalization and openness, such ministerial decrees are mosquito bites on the back of the globalization giant.

Until most recently, particularly for Syria, the investment environments of these countries have been minimally global and relatively closed off in comparison to countries like Thailand, Indonesia and Turkey. But with the new banking and investment laws of Egypt and Jordan we may see Egypt, and possibly Jordan, globalized in banking and investment even more than the former East Asian Tigers before their recent temporary fall.

Globalized trade

Clearly all three of these countries have had significant global and regional trade in merchandise and labor for many years. All three have been exporting to, and importing from, a large variety of countries for the time period 1973-1997.

Syria has been exporting labor throughout the world for a century. More recently, remittance income to Syria topped out at close to $1 billion in 1980. It had been dropping until just after the Gulf War to around $300 million. In 1993 it may have been 600 million. In 1996 it went up to $900 million. In 1997 it may have been as high as $1 billion. That is a pretty significant trade in labor for a country that had an economy of about $16-20 billion in 1997.

Egypt exports its labor mostly to the Gulf, Syria has remittances coming in from all over the world, including North and South America. For Egypt, remittances have been a large proportion of its GNP since the late 1970s. They accounted for about $2.1 billion in 1980, $4 billion in 1984, and over $6 billion in 1992. There was a sharp drop after 1992 to about $3-4 billion in 1993-1994. The 1992 upsurge may have been due to the remittance workers sending back more remittances than usual and some of their bank and other savings because of their perception of Egypt as a safer place to keep their money than the Gulf. This was likely a "one-shot."

More recently remittances have averaged about $3-4 billion. Egypt's remittances seemed to have defied the fall in the oil price in the 1980s. That may have been due more to economic diplomacy by the Gulf states than the necessarily increasing demand for Egyptian labor by the GCC and other Arab oil producers. Such increases against the trend in oil prices and oil revenues may have been a signal from the Arab oil states that they were going to support Egypt even in the face of the Arab embargo of Egypt and Egypt's signing of the Camp David Accords and the peace treaty with Israel. They may not have been that much against the treaty in the first place, possibly. The increased remittances may have been a subtle way to replace the aid that would have come from the Arab oil states had the peace treaty with Israel not been signed. However, the Arab oil states could not say this openly and publicly. They could say it by hiring more Egyptians, even though publicly they disagreed with Egyptian foreign policy. This is the opposite of what they did to the Palestinians, Yemenis, Sudanese and Jordanians after the Gulf War because of their countries' foreign policies with regard to Iraq (Sullivan, "Contrary views").

Like Egypt and Syria, Jordan's remittance trade really started to take off after the 1973 oil shock. There was another sharp upturn after the 1979 oil shock. Jordanian remittances boomed from $21 million in 1972 to close to $1 billion in 1981-82. By 1991 they were $450 million. However, there was already a significant and steady decline in remittances to Jordan before the Gulf War happened. The decline before and during the Gulf War was mostly due to the expulsion of

Jordanians, especially Palestinians, almost entirely from Kuwait, and many from Saudi Arabia. Many also left before and during the Iraqi invasion of Kuwait, and during the time period between the end of that war and the multi-national coalition invasion of Iraq. These drops in remittances, however, were mitigated by the remittance deposits into Jordan brought back by some of the "lucky" returnees. By 1993 remittances were back up to $1 billion. By 1996 they were $6 billion. These recent increases may be due to the return of some of the expelled Jordanians to the Gulf, although not many to Kuwait, and to the settlements of legal cases brought by Jordanians for lost assets because of the war and the expulsions.

What are other indications of global trade connections for the three countries, connections that could help them develop globalization strategies and successes in the future?

Total trade (imports and exports of goods and services) was 100% of GDP for Jordan in 1973. By 1980 it was 225% of GDP. Jordan saw a huge drop in trade/GDP from 1980-1986. By 1986 the ratio was back down to 100%. But it has bounced back. Over the last couple of years it has been at about 140-150% of GDP.

For Egypt, total trade had been between 50 and 80% of GDP from 1975 to 1997. There was a decline from 1980 to 1987 from about 80% to 50%. Since then it has bounced back to around 60-70% of GDP.

Even for a so-called isolated state like Syria, total trade has been hovering at around 50% of GDP from 1975 to date. For Syria it has been on a fairly even keel, unlike the trade/GDP ratios for Egypt and Jordan.

Putting these figures in per capita terms one can get a better feel for the situation. Trade per capita for Jordan has been over GDP per capita for just about every year since 1975. In 1981-83 trade per capita was around $3000 and GDP was around $1000. Trade per capita has dropped to about $2000 since then. Overall, after a steep decline to 1987, GDP per capita has risen slightly since 1983.

This, of course, was generated by global oil prices that generated regional remittances, that generated huge domestic imports during the time of the oil boomlet in the late 1970s and early 1980s.

For Egypt we see a still fairly trade-sensitive economy with GDP per capita trailing just under the total trade per capita. The closest points for these two data series were in 1980-1982, when they were almost equal. From that time period an increasing gap occurred, that is only recently being closed – unfortunately because of the huge increase in imports into Egypt over the last few years since the Gulf War.

Syria seems to be the least trade sensitive of the three. The gap between GDP per capita and trade per capita had been widening from 1973 to 1985-86. However, this gap was in the opposite direction to the gap that was being produced in Jordan. For Syria, GDP per capita was increasing much faster than trade per capita. After 1985-86 the gap was closing in Syria.

Interim conclusion: Jordan is by far the most trade sensitive. Egypt comes in a far second. Syria is a distant third. The charts for GNP per capita and total trade per capita show similar results (see the first three charts in this paper). Also in these charts one can see the trade sensitivity of these three countries. One can also see how internationally connected these countries have been.

Looking at the products these countries export may give us an idea of where globalization may help their economic developments in the future:

Syria's largest export markets in 1996 were the EU, Italy in particular, Spain, Croatia, Cyprus, Turkey, Jordan, Lebanon, Saudi Arabia, and, oddly, Costa Rica. Syria's largest import markets have been Italy, Japan, the People's Republic of China, Korea, the Czech Republic, Romania, Turkey, Ukraine, Egypt, Jordan, Saudi Arabia Argentina and Brazil. Now that seems like a global enough list for a small country like Syria. Syria's top export items are by most important country of destination the following (www.intracen.org/itc):

Product group for export	Top destination markets
Oil	Italy, Germany, France
Cotton	Italy & Spain
Petroleum products	Italy & Cyprus
Vegetables	Saudi Arabia, Kuwait, Italy
Fruits & Nuts	Saudi Arabia, Kuwait, Egypt
Apparel	Germany, France, U.K.
Live Animals	Saudi Arabia, Kuwait, Italy
Wheat	Tunisia, Germany, Belgium
Leather	Italy, China, Turkey
Women's Clothing	U.K., Saudi Arabia, Kuwait
Fertilizers	France, Romania, Yugoslavia

[Oil accounted for about 65% of Syria's exports merchandise exports in that year, and 20% of its GDP.] Many of these exports are not usually thought of as some of the driving forces of development. The linkages with the rest of the economy are limited in the industries associated with the production of these products, especially the oil industry.

Syria has not done well in connecting its exports to the basic needs of real development. For all of Syria's exports in 1996, primary products accounted for 93%, labor-intensive products 4%, technology-intensive products a measly 1%, human capital intensive products just 1% and natural resource intensive products only 1%. Primary product based development often has led to impoverishing growth in developing as well as developed countries.

Egypt's largest import markets have recently been the USA, the EU, the People's Republic of China, Japan, Malaysia, Singapore, Poland, Romania, Turkey, Saudi Arabia and Brazil. Egypt's largest export markets have been Italy, the USA, the UK, other large EU economies, Singapore, Romania, Turkey, Saudi Arabia, Japan and Australia. Just about all of the continents are in this list. Egypt's recent top articles of exports:

Product group for export	Top destination markets
Oil	Israel, Italy, Romania
Petroleum products	Italy, USA, Romania
Yarns	Italy, USA, Belgium
Vegetables	UK, Germany, Saudi Arabia
Apparel	USA, Germany, UK
Men's clothing	USA, Italy, Romania
Aluminum	Belgium, Germany, Italy
Women's clothing	USA, Italy, Romania
Cotton	Japan, Korea, Italy
Fruits & Nuts	Saudi Arabia, Kuwait, UK
Woven cotton	Italy, UK, Romania
Floor coverings	USA, Germany, Japan

Egypt also exports iron bars to Saudi Arabia, the USA and Japan. Again, many of these export items are not exactly related to the driving forces of modern development. But Egypt is doing a lot better than Syria in this category. Of all of Egypt's exports in 1996, 67% were primary products, 4% were natural resource intensive, 21%

labor-intensive (good for a labor surplus economy), 4% technology-intensive, and 4% human capital intensive products. If exports are to lead to development, Egypt does not seem to focusing on the most dynamic and competitive industries in the long run.

Jordan's largest export markets in 1996 were India, Saudi Arabia and Iraq. Jordan's largest import sources were the EU, the PRC, Turkey, Ukraine, Saudi Arabia, Iraq, Japan, Australia and Brazil. Notice that Egypt, Jordan and Syria share in some of the non-Arab markets for exports and share in sources of imports. When one looks at the export markets these three countries have outside and inside of the region, and the overlaps in the products that they export, one can also see some room for competition as well as cooperation.

Product group for export	Top destination markets
Fertilizers, processed	Malaysia, Philippines, Korea
Crude fertilizers	Netherlands, India, Japan
Live animals	Saudi Arabia, Kuwait, Netherlands
Medicines	Saudi Arabia, Tunisia, Iraq
Hides & skins	Turkey, Italy, Spain
Lime, cement	Saudi Arabia, Malaysia, Kuwait
Mechanical engines	UK, Netherlands
Petroleum products	India, Saudi Arabia
Men's clothing	USA, Italy, UK
Vegetables	Kuwait, Germany, UK
Aircraft	UK, Germany
Waste metal	Korea, Hong Kong, Japan

Fertilizers accounted for about 45% of all of Jordan's exports. In the 1980s they accounted for far more. Do these export items connect up with the rest of the Jordanian economy with linkages for development? Of all of Jordan's exports in 1996, 45% were primary products, 3% natural resource intensive, 6% labor-intensive, 40% technology-intensive and 5% human capital intensive.

Jordan seems to be doing a lot better job than both Egypt and Syria on the technology-intensive score and the human capital intensive score, but worse than Egypt in the labor-intensive score. In terms of development connections to exports, Jordan comes out on top. Because of this they may have the brightest future in development via globalized trade than the other two.

Globalized investment

What about globalized investment trends in these three countries? Fast food, communications, tourism, baby food, other food processing industries, pharmaceutical and business services seem to be the most likely candidates. The International Finance Corporation has been involved in tourism in Jordan and Egypt. It has also been involved in natural gas projects in Jordan, general investment in Jordan, the establishment of a risk management facility with the National Bank of Egypt, the aluminum industry of Jordan, Jordan's telecom sector, the establishment of an inter-Arab rating company with the Arab Monetary Fund, a tissue paper plant in Jordan, equity investments in Egypt, and the banking sector of Egypt.

Large trans-national oil companies have been involved in all three countries, but most of all in Egypt. Egypt has the largest potential oil reserves known and certainly has a more pro-business environment than Syria. Some of the companies involved in Egypt include Apache, Amoco, Arco, ENI-Agip, Exxon, BP and Mobil. Syria has attracted such companies as Tullow, Conoco, Elf and Total. An Arab-Israeli crude oil refinery in Egypt, called Midor, is still in the works it seems, with Spain's Repsol as the manager.

Egypt may have as much as $12 billion in assets to sell from its stock of public sector companies. This is another reason for foreign investors to take a closer look at Egypt. The Syrian Government may have billions of public assets to sell, but they seem to have little interest in doing so. The Egyptian Government seems focused on its privatization drive.

Petrobel of Egypt is a subsidiary of ENI of Italy. Seagull Energy of the USA is very much involved in joint ventures with the EGPC (Egyptian General Petroleum Corporation). BP Chemical is involved in the production and management of a polyethylene plant. The Sumed pipeline is owned by the Arab Petroleum Pipeline Company (APP), which is a multi-national joint venture: 50% Egypt, 15% Saudi Arabia, 15% Kuwait, 15% UAE and 5% Qatar. The International

Egyptian Oil Company (IEOC) is a subsidiary of ENI of Italy. IEOC is the leading producer of natural gas in Egypt. A nuclear research reactor was "finished" near Alexandria by an Argentinian firm in late 1997.

Egypt is looking into methods of getting more FDI into the country in electricity generation and distribution though BOOT (build-own-operate-transfer) project offerings. Natural gas company investments can be found in all three of the countries. One of the biggest natural gas investments, which unfortunately seems to have fallen apart, was to happen in Jordan. This was to be the construction of a massive LNG (liquefied natural gas) plant by Enron corporation of Houston, Texas. This liquefied natural gas was to be regassified and transported to Jordan, Israel and other markets. The gas to be regassified was to be Qatari liquefied gas, that is, LNG shipped by LNG tankers from Qatar to Jordan. The port of Aqaba was also going to be considerably changed by this investment. Now Israel has transferred this idea to a regassification plant to be built offshore near Ashkelon.

Now the biggest natural gas investment in Jordan is for the pipeline network that will bring gas from Egypt (but not just originating only in Egypt) to Jordan, the Palestinian Territories, and then up to Syria, Turkey and so forth. There are also plans to establish a natural gas loop almost encircling the Mediterranean. There are huge potentials for private sector investment here. Certainly the governments of the southern Mediterranean region cannot afford the entire cost of construction, maintenance, repairs, upgrades and whatever else will be needed to make this mega-project work. The World Bank and other development agencies may pay another part of the bill, but certainly in this political, economic and ideological environment, the private sector could find real opportunities in these power projects.

Jordan may have as much as 30 billion barrels of oil equivalent locked up in shale rock. In February, 1998, Shell Oil Corporation signed an agreement with Jordan to develop these shale oil reserves. US companies Westinghouse and Oil Shale Energy, Inc. are involved in the construction of an oil shale electrical plant near Lejjun.

The recent decision by Kuwait and Saudi Arabia to sell oil once again to Jordan at concessionary prices, as well as the relatively low price of oil recently, will make this project and many other energy projects less profitable for the time being, but they will likely still be built. They will also help Jordan develop energy independence to some extent.

India's Southern Petrochemicals Industry has a joint venture in Jordan for a $170 million phosphoric acid plant which came on line in August, 1997. The Arab Potash Company and a Japanese consortium led by Mitsubushi are building a fertilizer plant and an ammonia phosphate plant near Aqaba. Norsk Hydro is developing plans for a $400 million fertilizer project in Aqaba and Shidideh.

The Indo-Jordan Chemicals Company is a joint venture among Jordan Phosphate Mines Company, Southern Petrochemicals Industry Corporation and the Arab Investment Company of Riyadh, Saudi Arabia.

The Jordan-Japan NPK plant is joint venture among Jordan Phosphate Mines Company, the National Federation of Agriculture Association (ZEN-NOH), Mitsubushi Chemical, Asahi Industries and Mitsubishi Industries.

The Jordan Phosphate Mines Company and Fauiji Fertilizer of Pakistan signed an agreement in 1994 to develop a DAP and UREA plant. JPMC supplies phosphoric acid for the plant that has been built in Pakistan for 13 years.

Israel and Jordan have been developing a qualified industrial zone (QIZ). The companies who choose to join this joint venture will get exemptions from US taxes and tariffs if they can prove a certain percentage of joint Israeli-Jordanian production. They will also get other incentives from both Jordan and Israel.

In 1995, Malaysia's Petronas and Trans-Global of Houston, Texas, started exploring for gas and oil in northern Jordan. Jordan plans to privatize its oil sector. It is doubtful Egypt and Syria will consider such a move anytime in the foreseeable future. Jordan is in the process of privatizing its electrical power and transport sectors. There will certainly be opportunities there for FDI or even FPI (foreign portfolio investment).

On the other end of the liberalization spectrum, after 3 years of debate Syria has allowed Belgium's Tractabel and Lebanon's Sarabaki Group to build the first private power plant in the country, but it will only be a 600 megawatt plant. Even in the somewhat stifling environment of Syria, many Syrian investors in the textiles, pharmaceuticals, food processing and other light industries have backing from Gulf investors. Only 5 of the 14 oil companies that were in Syria in 1991 remained in 1998. These companies were Elf,

Marathon, Demenix, Tullow and Shell. The unsatisfactory business arrangements given by the Syrian Petroleum Corporation, as well as poor exploration results, corruption and problems with exchange regulations, drove most of the oil companies out. A somewhat surprising set of events occurred when Mitsubishi Heavy Industries was allowed to start construction on a 600 MW power plant near Al-Zara (with a soft loan to Syria from the Japanese Government) and a 1065 MW power plant near Aleppo (with a Saudi Development Fund loan to Syria).

Syria's crude oil exploration and production is dominated by Al Furat Petroleum Corporation, which is a joint venture among Syria's state-owned Syrian Petroleum Corporation, Royal Dutch/Shell, Pecten of the USA and Demenix of Germany. The marketing of crude oil in Syria is mostly done by Sytrol, which is a joint venture among Syrian public sector firms and Agip, Bayoil, Chevron, Conoco, Marc Rich, Oemu, Shell, Total and Veba. There is a $300 million service contract up for auction to develop associated gas in Syria. Conoco of the USA may have a good chance at winning it. Considering that oil is 55-60% of all of the export earnings of Syria, energy investments are vital. Natural gas may become much more important to Syria in the future. This is not only in the use of Syria's own gas reserves, but in the transmission of other countries' gas across Syrian territory. FDI will likely be needed for that to occur in the best fashion.

In Egypt, Hoechst Orient and the Arab African bank have floated bonds on the international markets to finance their future developments. About 50% of Egypt's most recent FDI inflows have been in manufacturing, another 30% has been in banking. This is a big change from earlier times when almost all of the FDI was in oil, with the rest going to tourism development. A good part of the new banking investment is due to recent changes in the business environment in Egypt as well as recent banking law changes that further opened up the potential for foreign ownership of Egyptian banks. This is a long way from Nasserism and Arab Socialism.

Most of Egypt's FDI stock is to be found in petroleum and natural gas joint ventures with the Egyptian General Petroleum Corporation (EGPC).

The Egyptian government has been floating bonds of around $250 million in the last year or so. Part of the funds from these bond floats may go to the development of the New Nile Valley, or the Toshkha Project in Upper Egypt. This is a major step away from

Nasser's way of partly financing the Aswan High Dam by national-
izing the Suez Canal. Could one imagine Nasser floating Aswan
High Dam bonds on Wall Street?

The Egyptian British Bank is now in a joint venture with the
Hong Kong and Shanghai Banking Corporation (HSBC). Egypt has
a baby food plant set up by Nestle and telephone exchanges set up
by AT&T and Seimens. These are hardly new examples of globalization. They were set up in the 1980s. The infrastructure projects
were mostly financed by globalized aid. If these projects were to be
done now, they might be financed in large part by the private sector.

The Egyptian data do not distinguish between Egyptian and
other Arab investors. This certainly leads to an underestimate of foreign investment stocks and flows. The non-Egyptian Arabs, especially Gulf Arabs and Libyans, have been very much involved in
investments in Egypt. Their investments can be found in banking,
construction, tourism, land reclamation (the New Nile Valley Project
or Toshka), oil and petrochemicals, for examples. Some of the nicest
hotels in Egypt are owned by Libyan and GCC investors. Arab
investors are a big part of the Egyptian privatization process.

One consider this as much a part of globalization as any investor
from Japan or Germany getting involved in Egypt. The non-
Egyptian Arab investors are foreign investors, all of the pan-Arab
Nasserism holding over in the statistical offices notwithstanding.
Real globalization for Egypt will include regional integration in
investment and trade, as well as more extensive global integration in
investment and trade. The regional integration and the global integration seem to be happening in these three countries at the same
time, albeit at different rates and directions for each country, with
mixed results.

For example, Arab investment in Egypt did slow down, but did
not stop, during the Arab "embargo" of Egypt (Lavy, 1984; Sullivan,
1998(2); Baradie). As the Arabs mostly kept away from investing in
Egypt, western firms like Amoco, Marriot, Sheraton, Elf, Agip, Le
Meridien and Movenpick moved in. Arab investment started up
again with gusto after the Gulf War. Many of Egypt's best businesses have Gulf Arab investors, partners or backers. More and more
western investors are showing interest in Egypt, but many investors
still have a sense of caution for the country. Given its political and
military past, as well as its weak legal system, they have good reason to be cautious.

Law Number 8 of 1997, put into force in May, 1997, was supposed to really open the floodgates of foreign investment with new and improved tax exemptions, free zone incentives and so forth. This law is far more business-friendly than its predecessor, Law 230. This law is meant to start the foundation of new businesses in Egypt. Venture capital markets may have reached the pyramids.

Recent improved taxation agreements also exist between Egypt and the USA and Egypt and the UK. This may add positively to the investment environment in Egypt for companies from the USA and the UK. The new Egyptian banking laws may also help in foreign banking investment, which may bring in new banking technologies, as well as new and better auditing and accounting procedures to Egyptian banks. They are certainly in need of such improvements.

However, the weak legal system, systematic official and private corruption, the low skills of much of the labor and management in Egypt, poor work ethics compared to East Asian competitors, somewhat opaque customs procedures, events such as what happened in Luxor in November, 1997, the faltering of the peace process, increased tensions due to what is happening in Iraq, and increased threats to many western countries' citizens, do not help the investment climate of Egypt – even with all of the improvements to the legal and economic environment of the country.

Jordan also has made some progress in opening up FDI in banking and in other fields. Syria is way behind the other two.

Egypt has 28 domestic commercial banks, 21 foreign commercial banks and 33 investment banks. Jordan has 15 domestic commercial banks, 5 foreign commercial banks and 12 investment banks. Syria has 1 domestic commercial bank, no foreign commercial banks and 4 investment banks. The banking system in Syria is so poorly run that many of the diplomats in Damascus, and their embassies, use banks in Lebanon. Jordan has the highest bank density per person of the three, followed by Egypt, and way down the list, with a lower bank density than the Sudan, is Syria.

We can get another view of the globalizing investment picture by looking at the total FDI figures over time in these three countries. From 1983 to 1988 average FDI inflows into Egypt were about $959 million per year. The peak years were 1984 and 1985 with about $1.2 billion. 1988-89 saw about the same amounts. After 1989, there was a steep drop-off, possibly because of the political uncertainties due to the Gulf War. For the 1990-1993 period FDI hovered in the $200 to $450 million range. In 1994 there was a tremendous leap to $1.4 billion. According to the IMF, it then dropped to $600 million for 1995 and 1996. According to the Economist Intelligence Unit, it increased in 1995 and 1996 to about $1.5 billion each year. 1997 may have been even higher, according to the EIU. Portfolio flows into Egypt have been erratic. There was just $5 million in 1981, $20 million in 1985, and back down to $2 million in 1989. In 1990 there were just $15 million, and $6 million in 1992. These are tiny amounts compared to overall international portfolio flows in the trillions of dollars, mostly to Asia, and particularly in the late 1980s and early 1990s.

EGYPT: FDI INFLOWS: SOURCE: IMF, BOPS

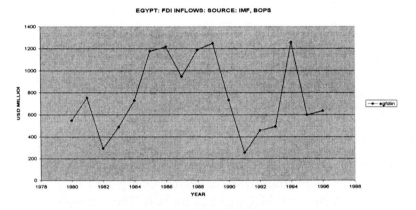

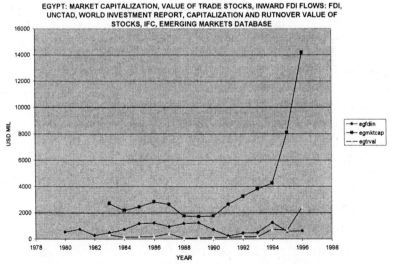

A measure of Egypt's ability to absorb FDI and FPI may be partially found in the capitalization of its stock markets. This was greatly aided by the Capital Markets Law of 1992 and Law 8 of 1997. Until the Capital Markets Law of 1992, the total capitalization of the Egyptian stock market was just $3 billion. By 1994 it was $4 billion.

By 1996 it was $14 billion. In 1997 it was a relatively staggering $20 billion. Egypt's stock markets have had some positively inspiring improvements since 1992. The first real upturn in the market was in 1991. This corresponds to the start of Egypt's ERSAP program and Egypt's beneficial international financial situation due to the Gulf War. However, only about 2% of Egypt's equity holdings on the stock market are held by foreigners recently. Most of this increase in the value of the stock market is due to Egyptians investing. The building up of this stock market is, however, a very good sign for potential increases in foreign investment in Egypt.

Turnover of stocks has also seen huge changes in recent years. Until 1994 turnover was only about $500 million per year. In 1994 it leapt to $700 million. By 1996 turnover in stock was about $2.5 billion. There is hope for globalization here, especially when one considers that over 60% of investment in Egypt is now private sector investment. But, then again, FDI is only .9% of GDP. Egypt has a long way to go. It has also come a very long way in the last 15 years.

Jordan's FDI inward flows, according to the IMF, have been in decline since 1981. They were $140 million in 1981. Most of these investments were from the GCC countries. By 1984 they were just $80 million. In 1990, FDI was $40 million. There have been years since the Gulf War when FDI was net negative. Part of the explanation for this in the pre-war years is that most of this FDI inflow has been from the Gulf Arab states. As their revenues declined, so also did their investments in Jordan. As Jordan showed its lukewarm support for Saddam Hussein in the invasion of Kuwait and as it tried to stave off the Gulf War of 1991, Gulf Arab investment dried up. Since the Gulf War most of the FDI into Jordan has been from Israel (since the 1994 signing of the peace treaty), the West, the EU and the USA, and very interestingly, the East, India, Japan and Pakistan. Still, it is paltry compared to what it could be. From 1991 to 1993 net FDI was on average -$5 million. From 1984 to 1988 it was just $37 million per year. For 1994 to 1997 FDI inflows averaged about $51 million per year. This is still very low, but at least an improvement over the previous years.

Jordan has very good potential for foreign investment. It may also be in a much better position to benefit from globalizing investment than either Egypt or Syria. Jordan's stock market may be the most modern and efficient in the Middle East. That certainly gives hope for investment inflows.

JORDAN: NET FDI INFLOWS: SOURCE: IMF, BOPS, VARIOUS YEARS

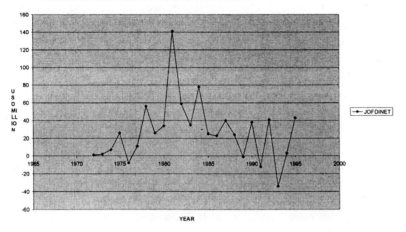

JORDAN: MARKET CAPITALIZATION (AFM) AND MARKET TURNOVERVALUE: SOURCE: IFC, EMERGING MARKETS DATABASE

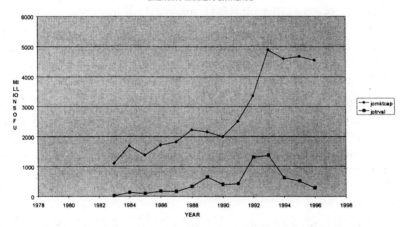

In 1983 the capitalization of the Jordanian stock market was about $1 billion. By 1990 it was $2 billion. By 1993 it had blossomed to $5 billion. Some of this money is likely a result of the inflow of funds from some of the Jordanians who returned from the Gulf because of the war and the expulsions. The Amman Financial Market (AFM) may be capitalized at around $6 billion recently.

There have also been significant improvements in the investment laws of Jordan since 1991. Law 16 of 1995, the "Investment Promotion Law," has brought in some foreign investment. Unfortunately, such investments have usually been under $100 million in the major industries in Jordan. There have been some very large investments by the Japanese and Indians recently, however.

As in Egypt, as government investment went down as a percentage of the GDP, the private sector and the stock market seems to have taken up the slack, even during some of the most difficult times, like during and after the Gulf War of 1991. Private investment is now 77% of all investment in Jordan. This is one of the highest in the Middle East. But FDI is only .2% of GDP.

A rather odd result is that the stock market capitalization of Jordan had its greatest growth period during 1990 to 1993. This is when Jordan was having some of its toughest economic crises in decades. It was also before the peace treaty with Israel. Since the peace treaty was signed, the capitalization of the stock market of Jordan has been relatively stagnant. The turnover of stocks also boomed in 1990 to 1993, from $400 million to $1.4 billion. Turnover has dropped off to under $200 million since then.

The pre-peace boom may have had a lot to do with changes in investment and tax laws. It may also have had something to do with the restrictive measures the IMF imposed on Jordan while it developed its ERSAP program. It may also have had something to do with the privatizations that were occurring at that time. But it also had a lot to do with the 400 000+ Jordanians who were mostly forced to return and start a new life, and new businesses in Jordan after 1990.

Another important fact about the Amman Financial Market (AFM), as reported by the Jordanian Embassy in Washington, DC, is that about 33% of the AFM's market value is owned by non-Jordanians. The Government of Jordan owns 26%. The Jordanian Embassy also reports that the private sector is 100% of construction, 94% of manufacturing, 95% of services like banking, business and other finance.

The Investment Promotion Corporation of Jordan, established as part of Law 16, "Investment Promotion Law," of 1995, gives the following data for investments in different sectors of Jordan for 1997. For industrial projects, 159.6 million JD were from domestic sources, 64.3 million JD were from foreign sources. For hotels, 74 million JD were from domestic sources, 54 million JD were from foreign sources. For agricultural investments, 12.2 million JD were from domestic sources, 4.9 million JD were from foreign sources. The exchange permits for that time period may also show who is doing what amount of investing. Persons or companies from the "Arab Common Market" countries were given 11.4 million JD in exchange permits. Other Arab persons or companies were given 5.3 million JD. EEC persons or companies were given 12.1 million JD. Persons or companies from the USA were, surprisingly, the highest at 32.9 million JD. Others had only 4.2 million JD total.

Syria seems to be a very different story. The annual average FDI inflows for Syria from 1983-1888 were about $38 million. This is a tiny number, like that for Jordan, compared to Egypt – and certainly compared to Singapore, Thailand, Taiwan and South Korea during the same time period. These numbers are also tiny compared to the Gulf Arab and other investments that could have gone to Syria if it had a more amenable foreign policy and if it had a more pro-business policy domestically. It may also have helped if Syria's banking system was not so corrupt, obsolete and inefficient. Syria's support of Iran in the Iran-Iraq war did not make many friends for Syria in the Gulf Arab states. The EIU report, quoting UNIDO (United Nations Industrial Development Organization) figures, estimated that as much as $8 billion in foreign investment might pour into Syria over the next few years if the government would allow the banks to go private, and the government regulations on these banks were liberalized.

The best year for FDI for Syria seems to have been 1994, with $200 million flowing in. 1995 and 1996 saw $100 million less. Many of these investments were in the oil industry. The drop off after this may have been due to most of these oil companies leaving Syria.

The data on FDI for Syria seem much more difficult to find than the data on Jordan and Egypt. Syria can sometimes be an opaque country anyway. Syria also has no stock market. Its financial markets are far behind those of Jordan and Egypt. It also has about half of the known oil reserves, and much less capacity for tourism than

RECENT FDI INFLOWS INTO SYRIA: SOURCE: IMF, BOPS

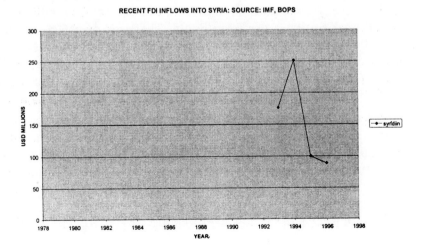

Egypt. Syria has many wonderful tourist areas, but not as many high quality hotels nor as much tourism infrastructure as Egypt has – or even as Jordan has per capita. Tourism investment in Syria seems to be mostly from domestic sources. There have been some considerable improvements lately. Now Syrian investors are focusing on building for the needs of wealthy Syrians, Gulf Arabs and tourists from the West. Tourism from France and Germany has increased considerably recently. Still, most tourists to Syria come from Lebanon and Jordan. The highest number used to be from Iran. But Iran has been having some economic difficulties lately. The Alawis, the ruling group in Syria, are an offshoot of Shia Islam. Iranians are also not hassled as much in Syria as they are in other countries in the region.

For Syria only .6% of the GDP is FDI, according to The World Bank, *World Development Indicators*. One might expect that the actual FDI is larger because the silent partners some Syrian businessmen have. Many of these partners come from the Gulf. They are also sometimes wealthy Syrians who now live outside of Syria. The textiles, pharmaceutical, food processing and other light industries have benefited from such outside backing. The opening of trade with Iraq in June, 1997, may also give some incentive for increased foreign investment. Some businessmen may be looking at Syria as a conduit for developing present, and possibly more important, future trading relations with Iraq.

For international equity issues, Egypt has been the only real player of the three. Outside of Kuwait it is the largest floater of international equity issues in the Middle East and North Africa. Before 1996 there were almost no international flotations from Egypt. There is still zero in Jordan and Syria. In 1996 there were $233 million in international equity issues from Egypt. That was over 50% of the international equity issues in the entire MENA region. The first and second quarters of 1997 saw over $200 million more international equity floats. These were using GDRs (Global Depository Receipts) and ADRs (American Depository Receipts).

When it comes to catching at least part of the wave of globalizing investments, Egypt seems to be the real winner and potentially the biggest winner of foreign FDI, FPI and international equity floats of the three. Jordan, however, should not be counted out. It still has chances of being the most agile economic "tiger" of the Arab world. Comparatively, Egypt is in a much stronger position for many reasons. Egypt's FDI stock is now over $4 billion. Egypt's pension funds bring in about $700 million annually and have a net worth of about $10 billion. There are real opportunities to develop global investing in Egypt.

There are various free zones being set up in all three of these countries. FDI and FPI may find a more welcoming, and more profitable environment in these areas than in other parts of the three countries.

Globalization of aid

Aid is another area in which these three countries have been "globalized" for many years. Aid for Egypt since Camp David has been mostly from the USA, but also from Western Europe, Japan, Canada, Australia, the People's Republic of China and more. For Egypt aid has dropped from 15% of GNP in 1990-1991 to about 3% of GNP recently. In 1980 it was just 6% of GNP. Jordan's aid is about 8% of GNP. Most of its recent aid has come from the USA, the EU and, somewhat surprisingly, Japan. In 1983 aid was 18% of Jordan's GNP. Most of this aid was coming from the GCC. In 1990-1991 it was 22% of GNP. From that year on aid from the GCC evaporated and the EU, the USA and Japan filled the aid gap, and actually increased the total foreign aid coming into Jordan considerably in 1990-1991. Syria's aid was about 1.4% of GNP in 1996. In 1980 it was about 16%. There had been a sharp drop off in aid during the decline of the price of oil in the 1980s, which corresponded with the time in which Syria supported Iran in the Iran-Iraq war. The collapse of the USSR is another reason for the decline of aid into Syria. After the Gulf War, aid to Syria increased dramatically from the EU, Japan and the GCC, but it was still not over 5% of GNP.

For these three countries most aid, be it from Arab, Western or Asian sources, has often been based more on global strategic concerns and economic (market) concerns of the donor countries. Egypt, Syria and Jordan were highly strategic countries during the Cold War. They were vital strategically during the Iran-Iraq war. They were also very important, especially to the GCC, during the Gulf War of 1991. Throughout the time period 1980-1997, they were continuously strategic for another reason, Israel. Egypt, Syria and Jordan have been important in the strategic quest to keep oil flowing smoothly and securely to both the east and the west. Egypt, Syria and Jordan are also considered important, or at the very least, potentially important transit and storage zones for international markets.

JORDAN: AID AS PERCENT OF GDI, GNP AND IMPORTS OF GOODS AND SERVICES (WDI)

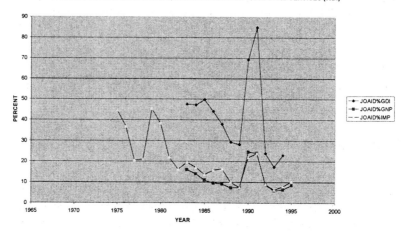

SYRIA: AID AS A PERCENT OF GDI, GNP AND IMPORTS OF GOODS AND SERVICES (WDI)

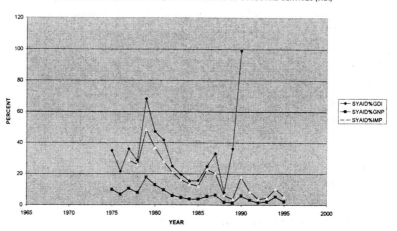

EGYPT: PERCENTS AID OF GDI, GNP AND IMPORTS OF GOODS AND SERVICES (WDI)

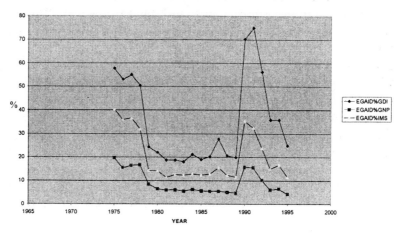

They may be relatively poor countries in economic terms. Militarily, they could hardly go to war with the USA or the PRC, but they are rich in strategic location. All three are essentially collectors of strategic rent called economic and military aid.

Most foreign aid has gone into infrastructure, and mostly large-scale projects. Some has gone to education, family planning and other quality of life issues. There has also been much aid directly sent to balance trade and government accounts, and to help establish industries. These projects may have long term effects on the overall development of these countries.

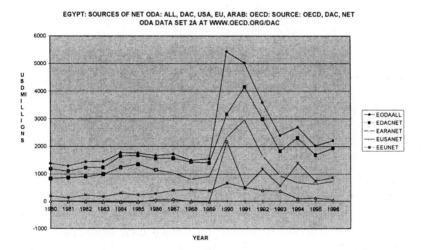

EGYPT: SOURCES OF NET ODA: ALL, DAC, USA, EU, ARAB: OECD: SOURCE: OECD, DAC, NET ODA DATA SET 2A AT WWW.OECD.ORG/DAC

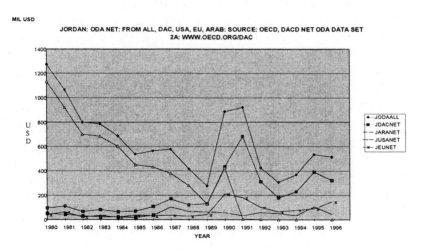

MIL USD

JORDAN: ODA NET: FROM ALL, DAC, USA, EU, ARAB: SOURCE: OECD, DACD NET ODA DATA SET 2A: WWW.OECD.ORG/DAC

SYRIA: ODA NET: FROM ALL, DAC, USA, EU

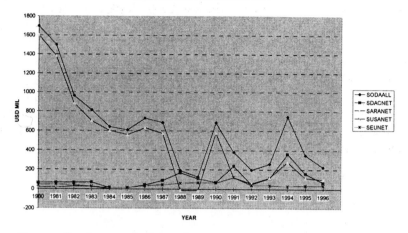

    Egypt, Jordan and Syria have received aid from the DAC (Development Assistance Committee) countries. Syria has not received aid from the USA since 1983, but that may start up again if there are any significant moves toward peace with Israel. Syria, Egypt and Jordan (mostly Syria during the time period of our study) also received loans from the USSR and the PRC. Most aid from the USSR was in the form of low interest, soft loans, and mostly directed toward the military or large publicity-laden infrastructure projects. Aid from the GCC was cut off from Egypt after the signing of Camp David. The aid to Jordan and Syria increased drastically in 1980-83, but then declined thereafter. Aid to Jordan and Syria declined in the 1980s due to the decline in oil revenues to the GCC, and hence a decline in their aid budgets and the aid budgets for Arab Agencies. Aid to Syria from the GCC also likely declined because of Syria's support of Iran in the Iran-Iraq war, as well as the drop in the oil price. A countervailing force that may have kept the money flowing to Syria was the fact that it was not about to sign a peace treaty with Israel anytime soon.

    Aid from the GCC to these two countries stayed positive mostly for inter-Arab political reasons, such as these two states being considered the last of the confrontational states after Egypt's departure from that group with the signing of the Camp David Accords and the peace treaty with Israel. Aid to Egypt from the GCC, however, took a "back door" after Camp David in the form of remittances. Remittances from the GCC to Egypt increased even as the oil price declined. Trade with Egypt also increased as the oil price, and the GNPs of the GCC, declined. For Syria and Jordan remittances declined as the oil revenues declined. Increased remittances to Egypt in the 1980s had been a subtle form of aid from the GCC that was counter to the Arab League embargo of Egypt (Sullivan, "Contrary views . . .").

Egypt was too important for the GCC to ignore or neglect even in the face of an Arab League embargo. Egyptian remittances, trade and aid with the GCC increased substantially after Egypt, the most militarily powerful country in the Arab world, supported the multi-national invasion of Iraq and the freeing of Kuwait. Aid to Jordan was cut after 1990. Syria supported the multi-national coalition and hence saw its aid from the GCC boom thereafter. The GCC pays its friends well and shuts off its alleged enemies, in a way.

Most aid from the USA to these countries, and even the cutting of aid to Syria in 1983, could be seen as mostly pushing the peace process with Israel and "pushing metal." "Pushing metal" means selling US products and services that were tied to the aid programs, both economic and military aid.

The benefits of such aid from the DAC countries, the USSR and so on, in many instances, are still unclear. But the new roads, dams, hospitals, factories, schools, clinics, agricultural extension centers, research centres and so forth bought with this aid money may have allowed these countries to develop better than they otherwise would have. Also, the results of these aid projects that are physically and permanently positioned in these three countries will remain in these countries.

If the governmental policies were more pro-development and pro-business in the first place, then some of these aid projects could have had even more of a positive impact on these countries. The results of aid are not only determined by the projects involved and the amount of money involved, but also by the politics and economics of the host and donor countries.

There are considerable differences in the aid history of these three countries. There are differences in where the aid comes from and what the aid has gone toward. For indications of these differences we can look at how much of the central government expenditures of these countries came from foreign grants. For Jordan this peaked in 1975 with about 55% of the government expenses being paid for by foreign grants. This dropped to about 48% in 1980, then to 18% by 1984. From 1992 to 1997 about 12-15% of Jordan's government expenses came from foreign grants. Jordan was the most foreign grant sensitive of the three when it came to its government's budget. Until 1990, most of these budgetary grants came from the GCC (Van den Boogaerde, 1989). Since the Gulf War, most of this aid has come from the USA and the EU. Jordan has been the most vulnerable when it came to paying its government's bills with outside help. A political decision, like signing peace with Israel and supporting Saddam Hussein, can drastically shift its government revenues.

Data on foreign grants to Syria's central government expenses are not available for the time period before 1986. After that they have fluctuated between about 10% in 1987, 12% in 1989, to 2% in 1990, to 12% in 1991 and sloping downward to under 3% for 1994-1996. Most of Syria's foreign aid seems to go to things other than directly into the government budget.

PROPORTION OF FOREIGN GRANTS AS PART OF CENTRAL GOVERNMENT EXPENDITURES: EGYPT, SYRIA, JORDAN: SOURCE: IMF, GOVERNMENT FINANCE STATISTICS YEARBOOK, VARIOUS YEARS

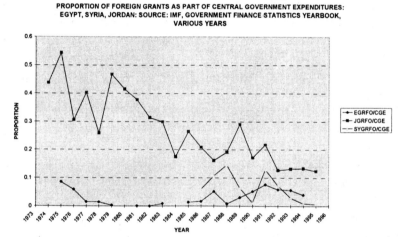

For foreign grants for budgetary purposes, Egypt has had the lowest proportion of the three. It may be the source of the grants that makes the difference in how the grants are used. Jordan got the majority of its aid from the GCC until the Gulf War. Syria got most of its aid from the GCC until 1991. From 1992 onward, much larger and larger percentages were coming from non-GCC sources. Most of Egypt's aid has come from the USA and western European countries. Arab donors seem more amenable to aid going to budget rather than to projects, it seems.

For most of the time period 1973-1991, from between 40% and 100%, depending on the year, of Jordan's deficits were financed from abroad. For Syria, very little, about 10% on average for the years since 1986, was financed directly from abroad – that is, for the years we can find data. Egypt is in the middle range of the three with a declining trend in the percentage of its government deficits being financed from abroad. It was 50% in 1979. By 1987 it was 0 with a slow angle of descent since 1979.

One could consider budgetary aid to a country as a globalization of public finance.

PERCENTAGE OF DEFICIT FINANCED FROM ABROAD

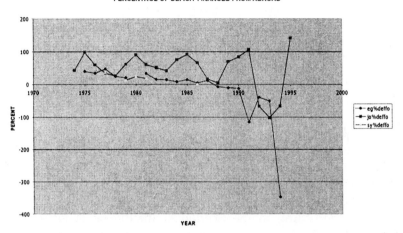

For Egypt almost all aid until the Gulf War came from DAC countries, mostly the USA (about 75%). Countries from Western Europe, and to an increasing extent, Japan, took up almost all of the rest. Arab aid was about nil from 1980 until the Gulf War of 1991. Just after the Gulf War Arab aid increased to over $2 billion for 1990. It then dropped rapidly to about $400 million. It was less than $100 million in 1996. This was a short, but vital, burst of aid from the GCC to Egypt. EU aid also significantly increased after the Gulf War from about $750 million in 1989 to average over $1 billion in 1991 through 1996.

Aid from the USA leapt from $1 billion in 1989 to $3 billion in 1991. It dropped back to about $1 billion yearly for 1994-1996. Indeed, Egypt was a major beneficiary of the Gulf War. Egypt got, excepting a brief couple of years just after the Gulf War, about 95% of its aid from the EU and the USA. About 75-80% of that came from the USA. After the Gulf War, Egypt saw a vast increase in net aid from Japan, which has given Egypt about $1.1 billion in aid.

Jordan is a completely different story. Most of its aid came from the Arab states until the Gulf War. There was a dramatic decline in aid from the Gulf states from $1.2 billion in 1980 to about $180 million in 1989. 1990 saw a brief increase to about $400 million. *It dropped to about nil after the Gulf War.*

Before the Gulf War Arab aid was about $300 million on average in 1989-1990. After the war DAC aid was about $700 million in 1991 and an average of about $300 million (what may have come from the GCC?) from 1991 to 1996. EU aid has been more than US aid after the war. These two sources have given on average about $200 million annually in 1991 to 1996. Japan has given about $1.4 billion since the Gulf War. The greatest increase in DAC aid after the war was from Japan.

Aid to Syria was almost entirely from the Arab states until 1988. That is, about 95% of it. Aid from the USA was cut off in 1983. Aid from the EU has been minimal at under $50 million per year on average for the period 1987-1991. There was a brief increase to over $100 million in 1991. From 1980 to 1987, aid from the EU was simply a trickle. Arab aid increased after the Gulf War, totaling from $2 billion to $4 billion for the time period 1991-1996, depending on what source you use. Japan increased aid to over $1.8 billion in the period 1992-1997, according to the Economist Intelligence Unit, *Country Profile: Syria, 1998-1999.* According to the OECD it was less than this, but still substantial, as the chart below exhibits. For Syria and Jordan the greatest rate increase in DAC aid during and after the Gulf War seems to have been from Japan. Now that is globalized aid.

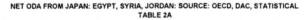

NET ODA FROM JAPAN: EGYPT, SYRIA, JORDAN: SOURCE: OECD, DAC, STATISTICAL TABLE 2A

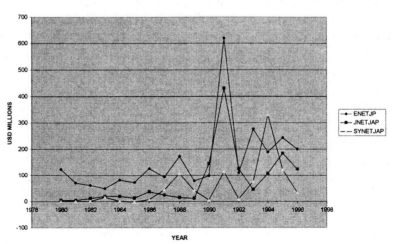

Conclusions and lessons learned:

Knowing the amounts, directions and types of trade of this group of countries gives us a part of the globalization to development puzzle. Knowing the amounts, sources and uses of aid to these countries gives us more of the pieces to the puzzle. Knowing the amounts, sources and type of FDI, FPI, international floats and other types of international investments in these countries gives us yet more. Knowing the typologies of how trade, aid and investment affect development is another part. Knowing the connections of trade, aid and development to the government policies of these countries is yet another part. Knowing the connections and linkages between trade, aid and investments and development of the key sectors of the economies of Egypt, Syria and Jordan is one of the last pieces. What will help to finish off the puzzle of development from these perspectives is an understanding of the synergistic and holistic natures of development. One cannot just throw money at a country's problems and expect development to happen. Integrative and holistic approaches are needed.

Domestic policies must correspond with international ones – or at least not contradict them. A pro-development and pro-economic freedom environment helped along by the government is best – with the usual legal and regulatory constraints that are often needed to take care of market failures, public goods, and so forth. Then the aid, trade and investment can have their greatest impact on development.

Egypt seems to be doing the best job on this. Jordan comes in second. Syria is a miserable third. From the result we have seen in this chapter, we can conclude that for these three countries development requires some form of globalization. The question isn't to globalize or not, but when. These countries need to improve their trade environments and their trade-development connections. They could benefit from considerably increased investments in those industries that are most connected with development, employment and increasing the standard of living and health; in other words overall development, human development, of their countries. These three countries could have used their development funds a bit better in the past. The question of the future is whether they will use those future funds more effectively toward development.

However, more research and analyses are required. Typologies for development that fit these countries must be individually constructed. That is, specific and detailed typologies of trade, aid and investment beyond what we have established here. Then typologies of each government's domestic and international economic policies can be constructed. Then there may be the overall typologies of the three economies in such areas as: the relative importance of certain economic sectors and how these have changed over the last 18 years or so; whether the country is labor exporting, oil based or not; the structure of the banking system and more. A decision-theoretic framework could then be developed to look into, first, the effects of trade, aid and investment on development in the past and what variables affected these links. Then some attempts at forecasting the important contributory variable in the future could be attempted. Only by piecing these typologies together can we get a sense of the economic development, and hence, of the economic security situations of these three countries in the past and in the near future.

What sort of things could be looked into? For example, what has hampered globalization's reach in Egypt, Jordan and Syria? One could look at the following explanations as they might be manifest in the trade, aid and investment connections: the slow development of the peace process, the Gulf Wars since 1980, corruption, poorly-designed and poorly-implemented economic policies, weak legal systems, Islamic militancy, inter-Arab politics and events, other regional and international politics and events, the vital domestic politics and events of each of the three countries, international economic events like the collapse of phosphate and oil prices, and domestic economic events.

The World Bank conducted a survey, *Private sector development in Egypt: The status and the challenge*, 1994, of Egyptian business persons about why FDI might be slow in moving into Egypt. The response they received indicated the problems were: unclear information about liberalization causing uncertainty among investors; complex and restrictive labor laws; weak protection of intellectual property rights, consumer rights (or rights in general, one might add to the list); inadequate antitrust and trade legislation; complex and prohibitive regulations on corporate approval and licensing, both at the national and local levels; inefficient and inadequate public institutions responsible for policy administration and enforcement; time-consuming and expensive litigation procedures that harken back to the days of a socialist planning economy. Add to this a weak legal system that is manipulated, if not controlled, by the powerful and corrupt; inadequate credit mechanisms for small- and medium-sized businesses; a limited securities market and virtually non-existent derivatives market; a lack of adequately educated workers and managers; cumbersome and time-consuming tax administration procedures, and more, believe it or not.

Law 8 of 1997 may have helped to solve at least a few of these problems. There has been some progress during the years since the government was changed and Ganzouri became Prime Minister. But there has not been enough change. Moody's rates Egypt as a BB-. This is better than Turkey, Hungary, India and Mexico and about the same as Greece and Oman. Thomson Bankwatch puts Egypt in the BB category, just below investment grade. This is about the same level as the Philippines and India. Thomson's reasons? The pound is overvalued. Egypt relies too much on historically volatile sources of income like oil, tourism and remittances. Egypt's bureaucracy and massive public sector are often not as productive as they should be, and are often a net drain on the economy. Militancy and high unemployment also add to investment risk.

Jordan has had its difficult times for many reasons: the drop in the real price of oil, the drop in the real price of phosphates, the Gulf War, increased debt, the difficulties of finding peace, and the rather mediocre return to the peace treaty with Israel so far, *inter alia*. Even so, it seems that Jordan has been heading toward greater export diversification. It has also been heading toward more development-oriented exports. The Amman Financial Market has been developing well. It may be the most efficient in the Middle East. A large proportion of the market value of the AFM is owned by non-Jordanians. Israeli, Indian, Pakistan, the EU and the USA have had more of their citizens and corporations investing in Jordan in recent years. The Arabs have shut Jordan off almost completely until most recently. Aid to Jordan has come from many locales and has been global indeed. Aid, trade and investment have been a part of the globalization of Jordan, particularly in recent years. Given the economic and political stress Jordan is under presently, one might expect that it will open up even more so to globalization. Jordan can benefit greatly from this opening up – with the appropriate safeguards in place.

Syria has been the laggard of the three. Investments have been very slow to move into Syria for quite obvious reasons: corruption, a moribund financial system, the tight grip the government has on the economy, confusing exchange restrictions, the no-war-no-peace situation with Israel, its weak and sometimes corrupt legal system, and on and on and on. Syria seems to be caught in the 1960s of

Nasser. The trade of Syria is the least diversified. Syria, however, has really no choice but to move from petroleum to other goods and commodities. Given the oil reserves known today they have very few years left. The dinosauric nature of the economic policy of the Syrian government may slow down the ability of Syrian businesses to respond to these economic changes. Yet, even the Syrian government has shown some signs of liberalizing its economy, if not its politics. Such liberalization will have to pick up pace if Syria wants to reap the benefits of globalization – and if Syria wants to stay away from being made a less than marginal economic player.

Aid to Syria, like aid to Jordan and Egypt, has found its bases mostly in politics. However, for all three countries, as the aid budgets of the DAC countries, especially the GCC, decline in real terms as many expect, they will have to turn to the private sector for many of their development needs and development funds. Syria may also benefit from a stock market, much as Egypt and Jordan have. It may also benefit from opening up its economy more at all levels. Clearly, Syrian socialism has had its benefits for the Syrian people, but its time is past.

It is time for Egypt, Jordan and Syria to rethink their economic policies and economic ideologies. Egypt and Jordan have been relatively dexterous on this. Jordan has been the most ambitious. Egypt has been cautious, but is becoming less so. Syria has been dragging its feet at almost all levels, politics, economics, law, etc. It has been paying the price. Yes, these are poor countries with some problems in income inequality. Pure capitalism could, therefore, never work in them. A more liberal and ambitious economic framework based on humane capitalism may be the way to proceed in order to gain the benefits from globalization, and yet keep the peace in these countries in the long run. The old ways are past. The shocks of the oil price declines, the wars, the end of the USSR, the economic diplomacy of the GCC, the massive buildups of debt, unemployment creep, periodical foreign exchange shortages and so forth have shown the weaknesses of these old ways of doing things. Globalization is like an economic freight train. If one is prepared to jump on board, then one can go far – if you pay the price for the ticket. Otherwise the freight train will pass you by and your competitor nations will be far ahead of you. Egypt, Jordan and Syria have the choice to jump on board or sit on the sidelines. Possibly, these countries could learn from the lessons of the years since Camp David to see the costs and benefits of change (and not changing), and the costs and benefits of globalization (or not catching the freight train). This chaper is simply a starting point of thinking about the issues. There is certainly more that needs to be said.

Bibliography

Albarak Investment and Development Company, www.albaraka.com.

Album, A. 1998. "Middle East Markets in Vogue," *Middle East*, September, pp. 34-35.

Alnasrawi, A. 1989. "The Rise and Fall of Arab Oil Power," *Arab Studies Quarterly*, vol. 6, nos. 1 & 2, pp. 1-11.

Alonso-Gamo, P., et al. 1997. "Adjusting to New Realities: MENA, the Uruguay Round, and the EU-Mediterranean Initiative," *IMF Working Paper*, WP/97/5, January.

Alonso-Gamo, P., et al. 1997. "Globalization and Growth Prospects of Arab Countries," *IMF Working Paper* WP/97/125, September.

"About AFM [Amman Financial Market]", www.accessme.com/afm.

Amerah, M. 1998. "Trade Liberalization and Foreign Investment in Jordan," in R. Safadi, ed., *Opening Doors to the World: A New Trade Agenda for the Middle East*, ERF and AUC.

Arab Authority for Agricultural Investment and Development (AAAID), www.haynese,winthrop,edu/mlas/xo6.htm.

Arab Business and Investment Journal, www.awo.net/newspub/abij, various issues.

Arab Company for Real Estate and Tourism Investment (an Egyptian joint stock company that is a subsidiary of the Saudi firm Dallah Albaraka), http://arti-eg.com.

Arab International Bank, www.mailer.datum.com.eg/aib/

Arab World Online, Tradeline, www.awo.net/newspubs/pubs/tradelin: "Country Profile: The Republic of Egypt"; Ambassador N. Veliotes, "Egyptian Construction Continues"; B. Heil, "Egypt Signs New Deals at Conference"; Y. Elguindi, "Power Sector Privatization: A Key to Economic Growth"; B. Heil, "Arab Capital Market Developments"; Y. Elguindi, "U.S. Companies Bubbling Over Egypt's Oil and Gas"; Y. Elguindi, "Egypt Offers Stake in Gas Grid to Private Sector"; B. Hiel, "Syria Devalue Exchange Rate"; Y. Elguindi, "IFC Investments in the Arab World"; J. S. Cramer; "Syria the Sleeping Giant"; B. Hiel, "Arab World's Free Trade Zones: Link to the Global Market"; Y. Elguindi, "IFC Invests in Jordan's Tourism Industry"; J. S. Cramer, "Industrial Estates Boost Jordanian Diversification."

Awartani, H. & Kleiman, E. 1997. "Economic Interactions Among Participants in the Middle East Peace Process," *Middle East Journal*, Vol. 51, no. 2, Spring, pp. 215-229.

Baroudi, S. 1993. "Egyptian Agricultural Exports Since 1973," *Middle East Journal*, Spring.

Barzagan, D. 1995. "Investments and Benefits," Inter Press Service, February 5, www.infoweb5.newsbank.com.

BBC Worldwide Monitoring, "Al-Bath," Damascus, May 11, 1998, Syrian newspaper reports oil, gas exploration, investment; www.infoweb5.newsbank.com.

BBC Worldwide Monitoring, "Al-Arab Al-Yawm," Amman, August 3, 1998, "Jordan: Experts Refute Figures on Israeli Investments in Jordan," www.infoweb5.newsbank.com.

Bisat, A., et al. 1997. "Growth, Investment, Saving in the Arab Economies," *IMF Working paper*, WP/97/85, July.

Blomstrom, M. 1997. "Regional Integration and Foreign Direct Investment: A Conceptual Framework and Three Cases," *Working Paper*, Stockholm School of Economics, NBER and CEPR, and Ari Kokko, Stockholm School of Economics, published as *World Bank, International Trade Division, International Economics Department, Policy Working Paper*, March.

Blomstrom, M. & Kokko. A. 1997. "How Foreign Direct Investment Affects Host Countries," International Economics Department, The World Bank, www.worldbank.org.

Blomstrom, M. & Kokko, A. 1996. "The Impact of Foreign Investment on Host Countries: A Review of the Empirical Evidence," International Economics Department, The World Bank, December, www.worldbank.org.

Canning, D. "A Database of World Infrastructure Stocks, 1950-95," The World Bank, Public Economics Division of the Development Research Group, and the Transport, Water and Urban Development Department, The World Bank, www.worldbank.org.

Chaffour, J., et al. 1996. "Growth and Financial Stability in the Middle East and North Africa," *Finance and Development*, March, www.worldbank.org/fandd/english/0396.

Cordesman, A. 1997. "Peace is not Enough: The Arab-Israeli Economic and Demographic Crises," Center for Strategic and International Studies, July.

Deen, T. 1996. "Expatriate Earnings Outweigh Aid Flow," Inter Press Service, June 23 www.infoweb5.newsbank.com/bin/gate.exe?f=doc&state=6k8csu.3.11.

DeRosa, D.A. 1997. "Agricultural Trade and Rural Development in the Middle East and North Africa: Recent Developments and Prospects," Policy Research Working Paper, 1732, International Economics Department, International Trade Division, The World Bank, February.

DiLuciano, D. "Banks to Redefine Role in the Arab World," Arab World Online, Tradeline, www.awo.net/newspub/tradelin.

DiLuciano, D. "Jordan Takes Initial Steps to Privatize," Arab World Online, Tradeline, www.awo.net/newspup/tradelin.

Driscoll, R.E., Hayek, P.F. & Zaki, F.A. *Foreign Investment in Egypt: An Analysis of Critical Factors with Emphasis on the Foreign Investment Code,* Fund for Multinational Management Education.

Easterly, W. 1997. "The Ghost of Financing Gap: How the Harrod-Domar Growth Model Still Haunts Development Economics," The World Bank, Discussion Paper, July.

Economic Research Forum (ERF), "Mena Indicators," www.erf.org.eg.

Economist Intelligence Unit, *Country Profile: Egypt,* various years, EIU.

Economist Intelligence Unit, *Country Profile: Jordan,* various years, EIU.

Economist Intelligence Unit, *Country Profile: Syria,* various years, EIU.

EFG-Hermes, "The Stock Exchange," www.efg-hermes.com/my_services/stockexchange.html.

EFG-Hermes, "Stock Market Indices," www.development.rite.com:8080/cgi-win/efg/efgindex2.exe.

Efrat, M. & Bercovitch, J. 1989. *Superpowers and Client States in the Middle East,* Routledge, London.

Egypt, Arab Republic, Investment Law 230-1989, gopher://iccuc.org:70/00/itc/dir4/dir44/dir443/dir4431/egjurisl.txt, written by Government of Egypt, General Authority for Investment, Cairo, Egypt

El-Erain, M.A. 1996. "Middle Eastern Economies' External Environment: What Lies Ahead?" *Middle East Policy,* vol. iv, no. 3, March, pp. 137-147

El-Erain, M.A. & Fennel, S. 1997. *The Economy of the Middle East and North Africa in 1997,* Middle Eastern Department, IMF.

El-Naggar, S. 1992. *Foreign and Intra-trade Policies of the Arab Countries,* IMF.

Ernst and Young, "Investment Profile: Egypt," http://mbendi.co.za/ernsty/cyegeyip.htm

Esfahani, H.S. 1990. "The Experience of Foreign Investment in Egypt Under Infitah," Department of Economics, University of Illinois at Urbana-Champaign, Faculty working paper no. 90-1710, December.

Hafidh, H. 1997. "Syria Takes Growing Share of Iraq's Border Trade," *Christian Science Monitor,* August 6.

Handoussa, H. 1997. *Economic Transition in the Middle East,* AUC Press.

Harvrylyshyn, O. & Kunzel, P. 1997. "Intra-industry Trade of Arab Countries: An Indicator of Potential Competitiveness," IMF, Middle Eastern Department and Policy Development and Review Department, IMF, Working Paper, WP/97/47, April.

Hashemite Kingdom of Jordan, "Investment Promotion Law," Law no. 16 for the year 1995, www.multiasking.com/jordanbiz/investment.html.

Hashemite Kingdom of Jordan, "Investment Promotion Law No. 16 of 1995," www.amon.nic.gov.jo:80/work/economics/laws/510.html

Hoekman, B. & Djankov, S. 1996. "Effective Protection and Investment Incentives in Egypt and Jordan During the Transition to Free Trade with Europe," Centre for Economic Policy Research, London, Discussion Paper, no. 1415, June.

Inter-Arab Investment Guarantee Corporation, www.moc.kw/users/aiig.

International Finance Corporation, *Emerging Market Database, 1998 Factbook*, IFC, also other years. Also used www.ifc.org.

International Finance Corporation, IFC Press Center, IFC Press Releases, "IFC Invests in Tourism Sector of Egypt," March 27, 1997; "IFC Invests US$1.4 Million in Jordan," March 25, 1997; "IFC Invests US$5 Million in Jordan," March 10, 1997; "IFC Invests US$10 Million in Tourism Project in Jordan," February 6, 1997; "IFC Signs Agreement for Industrial Gasses Project in Egypt," May 22, 1997; "IFC and NBE Establish Risk Management Facility in Egypt," May 21, 1997; "IFC Invests in Jordan's Aluminum Industry," March 29, 1996; "IFC Signs US$38 Million Deal for Jordan's Telecom Sector," October 30, 1995; "IFC Joins Forces with Arab Monetary Fund and IBCA to Launch Inter-Arab Rating Company," October 8, 1995; "IFC Approves Loan for Tissue Paper Plant in Jordan," September 19, 1994; "IFC Uses EC Equity Line to Invest in Egypt Fund," November 24, 1993; "IFC to Invest in Egypt's Tourism Sector," October 13, 1993; "IFC to Take Shareholding in Commercial International Bank, SAE, of Egypt," May 25, 1993; www.ifc.org.

International Monetary Fund, *Balance of Payments Yearbook*, various years.

IMF, *Direction of Trade Statistics Yearbook*, various years.

IMF, *Government Finance Statistics Yearbook*, various years.

IMF, *International Financial Statistics*, various years.

IMF, Middle Eastern Department, 1996. *Building on Progress: Reform and Growth in the Middle East and North Africa*.

IMF, Middle Eastern Department, 1997. *Financial Systems and Labor Markets in the Gulf Cooperation Council Countries*.

ITC, "Growth of International Demand for Leading Export Products of Jordan," www.intracen.org/itc/services/rau/jordan.htm.

ITC, www.intracen.org/itc/infobase/data/, "Imports Summary Table (1992-1996): Egypt"; "Exports Summary Table (1992-1996): Egypt"; "Imports Summary Table (1992-1996): Jordan"; "Exports Summary Table (1992-1996): Jordan"; "Imports Summary Table (1992-1996): Syria"; "Exports Summary Table (1992-1996): Syria."

ITC, "World Imports from Egypt," www.intracen.org/itc/services/rau/egypt-t.htm.

ITC, "World Imports from Jordan," www.intracen.org/itc/services/rau/jordan-t.htm.

ITC, "World Imports from Syria," www.intracn.org/itc/services/rau/syria-t.htm.

Investment Promotion Organization, Jordan, "Statistical Report: Jan 1st, 1997 to Dec. 31st 1997," www.arab-business.net/ipc/statisti.html.

Jordan Free Zone's Corporation, "Jordan Free Zone," gopher://iccuc.unicc.org:70/00/itc/dir4/dir44/dir443/dir4433/jojurisl.txt.

Kawash, N. 1996. "Arab Polices Seen as an Obstacle to Investment," Agence France-Presse, August 30.

Kanaan, T.H. 1998. "The State and the Private Sector in Jordan," in Shafik, N., *Economic Challenges Facing Middle Eastern and North African Countries: Alternative Futures*, ERF and MacMillan Press.

Khatib, F. 1988. "Foreign Aid and Economic Development in Jordan: An Empirical Investigation," in Rodney Wilson, ed., *Politics and the Economy in Jordan*, Routledge.

Khier el-Din, H. & El-Dersh, A. 1992. "Foreign Trade Policy of Egypt, 1986-1991," in S. El Naggar, ed., *Foreign and Intratrade Policies of the Arab Countries*, IMF.

Kiernan, P. 1998. "Jordan: State in Transition," *Middle East*, September, pp. 29-33.

Kleiman, E. 1992. "Geography, Culture and Religion, and Middle East Trade Patterns," The Hebrew University of Jerusalem, Working Paper #262, June.

Koch-Weser, C. 1994. "Economic Reform and Regional Cooperation: A Development Agenda for the Middle East and North Africa," *Middle East Policy*, Spring.

Lancaster, J. 1997. "Decades of Doctrinaire Policies Leave Arab Economies Stalled," *The Washington Post*, August 3, p. a1.

Lavy, V. 1984. "The Arab Economic of Egypt by Arab States: Myth and Reality," *The Middle East Journal*, vol. 38, no. 3, Summer, pp. 419-433.

Miller, R.R. et al. "International Joint Ventures in Developing Countries: Happy Marriages? Statistics for 1970-95," IFC Discussion Paper, Number 29, IFC, www.ifc.org/depts/ops/econ/pubs/dp29.htm.

NTDB (National Trade Data Bank). "Egyptian Investment Climate Statement," www.awo.net/business/invest/egy1.asp.

NTDB. 1997. "Jordanian Investment Climate Statement," November www.aow.net/business/invest/jor1.asp.

NTDB. 1997. "Syrian Investment Climate Statement," November, www.awo.net/business/inves/syr1.asp.

Nsouli, S.M. 1996. "The European Union's New Mediterranean Strategy," *Finance and Development*, vol. 33, no. 3, September, pp. 14-17.

OECD, DAC, Reference Section: total net oda (Dac2a-1997 partial) www.oecd.org/scripts/cde/cde_dac/datasets/total_net_oda.idc.

Petri, P. 1997. "The Case of the Missing Foreign Investment in the Southern Mediterranean," OECD, Development Center Technical Paper, No. 128, OECD/GD(97)196, December.

Petri, P. 1997. "Trade Strategies for the Southern Mediterranean," OECD Development Center Technical Paper, no. 127, OECD/GD(97)195, December.

Riordan, E.M., et al. 1995. "The World Economy and Implications for the Middle East and North Africa Region, 1995-2010," The World Bank, International Economics Department, June.

Safadi, R. 1998. *Opening Doors to the World: A New Trade Agenda for the Middle East*, ERF and AUC Press.

Shafik, N. 1998. *Economic Challenges Facing Middle Eastern and North African Countries: Alternative Futures*, Economic Research Forum for the Arab Countries, Iran and Turkey, and MacMillan Press.

Shafik, N. 1994. "Multiple Trade Shocks and Partial Liberalization: Dutch Disease and the Egyptian Economy," ERF, Working Paper 9503, November.

Share, M. 1998. "Jordan's Trade and Balance of Payments Problems," in R. Wilson, ed., *Politics and the Economy of Jordan*, Routledge.

Singer, A. 1994. "Aid Conditionality," University of Sussex, Institute of Development, Working Paper, DP 346, December.

SIPRI, www.sipri.org, "Egypt, Military Expenditure, 1988-97"; "Jordan, Military Expenditure, 1988-97"; "Syria, Military Expenditure, 1988-97."

Stewart, F. 1993. "War and Underdevelopment: Can Economic Analysis Help Reduce the Costs?" International Development Center, Oxford, No. 56, April.

Sukkar, N. 1998. "Syria: Strategic Economic Issues," in Shafik, N., *Economic Challenges Facing Middle Eastern and North African Countries: Alternative Futures*, ERF and MacMillan.

Sullivan, P.J., forthcoming. "Caveat for Peace: Some Notes on Palestinian Labor," *Research in Middle East Economics*, Vol. 4, JAI Press.

Sullivan, P.J. 1999. "Contrary Views of Arab Economic Diplomacy: Egypt," Arab Studies Quarterly, Fall, pp. 65-92.

Sullivan, P.J. forthcoming. "Iraq: The Pivot?" in T. Ismael, ed., *International Relations in the 21st Century.*

Sullivan, P.J. "Oil: Challenges and Prospects," *Cairo Papers in Social Sciences,* vol. 20, no. 2, pp. 55-90.

Sullivan, P.J. 1999. "Riding the Roller Coaster; Egypt's Regional Economic Relations Since Camp David," *Cairo Papers in Social Sciences,* vol. 22.

Syria, Arab Republic of, *Loi no. 10 du 4 Mai 1991 Portant Reglement des Investissements en Syria,* published by C.F.C.E, 10, Ave D'Iena, Paris 75873 Cedex 16, France, gopher://iccuc2.unicc.org:70/00/itc/dir4/dir44/dir4431/syrjurisl.txt.

The World Bank. 1993. *Arab Republic of Egypt: An Agricultural Strategy for the 1990s.*

The World Bank. 1998. "Middle East and North Africa," *Annual Report, 1998,* pp. 56-62.

The World Bank. 1998. *Assessing Aid: What Works, What Doesn't and Why.*

The World Bank, "Country Brief: Egypt," www.worldbank.org/html/extdr/mena/egyptbr.htm.

The World Bank. 1994. *Private Sector Development in Egypt: The Status and the Challenge,* A World Bank Report prepared for the conference: "Private Sector Development in Egypt: Investing in the Future," Cairo, October 9-10.

The World Bank. 1995. *Will Arab Workers Prosper or be Left out in the Twenty-first Century?* Regional Perspective in Development.

The World Bank, *World Bank Atlas,* various years.

The World Bank, *World Development Indicators,* various years.

The World Bank, *World Development Report,* various years.

The World Bank, *World Debt Tables,* various years.

The World Bank, *World Tables,* various years.

Tradecompass, www.tradecompass.com, (/library/books/com_guide/) "Jordan, Investment Climate Statement" (jordan07.html); "Syria: Investment Climate Statement" (syria07.html); "Syria: Trade and Project Financing" (syria08.html); "Syria: Commercial Overview" (syria01.html); "Syria: Economic Trends and Outlook" (syria03.html).

UN, Center on Transnational Corporations, "Courting Foreign Direct Investment in the Nineties," www.usis.usemb.se/ert/e02/4fdiuno.html

UN, ESCWA, *Summary of the Survey of Economic and Social Developments in the ESCWA Region, 1996-1997* (and other years), (gopher.un.org)

UN, UNCTAD, *World Investment Report*, various years.

United Nations, UNDP, *Human Development Report*, various years.

United States, Department of Energy, Energy Information Agency, www.eia.doe.gov/emeu/cabs: "Egypt", "Syria" and "Jordan" (Country Analysis Briefs).

United States, Department of Energy, Energy Information Agency, web page at www.eia.doe.gov/emeu/cabs/opecrev.html : "OPEC Revenues Fact Sheet," September, 1998.

United States, Department of State, www.state.gov, "FY 1998 Country Commercial Guide: Egypt"; "FY 1998 Country Commercial Guide: Jordan"; "FY 1998 Country Commercial Guide: Syria."

Van den Boogaerde, P. 1991. *Financial Assistance from Arab Countries and Arab Regional Institutions*, IMF, Occasional Paper 87.

Van Hear, N. 1995. "The Impact of the Involuntary Mass 'Repatriation' of Palestinians to Jordan in the Wake of the Gulf Crisis," Working Paper no. 84, April, Refugees Study Programme, Oxford.

Vittas, D. 1997. "The Role of Non-bank Financial Intermediaries in Egypt and Other MENA Countries," The World Bank, Development Research Group, November.

Wilson, R. 1994. "The Economic Relations of the Middle East: Toward Europe or Within the Region?" *The Middle East Journal*, vol. 48, no.2, Spring, pp. 268-287.

World Trade Organization, WTO Secretariat, "Trade and Foreign Direct Investment," 9 October 1996, www.wto.org/wto/archives/chpiv.htm.

Yeats, A. 1998. "Export Prospects of Middle Eastern Countries: A Post-Uruguay Round Analysis," in R. Safadi, *Opening Doors to the World: A New Trade Agenda for the Middle East*, ERF and AUC.

Yeats, A. "Just How Big is Global Production Sharing?" The World Bank, www.worldbank.org.

Marginalized Violent Internal Conflict in the Age of Globalization: Mexico and Egypt*

Dan Tschirgi

> Marginalization . . . is a condition resulting from prolonged function-
> al superfluousness. [Marginals] are deprived of virtually all the roles
> of which functioning society is composed. . . . Considered by the rest
> of the population as pariahs, morally and even perhaps biologically
> distinctive they. . . . remain more or less permanently on the perime-
> ters of society. . . .[1]

"Globalization" is here taken to mean the process through which economics, politics and technology unleash forces that increasingly make the societies of our world not only more interconnected, but also more susceptible to similar experiences. Among such experiences, violent conflict occurs in the context of rapid socio-economic-political change. Neo-liberal economic strategies, which figure so prominently in globalizing trends, are frequently blamed for much of today's violence in developing areas. Indeed, some would agree with Pierre Bourdieu's characterization of neo-liberalism as an "infernal machine" whose tentacles must produce structural violence wherever they reach.[2]

This sweeping stand is unsatisfactory, begging the questions of how and why neo-liberal globalization may generate conflicts and ignoring the patently obvious fact that neo-liberal policies have not invariably led to social violence. Nonetheless, substantial evidence indicates that globalization's neo-liberal dimension has been associated with the eruption of major domestic violence in developing areas. The real problem is to identify the circumstances and dynamics that may lead to this outcome.

Unfortunately, no generally accepted comprehensive typology of political violence exists. Still, it seems clear that such conflicts fall into broad categories that are essentially different. For example, a compelling distinction exists between international and internal con-

* I express appreciation to Jeffrey A. Nedoroscik and Dina Younis, who, as graduate students in a workshop I offered on Marginalized Violent Internal Conflict at the American University in Cairo and as leaders of a subsequent effort to apply a preliminary version of the analytical framework utilized here (cited below), provided many useful insights.

flicts involving developing states. In turn, the latter category is equally not all of one piece. Conflicts between the state and separatist movements as well as inter-ethnic conflicts in relation to which governments stand as involved – but nonetheless third – parties are also forms of sustained confrontations in developing countries

There also occur violent conflicts between governments and rebellious protagonists who neither seek separation from the state, nor challenge the state's essential validity, nor find their basic objectives in particularistic ethnic, tribal or regional demands. Insurrection is mounted in the name of the state itself and of its entire population. The polity's "true" values are claimed to be those of the insurrectionists. The existing government, or the existing political system in its entirety, is charged with betrayal of those values. Ethnicity, while possibly a practical factor in insurrectionary mobilization, is overshadowed by insurrectionary invocations of broader values within the state. Yet, in contrast to civil wars, conflicts of this sort do not produce relatively balanced warring parties who share the perception that a critical and decisive military struggle has been joined. Instead, the armed challenge to state authority emanates almost exclusively from mobilized elements of the most marginalized sectors of national society. The imbalance of power so overwhelmingly favors state authorities that the rebels' armed crusade fails to present a credible military threat. Authorities can therefore characterize the marginals' struggle as an irritating and misguided aberration of little consequence to the normal functioning of the state. Thus, the conflict is doubly linked to "marginality," pitting elements of the "functionally superfluous" against national governments in a struggle that is itself officially marginalized. There is, however, an important caveat to this: although the insurrectionary marginals have opted to reject the existing political process, their objectives are largely shared and supported – at least morally – by important dissenting actors within the political system.

I label this form of strife Marginalized Violent Internal Conflict (MVIC) and suggest that it may be particularly related to globalizing world conditions. While no claim is made that globalization may not also be a factor in other types of conflict, this article seeks to uncover the conditions and dynamics which shape the outbreak and development of MVICs by comparing the still unresolved insurrections launched by *Zapatistas* in Mexico and the *Gama'a al-Islamiyya* in Egypt.

At first glance, these cases appear to have little in common. The *Zapatistas'* struggle against the Mexican Government metamorphosed into sporadic violent confrontations and political maneuvers which have given its champions a romantic image in much of the world's mass media. The *Gama'a al-Islamiyya* has waged a bloody terrorist campaign that has not led to negotiations of any kind and is widely portrayed as a consequence of religious fanaticism. Yet, the contention here is that these conflicts are demonstrably generically similar in their origins and, moreover, that their glaringly distinct paths result from identifiable differences in a commonly shared dynamic.

The analysis supporting this conclusion focuses on the natures of, and interrelationships among, four groups of variables. These are: first, the "locus"[3] of each conflict; second, the impact upon the conflict of the "political institutional environment"[4]; third, the conflict's relationship to civil society; and, finally, its relationship to the international environment. At each level the analysis seeks to be both structural and cognitive, looking at established patterns of interaction among key participants as well as the outlooks that underlie them. Thus, of particular concern are the ideologies and decisions of principle actors.

In undertaking this task, Mittleman's observation that "globalization interrelates multiple levels of analysis: economics, politics, culture and ideology" is kept in mind.[5] So too is Grenier's admonition that a realistic understanding of conflict must avoid undue reliance on structural abstractions by recalling that "the eruption of internal war is contingent upon choices made by key actors."[6]

As it is clearly impossible to offer in this limited space the full analysis this framework implies, the following comparison primarily concentrates on the origins of the conflicts initiated by the *Zapatistas* and the *Gama'a al-Islamiyya*, although it also identifies and briefly explains major differences in their evolution.

Overview: The Mexican and Egyptian cases

On January 1, 1994 – the date of Mexico's entry into the North American Free Trade Association – some 2-4000 fighters of the *Ejercito Zapatista de Liberacion Nacional* (EZLN) seized several municipalities in the Highlands of Chiapas. This was accomplished with very little bloodshed and the rebels were quick to pledge that no harm would befall civilians, including tourists.

The rank and file of the *Zapatista* Movement were Mayan Indians, but the organization did not consider itself an "ethnic" actor. The *Zapatistas* proclaimed their cause to be that of the entire Mexican nation. The group's primary demand was for a fundamental change in the political system, the establishment of free and full democracy, to be preceded by the existing regime's resignation and the establishment of a transitional government. The plight of the country's Indian communities was stressed, but the EZLN plainly called for this to be remedied as part of overall revolutionary change that would respect Indian traditions.

Once the Mexican military began to move against the insurgents, fighting escalated. EZLN units withdrew to a series of valleys that link the Highlands to the Lacandon Jungle. By the time a cease-fire went into effect on January 13, perhaps as many as 1000-1500 persons had died.[7] In the aftermath of the fighting, the EZLN held its positions in what became known as the "Conflict Zone," in which many *Zapatista*-controlled villages have since since engaged in de facto local self government.

Shortly after the cease-fire began, steps were taken to resolve the conflict through negotiation. The Bishop of San Cristobal de Las Casas, Samuel Ruiz Garcia, was accepted as mediator by both sides. He became president of the legally mandated National Intermediation Commission (Conai), a small group whose members he picked as advisors. Its role was later seconded by the Commission of Concord and Pacification (Cocopa), a multi-party group of Mexican legislators.

Conai became the principle agent in a years-long mediation and negotiation process, during which the *Zapatistas* cultivated a strong presence in civil society and made extensive use of communications media to seek worldwide support. However, negotiations between *Zapatistas* and the government broke down in 1996 amid mutual accusations of bad faith – although mediation efforts continued. The ensuing years witnessed a deterioration of the mediation process as well as rising violence in Chiapas. Much of the latter was perpetrated by local anti-*Zapatista* paramilitary forces who appear to have acted with the knowledge and encouragement of state and national authorities, if not at their direction.

Against this dark background, Bishop Ruiz dissolved Conai and abandoned his mediating role in the early summer of 1998. Cocopa pledged to continue working for a peaceful settlement, but reliable sources portrayed that body as dispirited and suffering from internal dissent and a lack of coordination.[8] By the spring of 1999, no improvement was visible and the danger of renewed hostilities remained uncomfortably high.

In contrast to the *Zapatistas'* struggle, that of Egypt's *Gama'a al-Islamiyya* has not been tempered by negotiations of any sort. The bloodletting initiated by the *Gama'a* has been more prolonged and has exacted a higher cost on the nation than has its counterpart in Mexico.

Formed in the early 1970s, the *Gama'a* was inspired by the early militancy of the Muslim Brotherhood – an organization founded in the 1920s which has since renounced violence (although it is currently banned in Egypt) in favor of working politically for an Islamic state under *Shari'a*. Proclaiming these same goals, the *Gama'a* holds that Egypt's current political system and its leaders are religiously, morally and politically corrupt and have violated true Islamic and Egyptian values.

In the early 1990s, the *Gama'a* embarked on a sustained campaign of violence that made it the most prominent of Egypt's militant Islamic groups. Working through networks established over the years in poor neighborhoods of Cairo and other cities, the *Gama'a* was able to project its struggle, largely by terrorism, throughout much of the country. However, its focal point was Upper Egypt.

The Egyptian government adopted and maintained a hard line approach to the *Gama'a al-Islamiyya*, rejecting any possibility of negotiations. Instead, it relied on heavy security measures, including massive arrests, the death penalty and – after October, 1992 – the use of military courts to try suspected militants. A sustained corollary to the government's forceful response has been the use of the state-sanctioned "official" religious establishment as well as the mass media to undermine the *Gama'a's* claim to Islamic purity.[9]

By 1996, Egypt's government had clearly gained the upper hand. Militant attacks were in decline, though not ended, and this was paralleled by a resurgence of international tourism. Despite sporadic clashes in Upper Egypt, some *Gama'a* leaders suggested a cease-fire in the spring 1996, a call that was repeated a year later when six major *Gama'a* figures (and the group's spiritual advisor) proclaimed a "halt [to] military operations . . ."[10] These initiatives, which were rejected by the government, seemed to reveal a growing division in *Gama'a* ranks. This was confirmed in November, 1997, when members of the organization slaughtered 58 foreign tourists in Luxor.

The ferocity of the Luxor massacre brought the *Gama'a* to its lowest ebb. All indications showed that the overwhelming majority of Egyptians were outraged both by the carnage and its perpetration in the name of Islam. The split in the *Gama'a* became patent, with its main leadership apparently united in condemning the attack as a "violation" that proved "more damaging to the *Gama'a* than for the Egyptian government."[11] Although the government continued to arrest, try and sometimes execute *Gama'a* members in 1998, only a few relatively minor armed clashes occurred. By early 1999, Egypt's tourism, although not fully recovered from the blow of the Luxor attack, was solidly on the upswing.[12] For the time being, at least, it appeared that the *Gama'a* was cowed. It remained an open question whether this heralded the organization's final abandonment of its violent campaign or was simply a temporary lull.

The locus: Chiapas

The descendants of the first Spanish colonists in Chiapas have presided over an extremely stratified social configuration, at the top of which figure *Ladinos*, those claiming (not always accurately) a purely European heritage and, at the bottom, the region's Indians. Over the centuries, *Ladino* landowners and peasants pushed the original Indian inhabitants to less productive areas. The prevailing *Ladino* view of the Indian was – and remains – overtly and strongly racist, based on the conviction that the Indian is by nature not only inferior but also characterized by a potentially dangerous childishness.[13]

The Revolution that produced Mexico's 1917 Constitution did not substantially alter Chiapas' socio-economic structure. The Chiapas elite found its place in the clientalistic chains forged by the Institutional Revolutionary Party (PRI) as Mexico's post-revolutionary political system was consolidated. In turn, this elite extended its own control of the local state government through similar arrangements that at the lowest level co-opted or created village chiefs (*caciques*) who won tangible benefits by supporting the status quo. Chiapas' Indian communities are divided into several groups, all but one being Mayan. By the 20th century, the harsh realities of poverty and powerlessness had produced massive social deterioration. Alcoholism, violence, sexual abuse and similar ills plagued Indian communities.[14] The post-revolutionary establishment of communal landholdings (*ejidos*) generally did not provide peasants with more fertile or extensive fields than in the past, and the few attempts that were made to develop new lands were usually soon frustrated by the local elite who wished to extend their own holdings.[15]

Religion, that is, Roman Catholicism, played a major role in ensuring that indigenous identities and social structures were not completely lost.[16] Among Indian communities, however, Catholicism was mixed with pre-Columbian religious beliefs and practices. A major feature of this phenomenon is that many of the most important elements of the syncretistic outcome are related to the miraculous – to the supernatural manipulation of earthly reality in otherwise impossible ways.

Although Chiapas is rich in resources, this has not benefited most of its people. Chiapas is among the poorest – and in many ways *the* poorest – of the states in the Mexican Republic.[17] The largely rural population, mainly composed of Indian and Mestizo peasants, has steadily suffered from a high population growth rate and ensuing pressures on already scarce resources of available land. These pressures have been exacerbated by the local judicial system's traditional unresponsiveness to peasants seeking legal redress for lands taken by large landowners. These unhappy characteristics are found in exaggerated form in Highlands area, the region where the *Zapatista* rebellion unfolded.[18]

Few of Chiapas' rural population have not experienced non-traditional ways of life or false hopes of modernizing change. During the 1970s, the Highlands became the primary focus of the central government's attempts to include Mexico's Indian communities in national development efforts.[19] Although corruption and inefficiency severely limited their long-term impact, federal funds poured into the region at a rate that surpassed that of resources allocated to other areas of the country for similar purposes. International agencies also became heavily involved in attempts to further socio-economic development in the Highlands. At the same time, urbanization accelerated, as unstable conditions and lack of opportunities in the countryside drove peasants to the cities. Indeed, the extent of urbanizing movement was such that Chiapaneco scholar David Davila notes that the eventual outbreak of the *Zapatista* uprising must be understood as a "rejoining of urban peasants with rural peasants."[20]

The economic crises that gripped Mexico in the 1980s and the country's ensuing turn to neo-liberal policies severely affected the already precarious conditions of the small farmer in Chiapas and, particularly, in the Highlands. Declining federal investment in rural development led to the reduction or elimination of governmental organizations and programs designed to help peasant and Indian farmers. However limited or ineffective such aid had been in the past, its reduction further increased the level of misery in Chiapas. So too did decreases of subsidies to the agricultural sector and – particularly – the elimination of subsidies to coffee producers.[21] The peasants' plight was augmented as the liberalization of Mexico's trade policies led to an influx of cheaper foreign agricultural products into the domestic market. At the same time, the termination of large-scale government projects and the privatization of major agricultural concerns reduced employment opportunities for peasants.[22]

A bitter twist was added to the problems that engulfed Chiapas in the 1980s by the fact that the overall picture of the state's agriculture during the same period showed significant gains made by large landowners, who benefited from the De la Madrid administration's "Chiapas Plan."[23] However, the most striking step in the liberalizing drive to rationalize agriculture and facilitate movement toward agro-industry came in 1992, when the modification of Article 27 of the Mexican Constitution effectively halted land reform and permitted the sale of *ejido* land distributed under the old order.

It was in this context that the EZLN originated, recruited its membership and mobilized for the offensive that greeted 1994. The movement's development can partly be traced to efforts launched some 20 years earlier by Bishop Samuel Ruiz, of the Diocese of San Cristobal de las Casas. Ruiz was 36 years old in 1960 when he arrived in San Cristobal. The city's *Ladino* elites were initially charmed by the newcomer, but felt betrayed after a few years when he became actively concerned with the economic and social plight of his Indian flock.[24]

Ruiz and his subordinates fostered peasant organizations that sought to improve the lot of the rural population while remaining independent of government control. By the early 1970s, Ruiz's efforts were seconded by radical young Mexicans who arrived in Chiapas after fleeing the country's security forces. These individuals, augmented by a second generation of young radicals who joined them in the early 1980s, mobilized peasants in pursuit of objectives that were very similar to those pursued by the local Catholic hierarchy. The former's more militant approach led to the EZLN's foundation in 1983. Nonetheless, the Theology of Liberation adhered to by Bishop Ruiz and the Marxist orientation of the newcomers remained largely compatible. The result was that the two collaborated for several years in setting up a series of interlocking peasant organizations.[25]

During the 1980s, Chiapas' elites vigorously used state and national institutions to intimidate (and all too frequently liquidate) peasant activists. This intensified strains between Church-linked and Marxist-oriented activists in the budding peasant movement, with the latter steadily gaining adherents to the view that armed struggle was necessary. In the early 1990s, the two trends split. However, the sympathy of the non-violent followers of Samuel Ruiz for the EZLN remained strong and members of the EZLN visibly continued to hold the Bishop virtually in awe.[26]

From its inception, the *Zapatista* revolt attracted massive sympathy and vocal support throughout Mexico. But the support that Mexicans extended to the *Zapatistas* stemmed more from sympathy with the rebels' anger than approval of insurgency. The repeated economic and political crises suffered by the country since the early 1980s caused prolonged hardship to the lower and middle classes. By 1994, their increasing disaffection, and particularly that of the latter, was forcing the ruling establishment to yield reluctantly to demands for a more open and representative political system. Civil society – which had developed at an unprecedented rate over the preceding decade – as well as long-established opposition political parties ceaselessly pressed for effective political reform.[27]

In the five years since the cease-fire went into effect, the *Zapatistas* have taken great care to maintain their cause in the public eye and to enlist support from as wide a sector of society as possible. The issue of indigenous rights has gained prominence in the *Zapatista* discourse but remains cast in terms of broader national concerns. Active involvement in *Zapatista* decisions is sought through "national consultations" through which questions of *Zapatista* policy are placed before the bar of public opinion. Volunteer observers, both Mexican and foreign, are encouraged to visit *Zapatista*-controlled territory. Particularly extensive and effective use has been made of the internet, where a seemingly endless array of sites in various languages presents the *Zapatistas'* case to a domestic and international audience.

The locus: Upper Egypt

Upper Egypt comprises the country's eight southernmost governorates. As is true of Chiapas, the region's history is one of isolated removal from the center of national life. The local relationships resulting from this centuries-old condition gave Upper Egypt an identity of its own within the modern Egyptian state. Alongside the even more ancient presence of Copts, tribal groupings dating from the Arab conquest combined to form a hierarchical order that placed two groups, the *ashraf* and the *arab,* in dominating positions. These were followed by lesser tribes, with the *fellah* at the bottom of the social scale.[28] Southerners came to be stereotyped negatively in the rest of the country, widely held to be crude, prone to violence and lacking intelligence.

The authority of central governments in Upper Egypt was cemented through clientalistic ties with leading families of the *ashraf* and *arab* groups. Even the Nasserist regime did not substantially undermine this political-administrative arrangement. Although land reform benefited peasant farmers to a degree, members of the landed classes used a variety of means to retain much of their holdings. Cairo continued to staff the higher ranks of the local police and security apparatus with personnel from the *ashraf* and *arabs.*[29]

Religion was central to the development of Upper Egyptian society. The *ashraf* claimed direct descent from the Prophet, while the *arabs* traced their lineage to a group of tribes from Arabia. On the other hand, the status of the *fellahin* rested on the belief that they descended from Egypt's pre-Islamic community and had converted to Islam, a history that placed them inescapably beneath both the *ashraf* and *arabs.*[30] Copts have occupied an ambivalent position in the social scale; as Christians they are considered inferior to Muslims but their individual status effectively depends on more material criteria.

In Muslim as well as Christian communities, and particularly at the lower socio-economic levels, religious practices are strongly imbued with non-orthodox folk elements, some of pharaonic origin. Although orthodox Islam is well grounded in urban areas, the countryside is the domain of a rich folk-religion, replete with beliefs in the magical, miraculous and occult.[31] The influx of villagers into Egyptian cities and towns, which by the 1970s led increasingly to the "ruralization" of these centers, provided fertile fields for anti-modernist, fundamentalist movements. Urban mosques often became centers for the recruitment of rural migrants into militant organizations.[32]

Despite rich agricultural resources, Upper Egypt has long been the country's poorest region, whether compared in terms of rural or urban areas. By the mid-1990s, nearly 72 percent of Egypt's poor remained concentrated in the south.[33] Indicators related to health, population growth, social services and quality of life reveal similar disparities.[34]

The region has witnessed significant changes in the past four decades. The populist Nasserist years not only raised hopes for general improvement and a more equitable distribution of wealth, but also produced concrete achievements. Land reform, though not as sweeping as promised, brought some benefit to the *fellahin*. The opening of free universities in the 1960s seemed to promise an escape from poverty and the limitations of a rigidly traditional social hierarchy. With the government committed to employ all university graduates, the national bureaucracy provided a livelihood as well as a degree of prestige for sons of peasants who had no prospect of acquiring land of their own. However, it was not long before the ranks of university graduates outstripped possible placements. Moreover, when positions were available, *fellahin* graduates discovered that university credentials were frequently unable to overcome Upper Egyptian class bias or the general prejudice against southerners in other parts of the country.[35]

Other developments in the 1970s placed Upper Egypt's *fellahin* under increasing pressures. Anwar Sadat's reorientation of Egypt's economy through the liberalizing measures of *infitah* led him to seek the support of traditional rural elites. The renewed ascendancy of the landed notables – which sometimes resulted in officially sanctioned expulsions of peasant farmers from contested lands – not only menaced the *fellahins'* gains but also their aspirations. In the same decade, large numbers of *fellahin* who benefited from the oil boom by finding temporary employment in Arab Gulf states returned home with relatively significant capital, only to find the path to upward mobility still blocked by the traditional local power structure.[36]

Some, imbued by their experiences in Saudi Arabia with a more uncompromising and egalitarian vision of Islam, reacted to their mounting frustrations with greater religiosity – a phenomenon that helped produce a remarkable proliferation of private mosques in the 1970s. In Upper Egypt and among communities of southerners in urban centers throughout the country, returned *fellah* workers funded mosques in which an activist, socially-conscious interpretation of Islam challenged the status quo religious vision of the *ashraf* and *arabs*.[37]

The *Gama'a al-Islamiyya* developed as a movement, largely among students at Assiut University, in the early 1970s. Inspired by the early militancy of the Muslim Brotherhood, the group had links to, and shared a degree of overlapping membership with, similarly inclined groups in other parts of Egypt. One of these, the *Jihad*, would assassinate Sadat in 1981. Studies that focused on Egypt's Islamic movements in the 1980s concluded that Islamic militants came mainly from non-rural environments and lower-middle class backgrounds.[38]

However, Mamoun Fandy, "one of the first generation of peasant farmers' sons to benefit from Nasser's educational reforms" and an Assiut University classmate of many of the *Gama'a's* founders, argues that the *Gama'a al-Islamiyya* was marked from its inception by a distinctly Upper Egyptian *fellah* character which distinguished it from other militant Islamic groups. Most of its membership, he notes, "originally came from the *fellahin*."[39] While the *Gama'a* held the Cairo regime responsible for betraying Egypt's Islamic values and saw the solution as an Islamic state under *Shari'a*, it was also determined to alter power relationships in the south. In short, it aimed its fight "against southern tribal dominance, the Cairo government's role in this conflict, and the impact of this conflict, as well as [local culture], on the group's interpretation and use of Islam."[40] Fandy's recollections of the *Gama'a's* origins appear to be borne out by studies conducted after the organization gained prominence in the 1990s as Egypt's main militant Islamic group. Commenting on "the changing face of Islamic militants," Saad Eddin Ibrahim indicates that in comparison to militants studied in the early 1980s, those of the 1990s proved to be "younger and less educated . . . [many coming] from rural, small town and shantytown backgrounds."[41]

Anwar Sadat's assassination in 1981 was an immediate and serious setback for all militant Islamic groups. Government security forces carried out sweeping arrests and major clashes with militants took place, particularly in Upper Egypt. The *Gama'a*, however, survived and continued to mobilize support throughout the decade.

During the same period, as Hosni Mubarak gingerly pursued Sadat's liberalizing direction through steps that included reducing consumer and agricultural subsidies and decontrolling prices, the burden of poverty increased throughout Egypt's rural and urban areas.[42] Upper Egypt remained the poorest region. While "ultra poverty" was particularly high in Assiut, rural Upper Egypt continued to be the country's poorest agricultural area.[43] Additional regional misery hit after the 1986 downturn of Middle East oil economies reduced possibilities for migrant labor.[44] The 1990-91 Gulf Crisis, of course, produced a massive return of Egyptian workers from that region as well as deep uncertainties regarding that labor market's future. However, the worst fears of peasants seemed confirmed in 1992, when after a debate that had raged since 1985 the government enacted a measure that would effectively repeal statutes governing tenancy after a five-year grace period. Known by opponents as "the law for throwing out tenants from their land," this step profoundly disturbed what the rural poor considered "an important basis of a moral and political order."[45]

The *Gama'a's* major anti-government campaign developed in the early 1990s. No single event marked its beginning, but by mid-1992 there was no doubt that Egypt's government was facing a sustained offensive. Press accounts of the developing struggle revealed the extent to which the group was rooted in the rural countryside. The following, relating events in "a tiny village in Upper Egypt," is typical of such reports:

> *Since March, clashes between villagers and security forces have claimed two dozen lives. Farming is the only occupation . . . the district boasts few jobs and fewer public services. . . . It is fertile soil in which to recruit ardent young men for the Islamic Leagues [Gama'at al-Islamiyya], with their aura of romance and their programs of spiritual betterment and practical activism.*

> *In recent years the membership of such leagues has swollen into the thousands. In a dozen villages league enthusiasts have made themselves into enforcers of order and the providers of service.*[46]

Significant portions of Egypt's public agreed with the *Gama'a's* stated goals and values, though not with the means it chose to pursue them. This could hardly have been otherwise in a country where it is widely believed that, were free elections held, the non-violent, but banned, Muslim Brotherhood would emerge as the government's most serious challenger. The *Gama'a's* portrayal of the government as undermining Egyptian national and social values also found an echo in the hardships and frustrations of a population harried by growing economic disparities, cultural penetration and sharp changes in regional politics and Egypt's international standing.[47]

Nonetheless, the vast majority of Egyptians rejected the *Gama'a's* violent strategy. There is some evidence that even the small proportion of those who initially sympathized with the *Gama'a's* approach steadily dwindled as the violence progressed.[48] The cease-fire declared by part of the *Gama'a* leadership four months before the Luxor massacre seems likely to have been motivated by a growing conviction that violence had become politically counterproductive. The split that Luxor produced in the *Gama'a* appears to have led to the ascendancy, at least for the moment, of leaders who feel the organization must follow more moderate tactics if it is to achieve its aims. Among the newest tools employed to give both substance and recognition to this turn is a sophisticated Arabic language website, which went into operation in 1997.

The origins of MVIC

The conflicts that respectively pit the EZLN and the *Gama'a al Islamiyya* against the Mexican and Egyptian governments are products of a complex, but identifiable, interaction of factors. Among these are historical backgrounds that in each case created enduring local conditions which helped produce the violent outbursts of the 1990s; years of efforts by mobilizers who injected traditional local folk-religion with an new element that linked social justice and religious conviction to the "true" values of the nation as a whole; and, finally, the catalytic effects of neo-liberal economic and other globalizing forces.

The regions that gave rise to the EZLN and the *Gama'a al-Islamiyya* share histories of geographical isolation from the centers of national political, economic and cultural life. Over the centuries, Chiapas and Upper Egypt developed highly stratified societies that were largely left on their own by the national state, to which they were each linked through clientalistic ties between local and national elites. In each region an identifiable sub-group – the peasant/Indians of Chiapas and the *fellahin* of Upper Egypt – traditionally occupied the base of the socio-economic pyramid and was perceived as inherently inferior by the higher social orders. This perception was generally shared by the wider national populations.

Neither the Mexican Revolution nor the Nasserist experience radically altered the overall social, political and economic marginalization of Chiapas' rural peasantry or Upper Egypt's *fellahin*. Locally and nationally, the relative social, political and economic status of each remained much as it had been in the past. By the final quarter of the 20th century, economic deprivation and its typically associated social ills continued to afflict these groups. Official Mexican and

Egyptian statistics establish that in terms of income, poverty-levels, modern amenities, education and health, rural regions of Chiapas and Upper Egypt were not only mired in misery, but also among the poorest in their respective national contexts. Nor did internal migration guarantee relief. Whether in the shanty towns that urbanization brought to the outskirts of San Cristobal or in the poorer neighborhoods of Cairo, peasant *Chiapanecos* and Upper Egyptian *fellahin* were likely to find that deprivation still accompanied them.

However, neither group remained unaffected or unchanged by 20th century events. Decades of land reform failed to fulfill their promise but nonetheless led to some degree of relative improvement in Upper Egypt and Mexico. Upper Egyptian *fellahin* also benefited from Nasser's educational policies and, after the early 1970s, from opportunities to work abroad. During the same decade, the marginalized of Chiapas' Highlands not only found new, though temporary, employment in massive state-sponsored projects, but also became the focus of international efforts to upgrade their lives. Such factors involved changes that altered traditional life-styles and helped weaken traditional outlooks, including those elements of traditionalism that valued continuity above all. For many of the two groups considered here, change initially became seen as a welcome avenue that would lead to the satisfaction of raised hopes.

It was not long before such hopes yielded to fears that change might not only fail to produce improvement but actually lead to a deterioration of an already dismal situation. In Chiapas as well as Upper Egypt, rapid population growth steadily diminished available land for the marginalized and strained the capacities of existing social services. Budgetary crises in Mexico led to the curtailment of employment-generating government projects in the Highlands. In Egypt, the bloated bureaucracy proved unable to absorb university graduates and potential employees faced years-long waits before receiving positions. Graduates of newly established provincial universities in Upper Egypt at times felt the added weight of being discriminated against in their search for jobs because of their regional and social backgrounds. In both Egypt and Mexico, the increasing turns to national liberal economic strategies in the 1980s led to growing burdens on lower economic classes. During the same period, Upper Egypt's *fellahin* faced reduced possibilities of engaging in migratory labor as the oil economies of the Gulf contracted. In Chiapas, peasants learned that increased government expenditures designed to rationalize agriculture benefited large producers of export crops rather than small farmers.

Change, much of it emanating from sources far beyond the control or, in most cases, the understanding of the marginalized in Chiapas and Upper Egypt, appeared to have become not only threatening but almost overwhelming in its intensity, variety and malignity.

The unfolding of this perspective provided fertile ground for activist mobilizers who held state authorities responsible for the plight of the marginalized. Both in Upper Egypt and Chiapas, these mobilizers injected a new emphasis on social justice into prevailing religious belief systems, and linked the new interpretation to "true" national values. In Mexico, this role – initially filled by the socially conscious, non-violent, religiously-inspired mobilizers under Bishop Ruiz – came to be shared with the equally socially-conscious, militant, marxist-inspired mobilizers of the EZLN. In Egypt, social consciousness, religious inspiration and militancy were united in the mobilizers of the *Gama'a al-Islamiyya*. In both instances, the essential contribution, and attraction, of the mobilizer's message was that it offered, to those who accepted it, a credible promise of *both* change and resistance to change. This explains the emphasis given by *Zapatistas* and the *Gama'a* to demands for socio-economic change for the better and the preservation of cultural integrity.

In each case, the resulting militant movement has been closely linked to religious authority and belief. This is self-evident, of course, in relation to the *Gama'a*. Only an over-concentration on the secular discourse of *Zapatista* public pronouncements can obscure the fact that that movement's life – its values, origins, policies and membership – have all been influenced by the religiously-inspired activism of Bishop Ruiz and his cohorts, something that has been very well understood by the Roman Catholic establishment in Mexico as well as by the Mexican government. This is why dominant church authorities (including the Papal Nuncio) and government spokesmen have been so ready to accuse Ruiz of violating his true religious responsibilities. It is much the same discourse one hears when *Al Azhar* and Egyptian authorities accuse the *Gama'a* of being un-Islamic.

What made the mobilizers' message *credible* to those who followed their lead? Put another way, what caused these relatively small numbers of mainly impoverished Indian peasants in Mexico and lower stratum Upper Egyptians to believe they could force desired change despite the full military resources available to governing authorities? Undoubtedly, the answer is complex and probably includes an intensity of frustration, anger and desperation that galvanized some to conclude the effort must be made regardless of cost. But this alone cannot explain the conviction of those who took up arms that their cause would ultimately win.[49] Perhaps the answer also partly lies in the deep impact of a cultural context permeated by a syncretistic religious orientation in which the miraculous or magical is accepted as a normal part of life. The suggestion is that the folk-religions of the Chiapas Highland peasant Indians and Upper Egyptian *fellahin* fostered cognitive frameworks that were receptive to the notion that a just cause will eventually triumph, regardless of objective power relationships.

Globalizing economic, political and cultural forces merged with the impact of historically-derived conditions and the activism of mobilizers, tying local realities in Chiapas and Upper Egypt to wider world currents. The catalytic effects of neo-liberal policies undertaken by the Mexican and Egyptian governments in the 1980s were particularly direct. As indicated above, economically-marginalized populations of both areas were hurt by policies that reduced or eliminated social services, possibilities of government employment, agricultural and consumer subsidies and protected domestic markets. Policies designed to rationalize agriculture, especially steps to reverse the effects of earlier land reform programs, were perceived as major long-term threats to established ways of life and aspirations.

The impact of globalizing forces was not limited to sparking the violent campaigns of the EZLN and the *Gama'a al-Islamiyya*. It also appears to have been a significant factor shaping the terms in which their revolts were conceived. For although the marginalized in Mexico and Egypt may have suffered most acutely from the changes that affected their countries, they were hardly alone. In both Egypt and Mexico more integrated social sectors also saw their economic standing erode and their cultural values challenged throughout the 1980s. This was certainly true of the Mexican and Egyptian middle classes, who made their growing dissatisfaction known in a variety of ways. Thus, for example, the debates in Egypt and Mexico over specific domestic economic policies and the political and cultural implications of developments in those countries' international ties reflected national atmospheres of widespread dissatisfaction.[50] This, in turn, no doubt reinforced the conviction of the EZLN and the

Gama'a that their revolts did not imply a separation from the nation, but rather a reaffirmation of their commitment to the polity's "true" values.

Conclusion: Beyond the origins of MVIC

This article has tried to show that the generic similarity of the violent conflicts initiated by the EZLN and the *Gama'a al-Islamiyya* is evident in the dynamics that led to their outbreaks. It is, however, also evident that these conflicts have taken very different paths. The *Gama'a's* struggle has involved more sustained violence, and the group itself has perpetrated more grisly attacks against noncombatants. Finally, Egypt – unlike Mexico – has seen no effort to move toward a negotiated settlement. Do these differences mean that the two are not typologically linked; that they are, in fact, essentially different forms of conflict?

The answer suggested here is that such is not the case, that the distinct trajectories of the conflicts waged by the EZLN and the *Gama'a al-Islamiyya* reflect differences in interactions among three variables that together do much to shape the directions taken by Marginalized Violent Internal Conflicts. These are: the *political institutional environment*, the *civil society environment* and the *international environment*. In the final analysis, of course, conflicts do not "take directions" – they are given direction by leaders, who, in turn, opt for certain decisions rather than others through a process involving a constant interaction between ideology and action. Analysis must therefore focus not only on the interaction among the three variables indicated above but also between them and the decisions that leaders (both insurrectionary and government) make on the basis of ideological interpretation. In other words, the question is how the combination of factors emanating from the political institutional environment, civil society and the international environment affects the outlooks and consequent calculations and decisions of leaders. Such an analysis is well beyond the scope of this chapter, although it is possible to lay out briefly the main points to which it leads.

By 1994, Mexico's political institutional environment had bordered on the critical for over a decade. Governing institutions, dominated by the PRI, were largely discredited and the PRI itself was beset by fractious infighting. Opposition parties had emerged as real challengers to the ruling party's domination and the PRI's retention of its leading role was widely attributed to corruption. At the same time, however, the incumbent government of Carlos Salinas de Gortari (1988-1994) was widely – and as things turned out, incorrectly – perceived to be energetically putting Mexico on the path to renewed stability and prosperity. Continued positive economic indicators as well as the president's personal ambitions for the future depended upon the preservation of this image. The government, therefore, was prone to reject hard line advice – emanating particularly from the military and the established power structure in Chiapas – and instead accept the views of those who argued that neither the PRI's domestic position nor Mexico's economic policies would be served by pursuing a military solution in Chiapas.

Ernesto Zedillo assumed the presidency at the end of 1994, along with essentially the same conditions that had confronted his predecessor. Revelations of the extent of mismanagement and corruption that occurred under Salinas immediately plunged the new administration into a series of economic and political crises. Zedillo had emerged from relative obscurity only after the assassination of the PRI's initial candidate, Luis Donaldo Colosio. His political position as president was therefore uniquely weak in Mexico's recent history. Although Zedillo has on the whole adhered to the non-belligerent approach adopted by the Salinas government, his political debility appears to have been reflected over the years in recurrent vacillation as he occasionally yielded temporarily to more militant outlooks.[51]

That Zedillo's government has not decisively abandoned Mexico's non-belligerent approach to the *Zapatista* rebellion can largely be attributed to the impact on decision-making of civil society and the international environment. Both have served to constrain the military option. Civil society has not been unanimous in its reaction to the *Zapatistas*, but it has provided a constant forum for expressions of strong and widespread opposition to recourse to force. On the other hand, the international environment has also clearly urged the same message. Foreign governments, including that of the United States, as well as private investors, have feared the political and economic consequences of a major renewal of conflict in Chiapas.

The same factors that influenced the Mexican government's vacillating but essentially non-belligerent approach also help explain why the *Zapatistas'* have preferred the current stalemate over a renewal of armed hostilities. Both the weaknesses and strengths of Mexico's political institutional environment play a role in this. On the one hand, the political weakness that plagues Mexico's political system gives hope that *Zapatistas* may yet see their objectives realized through political means. On the other hand, the military strength that the government commands, and deploys in a threatening encirclement of the Conflict Zone, clearly helps make a revival of active hostilities unpalatable. Considerations related to civil society and the international environment act upon *Zapatista* calculations in much the same way. The networks of non-violent support that the *Zapatistas* have formed in Mexican civil society and abroad help fuel hope that *Zapatista* goals can eventually be realized through political means. These networks would be jeopardized, or at least seriously reduced, were the EZLN to assume responsibility for a resumption of major conflict in Chiapas.

The impacts of Egypt's political institutional environment, civil society and international environment contrast sharply with the Mexican case and explain the different course taken by the conflict between the *Gama'a al-Islamiyya* and the Egyptian government. Egypt's bureaucratic-authoritarian regime remains highly centralized and impervious to serious challenge within the existing institutional system. Although national elections are held and the legislative branch contains members from a wide variety of political parties, the government, as Noha Mikawy notes, has on the whole been reluctant to accept pluralist values even within that body.[52] In itself this ethos would have inclined the government to react forcefully to an extra-systemic challenge such as that posed by the *Gama'a*. Probably a more direct stimulus has been the *Gama'a's* historical links to the Muslim Brotherhood and espousal of the latter's objectives. Employment of the alternative to force – negotiation, mediation or some kindred conflict management technique – would at the very least redound to the credit of the Muslim Brotherhood's ideology and therefore to the credit of the very group that stands as the greatest potential political threat to the current regime.

Egypt's civil society has grown and developed over the past two decades but it remains highly controlled. Associational life is subject to a variety of legal constraints, all of which help shield the government from unwelcome actions or criticisms. Although relatively free in the context of the Arab World, Egypt's press has long functioned under stringent rules, and these have been strengthened in recent years. Under such circumstances, civil society's questioning of the government's hard line approach to the *Gama'a* could at best be only tentative while outright opposition could expect to be suppressed.

As in Mexico, Egyptian civil society is not of one mind but, unlike Mexico, it has been so muted that it is impossible to speak with much confidence about currents of public opinion. Nonetheless, available evidence – particularly the *Gama'a's* apparent soul-searching after the Luxor massacre – indicates that the group's methods, if not its objectives, became progressively more repugnant to the Egyptian public. Each of these characteristics of civil society enhanced the government's inclination to meet the *Gama'a* with force while eschewing opportunities to explore alternative approaches.

The international environment has exerted a similar influence. On the one hand, Egypt's principal Western allies are themselves committed to forceful stands against terrorism and all who practice it. On the other hand, Cairo had valid reason to believe that the *Gama'a* received some degree of support and encouragement from international actors whose primary motive was Egypt's destablization.[53]

The nature of Egypt's political institutional environment, civil society and international environment also explains the key decisions that have shaped the *Gama'a al-Islamiyya's* violent campaign. Faced by the government's firm control of the institutional political system and overwhelming military superiority, the *Gama'a* saw no alternative but violence, which it chose to project through terrorism in order to inflict the maximum amount of damage on the Mubarak regime by undermining public order and Egypt's valuable tourist industry. The government's ability to resist this strategy implied that its implementation must be drawn out and escalated. A growing suspicion that such a course would ultimately prove counter-productive seems to have moved some *Gama'a* leaders to call for a negotiated settlement as early as 1994. By mid-1997, key members of the group's upper ranks accepted this logic when they called on their followers to accept a unilateral cease-fire. In the post-Luxor period, the currently dominant, but not universally accepted, view among the *Gama'a* leadership appears to be that a change of strategy is in order. What this implies is still unclear.

Civil society and the international environment have also been key factors in the progression outlined above. If parts of the *Gama'a* came to perceive its strategy as counter-productive, it did so primarily by using as a yardstick the reaction of Egypt's public to the mounting ferocity of violence. If the Gama'a's violent campaign could not break the government's resistance, it was partly because the Mubarak regime's international support. And if another part of the *Gama'a* now feels that the original strategy must be retained, it is partly because they too are counting on international support and remain determined to sway the posture of civil society.

Political decisions are acts of ideological interpretation. The leaderships of the combatants examined here base themselves on declared ideologies (which for convenience's sake are identifiable as Zapatismo, Patriotism, Nationalism and Islamism) but have given them content through interpretive decisions. Those interpretations are largely – though not completely – understandable in light of the interaction of the four variables on which this analysis has focussed. Thus, much – but not all – can be understood of the various contending discourses: the *Zapatistas'* revolutionary discourse that emphasizes humanism and dialogue more than revolutionary violence; the Mexican Government's patriotic discourse that stresses the national duty to search for accommodation rather than the treachery of insurrection; the Egyptian government's nationalist discourse that emphasizes loyalty to the state and brands insurrection as treachery; and the discourse of the *Gama'a al-Islamiyya*, which stressed uncompromising Holy War against a treacherous regime (and which now appears to be changing).

The limits of the explanation offered here arise because neither leadership nor ideology can be considered totally dependent variables. Idiosyncratic factors have a role, and it must be kept in mind that *Zapatista* and *Gama'a* leaders have not simply responded to events. On the other hand, ideologies are not merely interpreted but also set limits to plausible interpretations. It may be that purely religious-rooted ideologies such as the *Gama'a's* have an elasticity that differs from the *Zapatistas'* secular-religious rooted ideology. What is called for is further study of leadership and ideology in the context of comparative conflict analysis.

With this caveat, the preceding comparison yields two further points. The first is that Marginalized Violent Internal Conflict appears to be a useful category, one that not only calls our attention to linkages between global forces and conflicts started by the least powerful members of society but also to levels of interaction that heavily shape the course of such conflicts. This has a direct bearing on the two cases studied here. The MVICs in Mexico and Egypt have yet to be resolved. Changes at any of the analytical levels examined here will determine whether their eventual resolutions will be through violence or through techniques of conflict management.

The second point is perhaps more basic, and more alarming. It is simply that as globalization touches the "Wretched of the Earth" in the world's most remote backwaters it may help trigger violent reactions from people who will not be dissuaded by even the most overwhelming objective evidence of the hopelessness of armed struggle.

Endotes

[1]D.E. Apter, *Rethinking Development: Modernization, Dependency and Postmodern Politics* (Sage Publications: Beverly Hills, CA, 1987), pp. 316-17.

[2]P. Bourdieu, "Utopia of Endless Exploitation: The Essence of Neo-liberalism," *Le Monde Diplomatique*, Dec., 1998, www.monde-diplomatique.fr/en/12/08bourdieu.html. Translated by Jeremy L. Shapiro, p. 3.

[3]Briefly put, this refers to *the confluence of the most immediate social dynamics impacting upon the insurrectionary groups.*

[4]Also briefly put, this refers to *the organized national system of decision-making and implementation*

[5]J.H. Mittleman, "The Dynamics of Globalization," in Mittleman, J.H. (ed.), *Globalization: Critical Reflections* (Boulder: Lynne Rienner Publishers, 1996), p. 2.

[6]Y. Grenier, "From Causes to Causers: The Etiology of Salvadoran Internal War Revisited," *Journal of Conflict Studies* (Fall, 1996), pp. 1-16, www.hil.unb.ca/

[7]Keesing's *Record of World Events*, News Digest for January, 1994, p. 39810. See also Arturo de Jesus Urbina Nandayapa, *Las Razones de Chiapas,* (Mexico: Editorial Pac, 1994), p. 74.

[8]Interview with confidential source. Chiapas, August, 1998.

[9]Jeongmin Seo, "Government Response to Radical Islamic Movements in Egypt During the Mubarak Regime," unpublished thesis, The American University in Cairo, 1996, pp. 39-56.

[10]"Disgruntled Militant Lawyer Stands Down," *Middle East Times*, January 25, 1998, p. 1 and "Foreign Emirs Shocked at Egyptian Militants' Cease-Fire Call," *Middle East Times*, July 14, 1997, p. 1. An earlier similar call was made by local *Gama'a* leaders in Minya and Sohag in 1994.

[11]R. Engle, "Militants Condemn Luxor Bloodbath," *Middle East Times*, December 7, 1997, p. 1.

[12]See, for example, "Tourist Numbers Recover," *Business Monthly: The Journal of the American Chamber of Commerce in Egypt*, Vol. 15, No. 3 (March, 1999), pp. 44-46.

[13]Interviews, Chiapas, 1995, 1996, 1998.

[14]See, for example, S. Tax Freeman, "Notes From the Chiapas Project: Zinacantan, Summer, 1959," in V.R. Bricker and G.H. Gossen, *Ethnographic Encounters in Mesoamerica: Essays in Honor of Evon Zartman Vogt, Jr.* (Albany: Institute for Mesoamerican Studies, The University at Albany, State University of New York: 1989), pp. 89-100; G.H. Gossen, "Life, Death and Apotheosis of a Chamula Protestant Leader: Biography as Social History," *Ibid.*, pp. 217-29.

[15]M. Serrano, "Civil Violence in Chiapas: The Origins and the Causes of the Revolt," in M. Serrano (ed)., *Mexico: Assessing Neo-Liberal Reform* (London, Institute of Latin American Studies, 1997), pp. 75-93; C. Tello Diaz, *La Rebelion de las Canadas* (Mexico: Cal y Arena, 1995), pp. 59-61.

[16]See Andreas Fabregas Puig, *"Los Pueblos de Chiapas,"* in Maria Luisa Armendariz (ed.), *Chiapas, Una Radiografia* (Mexico City: Fondo de Cultural Economica, 1994), pp. 172-97.

[17]See, for example, *Mexico Social, 1994-1995: Estadisticas Seleccionadas,* Division de Estudios Economicos y Sociales, Banco Nacional de Mexico, 1996, pp. 202-08.

[18]Daniel Villafuerte Solis and Maria del Carmen Garcia Aguilar, *"Los Altos de Chiapas en el Contexto del Neoliberalismo: Causas y Razones del Conflicto Indigena,"* in Silvia Soriano Hernandez (ed.), *A Proposito del la Insurgencia en Chiapas,* (Mexico: Asociacion Para el Desarrollo del la Investigacion Cientifica y Humanistica en Chiapas, 1994), pp. 83-117.

[19]*Ibid.*, pp. 83-84.

[20]D.R. Davila Villers, "Chiapas: Democratization and the Military in Mexico." Unpublished paper presented at the Latin American Studies Association XIX International Congress, Washington, D.C.: September, 1995, p. 6.

[21]Serrano, op. cit. To make matters worse, the international price of coffee fell sharply in the latter half of the 1980s.

[22]*Ibid.*

[23]Villafuerte and Garcia, pp. 85-86.

[24]A leading member of the San Cristobal *Ladino* community, an individual who also considers himself an *Autentico Coleto* – the label taken by the most racist of *Ladinos* – recalls Ruiz's social trajectory in the city as follows: ". . . it fell to me to welcome Samuel Ruiz. He was a very tranquil man [and] dined in the most honorable homes of San Cristobal. Yes, in those days he passed his time with *Autentico Coletos*. But then he slowly began to change. I think it's always been important for him to seek fame. . . ." Interview, San Cristobal de las Casas, 1995.

[25]Tello, op. cit., pp. 80-130.

[26]Interviews, Chiapas, 1995, 1998.

[27]Julio Labastida, "Mexico: Democratic Transition and Economic Reform," in D. Tschirgi (ed.), *Development in the Age of Liberalization: Egypt and Mexico* (Cairo: American University in Cairo Press, 1996), pp. 151-53.

[28]Mamoun Fandy, "Egypt's Islamic Group: Regional Revenge?" *Middle East Journal*, Vol. 48, No. 4 (Autumn, 1994), pp. 607-25.

[29]*Ibid.*, p. 615.

[30]*Ibid.*, p. 613.

[31]See W.S. Blackman, *The Fellahin of Upper Egypt*, London: Frank Cass & Co. (1968), pp. 183-200. See also M. Fandy, "The Tensions Behind the Violence in Egypt," *Middle East Policy*, Vol. 2, No. 1 (1993), pp. 25-27.

[32]Uri M. Kupferschmidt, "Reformist and Militant Islam in Urban and Rural Egypt," *Middle Eastern Studies*, Vol. 23, (October, 1987), p. 409.

[33]*Human Development Report Egypt, 1996*, (Cairo: Institute of National Planning, 1997), Table 2.2.

[34]J.A. Nedoroscik, D. Younis, El Sayed Gad Mohamed, M. Serrano, "Lessons in Violent Internal Conflict: Egypt and Mexico," *SYLFF Working Papers* (The Ryochi Sasakawa Young Leaders Fellowship Fund), No. 8, March, 1998, pp. 17-19.

[35]Mamoun Fandy, "The Tensions Behind the Violence in Egypt," pp. 27-28.

[36]Fandy, "Egypt's Islamic Group," pp. 616-18.

[37]Hamied N. Ansari, "The Islamic Militants in Egyptian Politics," *International Journal of Middle East Studies*, Vol. 16 (1984), p. 129; Fandy, "Egypt's Islamic Groups," p. 618.

[38]Saad Eddin Ibrahim, "Anatomy of Egypt's Militant Islamic Groups: Methodological Notes and Preliminary Findings," *International Journal of Middle East Studies*, No. 12 (1980).

[39]Fandy, "Egypt's Islamic Group," p. 613.

[40]*Ibid.*, p. 611.

[41]Saad Eddin Ibrahim, "The Changing Face of Egypt's Islamic Activism," in S. E. Ibrahim, ed., *Egypt, Islam and Democracy* (Cairo: The American University in Cairo Press, 1996), pp. 73.

[42]Karima Korayim, "Structural Adjustment, Stabilization Policies, and the Poor in Egypt," *Cairo Papers in Social Science*, Vol. 18, No. 4 (Winter, 1995-96), pp. 20-23.

[43]*Ibid.*, pp. 17, 18.

[44]D. Tschirgi, "Egyptian Labor Migration: Social, Political and Economic Effects," in M. Shtayyeh, (ed.), *Labor Migration: Palestine, Jordan, Egypt and Israel* (Jerusalem: Palestinian Center for Reg. Studies, 1997), p. 53.

[45]R. Saad, "State, Landlord, Parliament and Peasant: The Story of the 1992 Tenancy Law in Egypt," in A. Bowman & E. Rogan (eds.), *Agriculture in*

Egypt From Pharaonic to Modern Times, Proceedings of the British Academy, Vol. 96 (Oxford: Oxford University Press, 1998), pp. 387-89.

[46]"Upper Egypt: The Battle Against the Leagues," *The Economist,* July 4, 1992, p. 38. Similar accounts of conditions in rural Upper Egypt continued to be published throughout the early years of the *Gama'a's* campaign. See, for example, "Egypt Loses Ground to Muslim Militants and Fear," *New York Times,* February 11, 1994, p. A-3.

[47]Ibrahim, "The Changing Face of Egypt's Islamic Activism," pp. 76-79.

[48]Seo, pp. 39-58.

[49]This conviction was consistently expressed by militants in the jungles of the Conflict Zone, though in terms that recognized victory as a distant prospect that might not benefit the present generation of fighters. An EZLN leader,"Chus," for example, dismissed the possibility of his own death with calm eloquence and certainty: "They can kill 'Chus,' they can kill other leaders. But they cannot kill poverty and misery, and these will keep producing people like us." Interview. Chiapas, 1995.

[50]In Mexico, for example, the debate over the North American Free Trade Association (NAFTA) was cast in these, as well as economic, terms. In Egypt, multiple debates over American economic aid, peace with Israel and Egypt's strategic alignment with the United States had similar dimensions.

[51]Thus, in early 1995 Zedillo allowed the army to undertake an offensive in Chiapas, ostensibly to "arrest" the EZLN leadership, but soon reversed his position. For an account of relations between the army and Presidents Salinas and Zedillo during the early stages of the *Zapatista* revolt, see Stephen J. Wager and Donald E. Shultz, "Civil-Military Relations in Mexico: The Zaptista Revolt and Its Implications," *Journal of American Studies and World Affairs,* Vol. 37, No. 1 (Spring, 1995). Other temporary initiatives by the Mexican military occasionally occurred in subsequent years. A more important manifestation of the Zedillo administration's flirtations with hard line tactics appears to have taken shape since 1997 with the federal government's apparently increasing tolerance of paramilitary activity directed by elements in the Chiapas government and Chiapaneco *Ladino* elite. Interviews and personal observations, Chiapas, 1998.

[52]Noha Mikawy, *The Building of Consensus in Egypt's Transition Process* (Cairo: The American University in Cairo Press, 1999), p. 124.

[53]Egypt claims that the *Gama'a* has received support from the Sudan, Iran and Afghan Islamic groups.

Egypt in the Space and Time of Globalism

Raymond William Baker

With the earth and the life it supports imperiled by dangers beyond the capacities of the nation state and the world market, the most urgent task for the new century is to foster peaceful networks of trans-national cooperation in the planetary and human interest. The best hope for a just world order, responsive to the claims of the environment and human rights, flows from enhanced prospects for democratic participation that might yet create a framework of accountability for an unchallenged superpower and unrestrained market forces. As the 20th century draws to a close, this imperative defines my starting point in approaching Egyptian politics and all other issues of world politics. Driven by accelerated technological, financial and informational flows, over which only the single super-power can exercise any control at all, globalism today means unchallenged American dominance.[1]

The dominant globalism of the US hegemon and corporate capitalism dampens the hope for a global politics in the planetary and human interest. America's self-described commitments are to the free market and to democracy. It is now clear, however, that the tensions between these two goals will be resolved in favor of the market, with only a rhetorical nod to democracy, unless there is conscious intervention by democratic forces from below. The over-riding political and moral obligation facing citizens around the world is to use the new conditions and means of connectivity to work with others who share a global consciousness on behalf of projects in the common interest, driven neither by the power calculus or the cash nexus. Transportation and communication networks have created an enabling space-time compression that makes what was once a utopian dream of responsible global citizenship an experienced reality. Computer networks, Howard Frederick explains, are making possible the emergence of a global civil society to speak for "the Common Good of Humankind by loosing the bonds of the marketplace and the strictures of government on the media of communications. . . ." Around the globe, social forces that stand for peace, the environment and human rights are struggling to bend globalism to humane and principled ends. In this effort they rely on the new communication networks that are transforming international relations by strengthening global civil society.[2]

Trans-national social movements, leaning against nationalist and market pressures and organized around issues of peace, human rights and the environment, have been most effective in advancing this goal of creating a global consciousness and a worldwide arena for citizen participation in which it might find expression. The prospects of interaction for a common good have been extended to ordinary citizens, both at the center of American power and in areas where that power is felt, like Egypt. In short, new forms of association and cooperation are energizing a grassroots globalism that does hold promise of creating flexible webs of connection from which actions for the sake of safeguarding the earth and the human species can spring. Around the globe, prophetic minorities with a global consciousness have spontaneously arisen, committed to the peaceful remaking of themselves, their own societies and the global economic system originating in the "world revolution of Westernization."[3]

Such groups are the vanguards of grassroots globalism. In their ranks are those with Egyptian names, including those with identities shaped by their commitment to the universalistic values of Islam, interpreted for the late modern world. The creative, non-violent actions of these groups are local but with global import, related but not coordinated, and linked but not unified. These new trans-national social movements are inventing a post-modern global consciousness and politics with the potential to act against the violence that has marred the revolution of Westernization. They are creating projects of peaceful cooperation that advance human well-being and the health of the globe, projects driven neither by the realism of the nation state system nor the bottom line of the world market. Theirs, to borrow Inglehart's phrase, is a "silent revolution" that breathes life into the notion of a trans-national human social bond in the place and time of globalism.[4]

How does Egypt's political story play into this "silent revolution," if at all? What has been the impact of the strong American presence in Egypt for several decades now on the process of democratization? What contributions has the United States made to the strengthening of Egyptian civil society, from which such movements might arise? What steps might the United States take today to advance that goal? Who are the partners in Egypt who might respond and take advantage of any such opening that the United

States could strengthen? Do such partners include centrist Islamist forces?

Egyptians, whose consciousness has been awakened to needs more compelling than those of nationalism and consumerism, are initiating or making themselves available for collaborative political actions to address pressing issues of environmental degradation and failure to protect basic human rights and needs. For all the talk of the exceptionalism of the Islamic world, this hopeful trend has its Arab expressions, with some particularly promising manifestations in Egypt.

Interest in Egypt's politics will be sustained, as always, by the claims of her history and strategic geography and the ways in which those traditional strengths play into dominant power arrangements. Yet, Egypt's hold on our political imaginations will derive also from the inventiveness of Egypt's political class, including centrist Islamists, and their little-noticed role in elaborating the strategies of grassroots globalism in the Arab and Muslim lands. Egypt's political history is rarely told from this angle of vision. Most often, the Egyptian experience is appropriated for the dominant political narratives of the day; that is, we focus on those who conform to existing power arrangements rather than those whose contrary experience does not fit the mold. Egypt appeared as a "lead society" in the time of nationalism and non-alignment, and then was a valued strategic marker in the age of American-Soviet global rivalry. Today, Egypt's story is most often that of the exemplar of transition to market economy and formal democratization in the post-cold age of American hegemony and corporate capitalism, a story of transformation driven by the forces of corporate globalism. Egypt, firmly within the American orbit, is today most often seen as the emblem of the age, now the age of corporate and American-centered globalism.

The telling of the story of Egyptian politics is here set within the quite different horizon of the politic and moral possibilities created by grassroots globalism that haunts dominant corporate globalism with the subversive possibilities of a world-wide politics that demands superpower and market accountability. Viewed from this angle, the experience of Egypt provides some assurance that, behind the masks of mobilized masses for Mubarak and undifferentiated consumers of Big Macs, Pizza Hut and KFC, along side the willing subjects of USAID experimental projects, potential partners in the progressive projects of grassroots globalism have also appeared on the Egyptian political landscape. Their work on behalf of the institutions of civil society in Egypt is in many ways a disheartening one, with as many setbacks as advances. The last year has been particularly difficult, with short-term successes followed inexorably by failures that lead to prison and worse. The hardships experienced in recent years are part of the larger tale of the erosion of democratic advances and the disappointing record of American support for democratization in Egypt. Still, the very fact that centrist forces, including those with Islamist coloration, respond to repression with yet another moderate political party attempt or the founding of a newspaper with a genuinely independent stance keeps the hope of peaceful and non-coercive alternatives alive.[5] What must be celebrated is that there is such a story at all and that, even in defeat, it does carry important lessons for those moved by the hope of a global politics that encourages and enables citizen participation in a cross-grained politics that counters corporate globalism. Egypt's story is the tale of the resiliency and tenacity of the center, including the centrists groups of the Islamic wave.

The central thesis that emerges from this angle of vision is the American failure to exercise its influence on behalf of the forces of democratization. By that failure, whatever the rhetoric of support for democracy in the abstract, the American role in Egypt in fact hampers the fuller participation of Egyptians in global civil society by its failure to seize the opportunities open to it. Thus, the most important substantive conclusions from this study point to the steps that the United States might still take to help advance the prospects of democratization, including extending opportunities for full participation to moderate Islamists, that will, in turn, create a context supportive of all of Egypt's prophetic minorities who act on behalf of the larger prospects of a global civil society.

*   *   *

Today, the US dominates the world scene as the sole superpower. If the debate over policy toward Iraq is a measure, confirmation of that status comes most persuasively from those who have successfully urged that the US exercise its responsibilities by "quietly" bombing Baghdad. Violence, it seems, is the measure of superpower efficacy, just as it was the driving force of the worldwide revolution of Westernization to which the US is heir. By that standard, so full of tragic ironies, the United States role in Egypt must be judged consistent with earlier patterns of hegemony. Egypt resides fully within the American sphere and the Egyptian regime is so dependent on US support that the US role there provides an illuminating case to assess US post-Cold War global strategy and its impact on the "rest." For more than two decades now, US dominance has meant: 1) openness to global markets and utopian conditions for a very narrow but wildly flourishing middle class; 2) macro-economic improvement but mounting social tensions between the social elite and those Egyptians who can see, but neither taste nor feel, the new prosperity; 3) escalation of social violence, most often under a religious banner but no less driven by the deterioration of material and psychological conditions; and 4) erosion of the most promising democratic advances of the early Sadat/Mubarak eras, even as official rhetoric embalms the shells of increasingly fraudulent democratic practices.

What explains this record, so dismal from the perspective of an emerging global civil society? What, if anything, can be done to reverse or at least improve it? Equally important are questions prompted by the counter-intuitive emergence, in these dismal conditions, of such unexpected events as the emergence of human rights and environmental groups, as well as the creative and peaceful Islamist participation in the democratic institutions of civil society. What explains the surprising resilience of Egyptian social movements that stand against violence and for humane policies?[6] What, if anything, can be done to support and cooperate with them?

Despite the shocks, like the extremist violence in Luxor last year, the central but undramatic conclusion that emerges from sober reflection on Egypt's political system is the prospect of continuity. A mood of national depression has supplanted the sense of apprehension and crisis that the extended duel between the regime and the extremists had prompted. But the dark mood has not brought a decisive turning point. The most basic factor affecting stability – the Presidency as the center of ruling power, guaranteed by its unique relationship to the military – has withstood devastating defeat in war, popular upheaval, coup and assassination attempts, and jarring ideological reorientations and redefinitions. Even the tensions in the US-Egyptian relationship that had assumed a more public dimension have begun to recede. Once again, for the moment at least, it appears that the regime will suffer through, spared any collapse or diminution of its ability to play its regional security role and to "merit" the extraordinary US and international support it receives. However, the mood of national depression does register the very real damage that has been done in the last several years to the basic institutions of civil society and the extension of policies of repression from Islamist to other political forces. It coincides with a sense of the erosion of regime strength.

It is important to underscore forcefully that during these years, from the high point of Egypt's improved position as a result of the Gulf War, the regime has been pursuing a policy of repression without serious reform. In doing so, the government is drawing down three of its most precious resources: the reputation of the Presidency, the energies and talents of Egypt's youth, and the possibilities of national reconciliation offered by the country's moderate Islamists. As a result, the underlying violence built into the Egyptian-American connection is forcing its way to the surface. At the same time, the traditional Egyptian "investment in foreign policy" threatens to pay less of a premium. Egypt is increasingly taken-for-granted by an American administration that seems to believe that America's sole interests in the Middle East really just are oil and Israel. Egypt appears to have lost leverage with the United States. From the Egyptian point of view, an unprecedented level of arrogance and disregard has crept into the US stance toward Egypt, signaled by a whole series of incidents and issues – the Libyan human rights activist, the North Korean defector, the Israeli spy case, pressures around the Doha Conference and the reported intelligence background of the current Ambassador. There is, of course, some mileage to be gained from security assists for the Gulf, commitments to the global war against terrorism and help with the periodic jump starts for the peace process. But in today's Egypt, international posturing casts nowhere like the forgiving shadows that it did for Nasser and Sadat. Consequently, domestic politics matter more and the performance of the regime on that front is going from bad to worse.

Conventional wisdom makes sense of the Presidential regime's relationship to the Egyptian people in terms of contract theory. However useful this approach, it misses a great deal. Yes, the Nasser years were defined by a contract that provided economic and social security to Egypt's people in return for political passivity. Nasser proffered this contract and it was received in the context of a large national dream that inspired millions, not only in Egypt but in the Arab world beyond. In a world of bipolar competition, Egypt would be a major player with a pan-Arab, nationalist agenda that placed it in the forefront of the Third World. In the changed circumstances of superpower détente, Sadat leaned to the ascendant Americans. Now the same contract offered Peace and Prosperity, with the explicit promise of democratization, as Egypt linked its destiny to the West. In today's post-Cold War era, with peace so diminished in its consequences for Palestinians and all Arabs and prosperity more elusive than ever, Mubarak could promise only a lowering of the voice, personal probity, a curbing of regime corruption, a deepening of democracy and a realistic engagement with Egypt's economic travails – all made plausible by the backing of the only superpower left.

After the long years of Mubarak's rule, all of these "dream substitutes" are unraveling. The lowered voice now registers inertia at best, the regime and the President's family is no longer regarded as being above rampant corruption. The telltale jokes about the President have shifted from his lack of intellectual acumen to his corruption. The democratic process has halted and there have been some important markers of reversal in the last years: intrusions into the workings of such key institutions of civil society as the professional unions; increased official violence, including an unprecedented level of violence around electoral politics that killed, incidentally, just about as many Egyptians as the foreigners who were murdered at Luxor; the extremists; the toleration of a climate within which candidates in the last elections, including some backed by the regime, attacked Copts in the most ugly and dangerous manner; the failure of the regime to nominate Copts as part of its own slate; and a clumsy and soon abandoned assault on press freedoms. The situation has worsened to such a degree that economic restructuring, too, has yet to produce any tangible improvement in the conditions of the mass of Egyptians, however upbeat the macro-economic indicators have become.

Dreams are most important to the young, for they promise a better future and that future belongs to the young. Yet, look at the future that awaits Egypt's youth. Their education today takes place in a crumbling and corrupted public system. They graduate from overcrowded institutes and universities to swell the ranks of the unemployed. The humiliations of continued reliance on the family dole is aggravated by the terrible frustrations of deferred employment, delayed marriage, and a decade and more in search of the money for the most modest housing on their own. These painful conditions, national and personal, make thousands upon thousands of Egypt's best youth candidates for desperate migration or violent militancy. In either case, their enormous talents are lost to Egypt.

This dismal picture is made all the more depressing in that Egypt's lost youth has been the target of the rising tide of human rights abuses that now leave a large stain on Egypt's reputation. The regime has not found a way to confront violent militants without committing human rights abuses as savage or more so than the violence they seek to contain from the ranks of the militant Islamists. Disgusting levels of torture are commonplace in Egyptian jails. My own estimate would be that there are now about 20 000 young Egyptians in these brutalizing training schools for producing the next generation of militant theorists like Sayyid Qotb and the bands of terrorist followers who will give us more slaughters like those in front of the Egyptian Museum and Hatshepsut's tomb in recent years. The United States has failed to deliver an unequivocal condemnation, with Presidential imprimatur, of these abuses. Even lesser steps, such as a moderation of the sweeping emergency laws that give sweeping powers to undisciplined police and security forces and no legal protection at all to their targets, are not taken.

We in the West have been ill equipped to understand the issue of Islamic militancy and we have been too quick to accept the characterizations of its meaning offered by compliant regimes. Ideological formulations such as "Muslim Rage" and the "Clash of Civilizations" mask the politics and policy dimensions that underlie the clash between established regimes and Islamist extremists. However, simply acknowledging the political dimensions is not enough. It is important to get the political story right.

The Egyptian regime has its own self-serving version: the battle of a secular, pro-Western government to stave off the atavistic assault of an Iranian-style fundamentalist threat in the interest of preserving a democratic political and liberal economic experiment.

A second, somewhat more sophisticated version often adopted by Western analysts recognizes the regime's role in the freeing of the Islamists from the prisons and unleashing them on the left. That move is seen as a bold strategy that backfired when the Islamists turned against the regime for the sake of its own agenda, with murderous effect. The problem here is the underestimation of the wellspring and the force of the destructive Islamic political impulse.

A third version of the political story line, adopted as the self-understanding of key moderate Islamist figures speaking for the Islamic moderate mainstream or *wasittiya*; they have a strikingly different view of the Islamic wave and its political and social import: An Islamic Awakening, temporarily eclipsed, is reasserting itself with a long range educational and cultural project for Egypt's transformation, at times accommodating and at times clashing with the regime. The Islamic Awakening, with its emphasis on a national project built on the foundations of Egypt's distinctive Islamic legacy, indicts the entire Free Officer experience as a vehicle of anti-Western Westernization, devoid of any authentic link to Egypt's heritage. According to these centrist Islamists, at the very heart of the Free Officer project, from Nasser through Sadat to Mubarak, lies a deadening cultural and spiritual void.[7] Elsewhere I have argued in detail that in a liberalized Egypt, Islamic intellectual and social forces that are emerging from the broad center of the Islamic wave could emerge to take their place with other social forces as part of a global, humanizing force, struggling for a politics in the human interest.[8] For my purposes here, it is enough to register that this broad, centrist current is feeding the Islamic intellectual and social groupings that bear comparison with the "prophetic minorities" emerging elsewhere around the world.

Even without accepting fully this Islamic, centrist version of the key political narrative of Egypt today, it does seem reasonable to recognize that the Islamic factor goes far beyond the militants. Just for that reason, unless and until an effective regime alternative to the very powerful and deeply rooted Islamic vision of Egypt's future is put forward, regime successes in containing the militant fringe of the wave will most likely assume a pattern of ebb and flow. Effective containment of the militant challenge is unimaginable while the central government continues to fail to respond to the terrible predicament of Egypt's youth. From a different angle of vision, the assault on the moderate Islamists does seem to have the potential to split the political elite and perhaps cause a fracture that would extend into such key institutions as the bureaucracy and the military. What's behind the regime's willingness to take this risk of moving against the centrist Islamists?

For the last several years, regime policies make sense only by concluding that the overt war against the Islamic militants is only a tactical cover for a much more sweeping attack against this broader Islamic wave. The regime consciously adopted a broad strategy of "drying the springs" – that is, attacking what are presumed to be the moderate well springs in civil society that allegedly feed the militant waves.[9] Among these policies are the measures designed to restrict the international linkages of parties and to curtail the activities of Islamists in professional associations by manipulating voting procedures. At the same time, and as a direct consequence, opportunities for the sound religious education of a new generation of Egyptians in a centrist reading of the Islamic legacy are diminishing, leaving only the sterile pontifications of official Islam tied to the regime or the gross and dangerous simplifications of the radicals. The arrest of such prominent moderate Islamist figures as Essam al Eryan provides a face, while not known internationally, still sufficiently prominent and respected in Egypt and the Arab world to call into question the whole regime's effort to curtail the moderates. These policies point unmistakably to the conclusion that the current regime regards the only real threat to its grip on power to be an Islamic moderate one. The war against the terrorist serves at once as a response to the criminal violence of a militant minority and at the same time and in perhaps a more important way, as simply a tactical cover for the elimination of this moderate "threat." Regime violence, legitimated as strikes against terrorism, is taking consistent aim at the most promising of Islamic centrist currents that, in turn, find common cause with other humane and democratizing elements on the Egyptian scene.

This regime strategy points to a deepening of authoritarianism rather than democracy. More importantly, it sacrifices an important moderate Islamist alternative for Egypt and the Arab world. Egypt is not Iran. Egypt is not Algeria. There is an Egyptian Third Way, an Egyptian alternative of reform and reconciliation, unworkable without the active participation of the moderate Islamists. But neither reform nor reconciliation is possible in the context of a state-sponsored war against the Islamic trend that is profoundly damaging to all elements and institutions of civil society. Reform means political restructuring. Reform means a genuinely pluralistic ruling party. It demands the routinization of presidential succession and limits on the tenure of the President. Reform is impossible without the incorporation of the Islamist mainstream into public life, whether by a political party or participation in civil society. To work, the broadening of democracy would have to extend to a conscious effort to revitalize the almost moribund political opposition parties. Some parties are at this point little more than newspaper-centered clusters of aging intellectuals, with little influence or even ties to the masses.[10] To make matters worse, they are deeply divided. Reform is inconceivable without a vigorous anti-corruption campaign that retrieves the image of the Presidency and its military guarantor as a force that carries a national vision that rises above corruption and brutality. Reform and reconciliation may not be as sweeping a vision as Nasser's and Sadat's, but it just might be the most hopeful way out of the present deteriorating situation, from a long-term perspective.

The regime, however, gives no signs of moving in this direction. In a regional context where the United States continues to put all its eggs in the greatly diminished "peace process," the regime will get no serious prodding for political or, for that matter, economic reform that improves the lot of the mass of Egyptians. The gap between the very rich and the very poor is growing. Egypt's President will make his political calculus secure in the knowledge that what counts to the Americans is support for the peace process – not democratization, not a broader national project of serious economic reform, but political reconciliation.

In the absence of such a project, the radical Islamists and their violence is a godsend for the President. With no vice president standing by, any attack on the President can be projected as a dangerous invitation to the discredited militants to assume power. When the attempt to assassinate the President took place in Ethiopia, there was relief that a succession crisis had been avoided. Should the next attempt be successful, it is most likely that Egyptians would look to the military to act to stabilize the situation.

Barring assassination, it is most likely that, despite the mounting costs, the regime will continue to muddle through. Egypt's youth will continue to turn to migration or militancy. There is, then, a certain short-term, surface logic to the American hopes for Egyptian regime stability and the "peace process," just as those deep-seated American fears that center on the "terrorist" and the "immigrant" have their own long-term, self-fulfilling justification.

From a vantage point that highlights the prospects of grassroots globalism, it is impossible to end Egypt's political story with such depressing realism. The hopes for a more positive American role have not been realized. But just as moderate Egyptians unrelentingly assert themselves in the face of repression, it is critical to hold the US to a higher standard. The opportunity is there. Since America is so closely tied to the current regime, there are things that can and should be done with an eye to the longer-term reform and regeneration of the regime. On the American scene, it is critical to make the point that the collapse of what is left of the peace will mean the loss of leverage over the regime for democratization, i.e., the government can use Egyptian distress at a failed process and Israeli intransigence (with American support) to re-legitimize the unreformed regime.

On the Egyptian scene, it will be important to:

1. Press for a regeneration and deepening of the process of political liberalization, providing openings to all political forces – left, right and Islamist. The only real strategy to contain the radical is an opening of the political process that would allow the minority status of the Islamists in general and the radical Islamists in particular to become clear.

2. Convey a sharp sense of the inadequacy, even illegitimacy, of the current Parliament. In the next parliament, the opposition must win at least 100 seats; elections free from official coercion will ensure that result.

3. Recommend a cessation of the hostility and even repression of the Professional Associations and recognize them for what they are, critical arenas for emergent civil society.

4. Argue for a more pluralistic media, including television, to give a variety of reformist voices the opportunity to counter the radicals.

5. Advise the regime to act immediately to improve the image and reputation of the police, increasingly viewed as "enemies of the people" as a result of the violence against the radicals and general arrogance of their disregard for the rights of average Egyptians.

6. Advise that labor unions be given more say to balance the negative social effects of privatization.

7. Urge the regime to take pre-emptive action on the issue of national unity and to remove the scandal of the non-representation of Copts in national institutions. Drop even the hint of US intrusion into the Coptic issue, misunderstood as one of minorities; assiduously avoid use of the threat of cessation of US foreign aid.

8. Advise that the government launch an effective anti-corruption campaign or risk leaving this powerful issue to the Islamists alone.

9. Recommend strongly and support in whatever ways possible efforts to provide rehabilitation and support for Egypt's abandoned youth.

10. Urge reconciliation with moderate Islamic forces.[11] The government should proceed in two stages: first, recognizing the legitimacy of the Islamist opposition centred in the Labor Party, and then creating a real opening to the Muslim

Brothers. This could be done cautiously, first by recognizing the youthful spin-off Wasat Party and releasing prominent Islamist political prisoners, notably Essam al Eryan, and then turning directly to the Brothers as potential partners in a broadened liberalization.

The American role in Egypt has made the country safer for the multi-nationals; it has made possible a more repressive style of regime rulership. At the same time, despite the concrete opportunities for constructive action that exist, the United States has done little of what it might do to advance democratization. The issue is not the abstract one of American interference in Egyptian affairs. In the age of globalization, America everywhere wields influence. In Egypt that influence could serve to strengthen the generative context for the kind of planetary citizens who are emerging around the world to speak and act together for the earth and its people in the space and time of globalism.

Endnotes

[1] For a recent account celebrating American-dominated, corporate globalism, see Thomas L. Friedman, "What the World Needs Now," *The New York Times Magazine*, March 28, 1999.

[2] See Howard Frederick, "Computer Networks and the Emergence of Global Civil Society," in Linda Harasim, *Global Networks* (Cambridge & London: MIT Press, 1993), 283.

[3] This phrase was coined by Theodor Von Laue in his *The World Revolution of Westernization: The Twentieth Century in Global Perspective* (New York: Oxford University Press, 1987). Von Laue's global history of the 20th century is structured by a "culturalist" perspective that I do not fully accept, although he offers a compelling account of the making of the modern world and, in particular, the role that violence has played in it, especially in the hands of "anti-Western, Westernizing forces."

[4] Ronald Inglehart has developed his conception of the "silent revolution" in *The Silent Revolution: Changing Values and Political Styles Among Western Publics* (Princeton: Princeton University Press, 1977) and *Culture Shift in Advanced Industrial Society* (Princeton University Press, 1977).

[5] For an account of one such incident, the founding of the *al-Wasat* party, see Nabil Abdul Fattah, *Al-Wafd*, 18 January 1996.

[6] For an account of Egyptian politics that centers on such contrary movements, see my *Sadat and After: The Struggle For Egypt's Political Soul* (Cambridge: Harvard University Press, 1990.)

[7] Both intellectuals and activists, body and mind, speak and act for centrist Islam. In my view, the most compelling statement of the centrist Islamist position is Kamal Aboul Megd, *A Contemporary Islamic Vision: Declaration of Principles* (Cairo: Dar al-Sharuq, 1991).

[8] See, for example, my chapter "Invidious Comparisons: Realism, Postmodern Globalism, and Centrist Islamic Movements in Egypt" in *Political Islam* (Boulder & London: Lynne Rienner, 1997), edited by John Esposito.

[9] Fahmi Huweidi, the gifted Egyptian Islamist journalist, has popularized this characterization of the regime strategy for containing and undermining the Islamist current. See, Huweidi, *al-Ahram*, 2 February 1993.

[10] For a wonderful, satirical account of the lack of life in Egypt's political parties, see Manar al Shorbagy, "For the Sake of – Soap!," *al Nidaa an Jadid*, March 1996.

[11] Civil Society institutions in Egypt, notably the human rights groups, have on occasion boldly recognized the importance of incorporating the Islamists into political life. For an informative account of one symposium where this imperative was candidly discussed, see *Al Wafd*, 5 July 1996.

Westernization as a Prelude to Globalization: The Turkish Experience

Seymen Atasoy

Turkey's enthusiastic embracing of globalization in the 1980s was mainly forced by economic necessities. Yet, the rapid and extensive adoption of a corresponding public discourse remains in need of further explanation. The Republic of Turkey emerged out of an anti-imperialist liberation war, and made "complete independence" a fundamental principle of its political culture. Under these circumstances, the recent acceptance of "integration with the globalizing world" as a basic state objective appears to be a deviation from the established pattern. However, a survey of relations with the West and modernization efforts during Ottoman and Republican eras illustrates a remarkable degree of continuity, indicating the historical roots of the current globalization phase in Turkey.

Globalization and Turkey[1]

"Globalization" remains a popular yet controversial concept of the last two decades. Basically, it refers to increasing global interconnectedness in economic, social, cultural, ecological and other matters. Regarding its consequences, academics from different schools of thought present conflicting interpretations, while policymakers use these to legitimize or oppose a wide range of divergent choices.[2]

According to liberals, the expansion of a single world market, the proliferation of communication and transportation technologies, the spreading of a cosmopolitan culture and the mushrooming of international non-governmental actors are totally transforming the state-centric nature of world politics. Realists disagree that the status of states as the determining actors of international affairs is changing. They claim that economic, technological, social and cultural phenomena associated with globalization do not alter the fundamental competition for power among states, but rather change the environment wherein this competition takes place. Neo-Marxists perceive globalization as the latest phase of international capitalism that favors the rich West at the expense of the poor South.[3]

The dominant interpretation in Turkey during the last 20 years perceives globalization as supportive of the long-standing modernization objective of the country. The concept was utilized by successive governments as a guiding principle for policy analysis, and as a tool for the legitimation of market-oriented macro-economic reforms. On the other hand, opposers to these structural changes (at times as coalition partners in governments) used alternative interpretations of globalization to moderate measures towards economic liberalization in Turkey.

Küreselleşme, the Turkish version of globalization, was essentially perceived to be an external force demanding change at the domestic level. Those countries that promptly understood and implemented the adjustments globalization required were assumed to be the likely winners of international competition in the future. Thus, a mostly realist interpretation of globalization became popular, as neo-Marxist and Islamist critiques sought to challenge it.[4]

A purely liberal understanding of globalization was rather uncommon.[5] This seems to be due to the status of the business elites. Unlike most European countries, where capitalists developed independently from the state, the entrepreneurial class of the Republic flourished under state tutelage and sponsorship. Civilian and military bureaucrats maintain significant influence in major macro-economic policy choices and politicians have to be sensitive to the preferences of these state elites, which at times diverge from those of the business community.

Reforms in the Ottoman Empire as well as the Republican Turkey were initiated from above and in response to external challenges. Successive defeats on the battlefields against the superior armed forces of European industrialized powers had forced the Ottoman Sultans to military reforms on the western model. Westernization gradually spilled over to economic, social and political spheres, preparing the basis for the formation of the modern Republic.

Main lines of Ottoman-European relations[6]

During the three centuries after AD 1050, various Turkish tribes from Central and Western Asia migrated into Asia Minor. When the Seljuk Sultan Alp-Aslan defeated the Byzantine army at Manzikiert in 1071, Anatolia was further opened to the migration and settlement of Turks. On their centuries-long migration towards the West from Central Asia, Turks had met Muslims and accepted Islam. Thus, the turkization of Asia Minor blended three distinct civilizational heritages: i) the indigenous and ancient civilizations of Anatolia that had earlier been overlaid by Christianity; ii) the nomadic culture Turks brought from Central Asia; and iii) the Islamic civilization again brought in by the Turks.[7]

Reliable statistics regarding the indigenous population of Anatolia and the number of the migrating Turks are not available. The indigenous Anatolian population of the period is predicted to have ranged from 3 to 13 million people, while the number of the incoming Turks was likely only a fraction of it. But, the three states founded by the Turks decisively shaped the political and cultural evolution of Asia Minor: The Seljuk Empire, the Ottoman Empire and the Republic of Turkey. These states inherited and used Islamic, Byzantine, Turkish and Western administrative traditions in varying combinations.

Thus, Muslim Turks captured the land that was then the core of the Christian world and made it their own. Waves of Crusades from Europe seeking to recapture the holy lands in Palestine and other formerly Christian territory failed in the long-run. The Ottoman Empire that replaced the Seljuks started conquests in the Balkans in the early 14th century and controlled a quarter of the territory of Europe until the 18th century. The second failed attempt by the Ottomans to take Vienna in 1683 formed a turning point in Ottoman-European relations, one from conquests by the Turks to their gradual withdrawal.

During the early 16th century, The Ottomans had reached the gates of Vienna. Perceiving the Habsburgs as the main barrier to their Westward expansion, they entered an arrangement of military, political and economic cooperation with the French under Francis I. In the words of Adam Watson, "through French contacts with the Protestant princes opposed to the Habsburgs, the Ottomans developed a general policy of fostering disorder in Christian Europe and weakening their Habsburg enemies by offering political and military cooperation and economic inducements to anti-hegemonial states and rebellious movements there."[8] The Ottomans achieved their diplomatic objectives in Europe during the 16th century, acting as a part of and shaping the evolution of the European state system to a significant extent.

Expanding the dar al Islam was an important religious justification for conquests in Europe, as were the struggles with the shia

Safavids in Persia. Being between two distant fronts, the Ottomans arranged temporary truces with the enemies and sought allies especially from among emerging Christian states, and became diplomatically engaged with them.[9] The defeat of the hegemonial attempt of the Habsburgs and the development of the Westphalian system were made possible by Ottoman pressure. Later, when Louis XIV developed hegemonial aspirations, the Ottomans joined sides with the Habsburgs in the corresponding anti-hegemonial coalition.

Alongside diplomatic and strategic involvement, the institution of capitulations beginning in the 16th century formed a body of common rules regulating relations between Europe and the Ottoman Empire. Starting with France, they were gradually extended to Britain, the Netherlands and Russia. Originally, the capitulations were unilaterally declared regulations of the Ottoman Sultans to manage trade and issues of extraterritorial jurisdiction with the European states. European aliens were under the jurisdiction of the consuls of their states, and the European concept of consulates developed thus.[10] Under this system, the European states enjoyed economic advantages in the large Ottoman markets and freely developed their influence on the Christian minorities of the Empire.

As the Europeans became stronger and the Ottomans weaker, the nature of the capitulations changed drastically: from unilateral grants of concessions subject to withdrawal, they turned into permanent mechanisms for the maximization of European interests in Ottoman realms at the expense of indigenous objectives. Playing a key role in the economic underdevelopment of the Ottoman Empire, and in its fatal weakening by the revolts of Christian minorities with European urging and support, the history of capitulations still continues to influence Turkish perceptions of economic and legal engagement with the West. Dealings with the Ottoman Empire formed the European model for later relations with other non-European cultures.

The Ottomans and the Europeans perceived each other as too alien for the Ottoman Empire to become a full member of the European society of states, despite extensive interactions. A separate and more restricted set of institutions were developed to manage these inter-civilizational interactions.

The Ottoman Empire was only marginally touched by common European experiences such as reformation, renaissance, rationalism, enlightenment, scientific and technological progress, and the industrial revolution. It was rather the military superiority of Europe and

Ottoman failures on the battlefield that caused the initiation of Westernizing reforms under the Sultans in the 19th century.[11] In an effort to defeat European armies, Ottomans started to reform their armed forces and military academies after the Western model and by employing European experts. With the transfer of new ideas from Europe into the Empire through the efforts to modernize the military, reform spilled over into areas of education, law and statecraft. Limited experiments in democracy and in the assurance of human and minority rights were undertaken during the 19th and early 20th centuries.

The collapse of the Ottoman Empire with World War I and the establishment of the Turkish Republic under Atatürk's leadership was followed by a comprehensive reform effort. A political and cultural revolution from above was initiated in an effort to raise Turkey to the standards of contemporary civilization. The West, from the imperialist designs and the occupation of which Turkey saved itself through a costly liberation war, was again the ironic model for this comprehensive change. The Latin alphabet replaced the Arabic one, European legal codes replaced Islamic law, the education system was unified and reformed, traditional local and religious legitimacies were suppressed, and the dress of the people was changed along Western lines with the adoption of the hat and the banning of the fez and the veil by law.

Turkish-Western relations in the Republican era

During the inter-war period and WW II, Turkey continued a rather isolationist and inward-looking foreign policy along the Kemalist principle of "peace in the country, peace in the world."[12] The priority was the consolidation of the Republic and the reforms. Under these circumstances, Turkey stayed out of World War II with determined effort and maintained its neutrality until the last days of the War, then siding with the allies. The territorial demands and other pressures of the Soviet Union in the aftermath of World War II made a neutral Turkish foreign policy impossible, forcing Turkey to join the Western alliance against Soviet expansionism. It became a member of NATO in 1952, in addition to memberships in the Council of Europe and the Organization for European Economic Cooperation (OEEC). It enjoyed US military and economic assistance under the Truman doctrine and the Marshall Plan.

Stressing the geopolitical location and strategic importance of Turkey for Western collective defence, Turkish governments have generally sought to increase the amount of the military and economic assistance they received from the US-led West. The door was left open for occasional rapprochements with the Soviet Union to increase bargaining power vis-a-vis Western partners.

Turkish disappointments with the West and the assumption that the West was culturally biased against Turkey increased when the US was perceived to support the Greek side in the Cyprus conflict surfacing in 1963, and when President Johnson threatened Turkey in 1964 by implying that it could be left alone in the case of Soviet aggression emerging within the context of a Turkish involvement in Cyprus. This episode led to a review of relations with the West by Turkish leaders and the initiation of closer relations with the Soviet Union. Despite these developments, Turkish-Western relations generally remained intact and robust. The military regimes coming to power in 1960 and in 1980 started business by proclaiming and assuring the continuation of Turkey's Western-oriented foreign policy.

Yet, the historically- and culturally-conditioned Greek enmity towards Turkey has been and remains a key barrier to the deepening of Turkish-Western cooperation.[13] The turkization of Anatolia starting in the 11th century involved the replacement of the Helenic civilization with a Turkish-Islamic one in Western and Coastal Anatolia. The Greek military adventure to recapture Western Anatolia after WW I ended with a devastating defeat in the Turkish liberation war of 1920-22. Unable to forget this set-back, certain post-WW II Greek leaders imagined a new Greek Eastward expansion at the expense of Turkey that was to start with the unification of Cyprus with Greece.

Because of its strategic position controlling Turkish access to the Mediterranean and the existence of a Turkish minority on the island, Greek plans on Cyprus were vehemently opposed by Turkey. Conflicts regarding the Aegean Sea, the extent of territorial waters, and Greek violations of the rights of the Turkish minority in Western Thrace continued to complicate relations. These problems were enhanced by cultural differences. Greece sought to sever Turkish-Western cooperation, succeeding in this to a considerable extent. The US Congress, under the influence of the Greek lobby, then imposed an arms embargo on the NATO ally Turkey for its military intervention in Cyprus in 1974 to thwart an attempt of a group of

Greek Cypriots to establish a dictatorship on the island with the help of the colonels' junta in Athens.

Presently, one of the main barriers to the establishment of closer relations between Turkey and the European Union is Greek resistance, which seems to be based on historical/cultural factors rather than rational ones. As the strategic necessity for maintaining stability in the South-Eastern flank of NATO is perceived to be declining, Greek activities in the West against Turkey find more room for action.

Alongside security cooperation with the West within NATO, extensive economic cooperation was undertaken through various mechanisms. Between 1948 and 1952 Turkey received economic assistance from the US within the framework of the Marshall Plan. After the ending of the program in 1952, Turkey continued to receive military and economic assistance from the US, and participated as a member in the OEEC, which evolved into the Organization for Economic Cooperation and Development (OECD), and worked closely with the International Monetary Fund (IMF) and the International Bank for Reconstruction and Development (IBRD).

In response to Turkish requests, amounts of assistance provided were gradually increased. But the enlargement of the Turkish economy decreased the importance of foreign aid in national development. American aid that financed most of the investments in 1950 corresponded to only 10% of the investments in 1955.[14] Aid came in under the principle of defense support and consisted of credits and donations. The share of donations compared to credits declined gradually and became marginalized. With the shift to planned development in Turkey in 1960, credits were increasingly tied to the importation of capital equipment for specific public and private investment projects.

An important milestone in the evolution of Western-Turkish economic cooperation was the establishment within the framework of the OECD in 1962 of a Consortium for assistance to Turkey. Consisting of a grouping of 14 Western states, the IMF, the IBRD and some other European international economic institutions, the consortium formed a forum for dialogue and for the generation and implementation of Western policies regarding program credits, project credits and debt restructuring regarding Turkey. At the same time, Turkey continued to obtain development assistance from Western multilateral economic institutions, notably from the IMF, IBRD and the European Investment Bank. Western states other than the US have also developed bi-lateral economic assistance schemes of various sizes for Turkey.

Economic crisis and reform

The economic crises of the 1970s forced Turkish governments to a major overhauling of the fundamental economic philosophy of the country.[15] Acute balance of payment deficits brought about by OPEC oil shocks and the US arms embargo hastened the bankruptcy of the traditional import substitution strategy in Turkey, and made inevitable the adoption of economic liberalization.

Upon a brief experimentation with economic liberalism in the 1920s, statism had been adopted as the main economic development strategy of the Republic. The experience of the 1920s had indicated that the country lacked sufficient private capital accumulation and an effective entrepreneurial class existed no longer. The great depression and the onset of the World War II were international developments of the period necessitating state leadership in development and industrialization.

For about half a century, state-led import-substitution policies based on protectionism and a semi-closed economy were maintained. At the end of the 1970s, the inability to import needed oil, the absence of investment credits and proliferating labor strikes had brought the economy to a standstill. The absence of basic consumption goods, rising inflation and soaring unemployment led to political polarization and massive social unrest. The death toll of street clashes and terrorism reached several thousands a year in the second half of the 1970s. Short-lived coalition governments failed to cope with these massive problems.

With the hope of overcoming the financial deadlock and regaining access to international credits, the Demirel government announced a program for economic liberalization in January 1980. During September of the same year the Turkish armed forces captured political power and established a military regime. They maintained the new course in macro-economic management and put in charge of the economy Turgut Özal, who had prepared the liberalization package as a high ranking bureaucrat under the Demirel government.

The main idea behind the new approach was to replicate in Turkey the earlier successes in economic growth of the South East Asian economies.[16] Export promotion was to replace import substitution as the main industrialization strategy. The main measures towards this end were reductions of tariffs and import restrictions, installment of temporary incentives for exports, freeing of international financial movements from bureaucratic controls, and simplification and reduction of regulations for foreign investments. Privatization of the unprofitable state economic enterprises was declared as a critical measure to reduce inflation and to raise the international competitiveness of the Turkish economy.

Despite ups and downs in implementation, this program for liberalization was maintained up to the present. As a result, a remarkable performance in economic growth was achieved, while the social and cultural consequences of such rapid integration into the world economy remains debated. It has often been claimed that globalization causes collective identity crises and cultural fragmentation within states.[17] It is noteworthy that Turkey faced growing challenges from Islamic fundamentalism and Kurdish nationalism during the last two decades as well.

The supporters of the change of course in economic development often made reference to globalization, arguing that pursuing a national industry with protection could only generate an inefficient and uncompetitive industrial sector ultimately doomed to failure. Globalization was an inevitable reality to which individual countries had to adjust in order to survive and thrive. Delaying this process was perceived to only cause a loss of valuable time, creating major disadvantages in long-term international economic competition.

A minority of the state elites, social democratic parties, labor unions and leftists argued that the reforms declared to integrate Turkey into the global economy mostly served the narrow interests of Western and domestic capitalists, neglecting the serious deterioration of economic and social conditions for large segments of the population. They claimed that privatization was transferring the nation's long-term savings to a few politically favored entrepreneurs without regard to the unemployment that followed.

Some Islamists and ultra-nationalists also opposed state-sponsored programs for adjustment to globalization on cultural grounds. They criticized the intrusion of foreign consumer tastes and lifestyles which inevitably followed the flooding in of imported products. In their view, the cultural and spiritual foundations of the country were sold out in the name of economic growth and materialistic progress.

Regarding foreign policy, the Refah Party often made references to strengthening ties with Islamic countries rather than remaining a second class member of the Western world. Nationalists focused on the Turkish zones of the former Soviet Union and sought to deepen cooperation with the newly independent Central Asian republics and Azerbaijan. Ecevit and other leftist thinkers have occasionally proposed a foreign policy that emphasized regional ties, instead of an approach submitting itself to Western interests alone.[18]

Despite these divergent views, no serious clashes on foreign policy have taken place and a common front to the external world could be maintained. Most Turks have seen no contradictions in promoting closer ties to Western, Turkic and Islamic countries at the same time, while trying to adjust to globalization. Leaders like Özal and Demirel were typical examples. Both had traditional values, including Islamic ones, and were keen to develop relations with the Turkic world. At the same time, they were the champions of the globalization/liberalization effort in Turkey and have worked for deeper cooperation with the West.

Efforts to adjust to globalization were not restricted to the economic domain in Turkey. English as the prominent language of the globalization process has been promoted throughout the education system. The proliferation of English-speaking foundation universities has been most dramatic. Before the 1980s, Turkey had two state universities using English as their medium of instruction.

In 1987, state monopoly in university education was given up with the establishment of Bilkent as a private non-profit institution. Since then, these so-called foundation universities mushroomed with state support, approaching 20 in number. All use English as their medium of instruction and employ Turkish and foreign faculty members, mostly with Ph.D.s from the US and the UK. Even the *Fetullahçilar*, an Islamist grouping, set up an English-speaking university in Istanbul. They also established several hundred Turkish-speaking high schools around the world, which emphasize English as a second language.

This openness to globalization in Turkey may appear surprising in the face of the historical legacy of the country. Turkey and its predecessor, the Ottoman Empire, had vigilantly maintained their independence throughout their history. Turkey stands out within the non-Western world as a country the Europeans failed to subdue and colonize. The Turkish Republic was born out of a successful liberation war which thwarted European imperialism.

Alongside the historical commitment to independence, the Ottoman experience with capitulations formed another set of historical experiences that could be expected to turn Turkey against globalization. Given by Ottoman sultans as unilateral grants of concessions to European powers starting in the 16th century, capitulations had become tools of exploitation. Originally voluntary and subject to withdrawal by the Sultan, their nature was altered to the detriment of the Ottoman economy as the power balance between the Ottomans and Europeans changed in latter centuries.

A main economic goal of the founders of the Republic was to free Turkey from capitulations that formed structures of unfair competition between foreign and domestic producers, privileging the former. Earlier, they had led to the destruction of traditional artisanship in Ottoman lands by permitting the penetration of European mass-produced goods without any control. These historical experiences were maintained in the institutional memory of the Republic, and still continue to influence macro-economic decisions to some extent.

Conclusion

The preoccupation with total independence of the Republican political elites is clear. Under these circumstances, one is likely to wonder what made globalization and policies to adjust to it so acceptable in Turkey. The answer probably lies in the long-standing modernization orientation of the country, which is free from any colonial complexes.[19]

Atatürk had initiated westernizing reforms after scoring clear victories on the battlefield against the intrusion and occupation of Western powers. Turkish reforms were not implemented by a colonized elite mesmerized by Western civilization, but by committed nationalists who had proven themselves on the warfront. This fact provided the Kemalist elite with the needed legitimacy to introduce radical and ambitious reforms, which were not intended to please the West but to strengthen the Turkish nation.

The long-term target of these reforms was defined as bringing Turkey to the level of the highest "contemporary civilization." Theoretically, if this was perceived to be in China, Turks had to learn from the Chinese. In reality, with the level of prosperity, individual freedom and power it created, the West formed an obvious model for Turkey.

Unlike formerly colonized developing countries, Turks had experienced Europe at a more or less equal footing. In fact, European traditions for dealing with the world outside their cultural domain developed on the basis of interactions with the Ottoman Empire, which remained an important actor of the European international system for centuries.[20] Turkey's membership in NATO and other Western international institutions illustrates the continuation of this role.

In the words of a leading historian of the Ottoman Empire, Turkey represents a Turkish-European synthesis alongside a Turkish-Islamic synthesis.[21] Coupled to its historic roots in Asia and the Middle East, there is a solid European dimension within the Turkish national identity which strengthens the dedication of the Republic to remaining on its modernization course in association with the West. Turkey is likely to continue perceiving globalization as an opportunity within the foreseeable future, as it will have to cope with the challenges and internal contradictions this process generates for all countries.

Endnotes

[1] This discussion of globalization is adapted from an earlier work of mine: "Globalization and Turkey: From Capitulations to Contemporary Civilization," paper presented at the international conference on "Globalization: Socio-Cultural, Business and Political Dimensions," International Center for Contemporary Middle East Studies, Eastern Mediterranean University, Gazimagusa, TRNC, November 19-21, 1998.

[2] For examples see, Dani Rodrik, "Sense and Nonsense in the Globalization Debate," *Foreign Policy*, Summer 1997. For a harsh and popular critique of globalization from Germany, see: Hans-Peter Martin and Harald Schuman, *Die Globalisierungsfalle: Der Angriff auf Demokratie und Wohlstand* [*The Globalization-Trap: Assault on Democracy and Welfare*] (Hamburg: Rowohlt Verlag), 1996.

[3] Liberal, realist and radical interpretations of globalization are discussed in: John Baylis and Steve Smith, (eds.), *The Globalization of World Politics*, (Oxford: Oxford University Press) 1997.

[4] For an authoritative neo-Marxist critique of the effects of globalization on Turkey, see: Gülten Kazgan, *Yeni Ekonomik Düzen'de Türkiye'nin Yeri* [*Turkey's Place in the New Economic Order*] (Istanbul: Altın Kitaplar), 1994.

[5]Popular business magazines form a deviation from this pattern. For instance: *"Türkiye Global Dünyanm Neresinde?"* ["Where is Turkey in the Global World?"] in *AD Business* (September 1998).

[6]This section is based on an earlier work of mine: "Are Multilateral Orders Trans-Civilizationally Expandable? Insights from Turkish-Western Relations," paper presented at the 36th Annual Convention of the International Studies Association, Chicago, IL, 21-25 February 1995.

[7]For a comprehensive study of the subject, see: Bozkurt Güvenç, *Türk Kimliği: Kültür Tarihinin Kaynakları* [*Turkish Identity: Sources of Cultural History*] (Ankara: Kültür Bakanlığı), 1993.

[8]Adam Watson, *The Evolution of International Society: A Comparative Historical Analysis* (London and New York: Routledge), 1992.

[9]Watson, 1992, p. 178; and Thomas Naff, "The Ottoman Empire and the European States System," in Hedley Bull and Adam Watson, (eds.), *The Expansion of International Society* (Oxford: Clarendon Press), 1989.

[10]Watson, 1992, p. 218.

[11]A classic study of Ottoman and Turkish reform is: Bernard Lewis, *The Emergence of Modern Turkey* (London: Oxford University Press), 1961.

[12]A comprehensive survey of Turkish foreign policy in the Republican era is: Mehmet Gönlübol, et al., *Olaylarla Türk Dış Politikası* [*Turkish Foreign Policy*] (Ankara: Alkım), 1989.

[13]Nicholas X. Rizopoulos, "Pride, Prejudice, and Myopia: Greek Foreign Policy in a Time Warp," *World Policy Journal*, Fall 1993.

[14]Gönlübol, 1989, p.452.

[15]Atasoy, 1998.

[16]For a popular presentation of this approach, see: Cem Kozlu, *Vizyon Arayışları ve Asya Modelleri* [*Searches for Visions and Asian Models*] (Ankara: İş Bankası Kültür Yayınları), 1995.

[17]See, for instance: Bassam Tibi, *"Strukturelle Globalisierung und Kulturelle Fragmentierung"* [Structural Globalization and Cultural Fragmentation], *Internationale Politik*, January 1996.

[18]For example: Bülent Ecevit, *"Bölge-Merkezli Dış Politika"* [Region-Centered Foreign Policy] in the special issue on Turkish foreign policy of *Yeni Türkiye* (March/April 1995).

[19]Atasoy, 1995.

[20]Elaborate explanations on this matter are presented in: Adam Watson, *The Evolution of International Society: A Comparative Historical Analysis* (London and New York: Routledge), 1992.

[21]Halil Inalcık, *"Türkiye, Milli Kültür ve Küreselleşme,"* unpublished manuscript, Bilkent University, Department of History, 1993.

Globalization, Identity and Social Work Practice: Insight from Working with Bedouin-Arab Peoples

Alean Al-Krenawi & John R. Graham

Globalization, like other complex concepts, is not without paradox. On the one hand, pervasive structures of international finance and political arrangements may seem, to some, to flatten intranational, intra-community and intra-positionality differences. Likewise, on ideological grounds, observers such as Francis Fukuyama argue that the world is increasingly adopting a liberal, capitalist stance in the aftermath of the Cold War's end.[1]

On the other hand, powerful forces of identity emerge at the level of community, region, ethnicity, race, sexual orientation, gender, politics and other forms of positionality differences.[2] The present chapter on ethno-racial aspects of social work practice expands upon part of this latter aspect of globalization – highlighting identity and difference. It does so through the prism of the authors' experiences writing about, and reflecting upon, intervention with Bedouin-Arab peoples in the Middle East.

The chapter begins by making the case that social work epistemology remains a largely Western conception, but is nonetheless beginning to add space to non-Western voices and perspectives. The next section analyses three culturally specific facets of Bedouin-Arab life – blood vengeance, polygamy and traditional healing – that can well enhance social work's efforts to understand and act upon differences between Western and non-Western peoples. A concluding section considers the common ground that exists between social work and important leaders in Bedouin-Arab communities; principles for integrating social work professionals; and non-Western cultural ways of looking at social work intervention; and the significance of these facets to globalization.

Much of the discussion focuses on Bedouin-Arab people in the Negev region, Israel. This community, in our view, lives a dialectic of globalization versus localization. On the one hand, there are attempts to protect indigenous cultural/religious belief systems. On the other, there are pervasive forces of modernization; cultural, social, economic and political transformation; and exposure to Western values. In some respects, many in the community perceive a struggle between a dominant culture and a minority. At the very least, as we point out in the conclusion, since every intervention is on some level referenced to these forces, social work cannot avoid being part of such intra-cultural relations.

Reflections on social work scholarship

On the surface – given the public rhetoric and growing presence of the literature – social work's commitment to racial and ethnic plurality seems firmly established. Scratch beneath the surface, however, and a Western epistemology continues to prevail. The reasons are several-fold. One of the most significant is the Western origins of the profession and the commensurate biases that endure. A wonderfully illustrative benchmark is the 1945 publication by the eminent University of Chicago social work scholar Charlotte Towle. Towle's *Common Human Needs* was a landmark textbook that was used by successive generations of students in North America and Europe. That book, like psychologist Abraham Maslow's hierarchy of needs, represented the thinking of her generation, highlighting those requirements that were considered universal to the human condition. Over a half century later, social work, like other helping professions, has allegedly modified its knowledge base, attempting to take into account social diversity on the basis of race, ethnicity, range of ability, gender, religion, creed, sexual orientation, nationality and geography, among other parameters. Perhaps most scholars and practitioners would concur that an early 21st century version of Towle's classic would surely emphasize differential, rather than common, human needs as an analytical framework.

And yet much of the multicultural literature emphasizes ethno-racial considerations within particular countries – such as the United States or United Kingdom, where scholarship is arguably the most advanced. Potocky's and Rodgers-Farmer's 1998 book is one of many examples.[3] An excellent work, providing a range of practical and rigorous insights into the art and science of the profession, it is subject to one fundamental – and all too pervasive – critique. Its scope is far too oriented to one single country, in its case, the United States. Both editors and all contributors have an American affiliation. Policy directives and trends in practice are referenced exclusively to the United States. Data focuses on such ethno-specific and minority groups as African-Americans and Latinos, among others. The ultimate effect is to portray an exclusively American and therefore limited conception of minority and oppressed populations.

The examples of similar biases in teaching, research and practice are legion. The first author portrays, in vivid detail, his experiences trying to reconcile his social work training within Western-based universities, on the one hand, with his own lived experiences as a practising professional and community member of the Bedouin-Arab city of Rahat, Israel.[4] His father compelled him, through culturally-constructed analogy and metaphor, to integrate, rather than overlook, the thinking and practices of his home community. This, perhaps, was the most germane advice the author received. Both authors, like other academicians, are well familiar with experiences of students from ethno-racial communities that are not dominant. These include the feelings of marginality; and the lack of perceived reinforcement to integrate the formal theories of social work with the informal, and equally legitimate, theories that constitute the cultural assumptions of a non-Western community.[5]

To this end it is helpful, if not essential, to recover the profession's engagement with diverse interdisciplinary thinking – which may be perceived, ultimately, to have much relationship with post-modernism, and the latter's commitment to a plurality of voices.[6] To its credit, a nascent social work literature is beginning to portray authentic diversity. The profession's leading theoreticians incorporate significant attention to diversity theory,[7] and traditional healing as a legitimate core of the profession's theoretical constructs.[8] But the struggle has been up-hill, and in our view the continued differentiation between multicultural practice and theory, on the one hand,[9] and international practice and theory, on the other,[10] obscures and neglects as much as it explains and illuminates. True, there are important social, political, cultural, economic and legal differences between multicultural practice in, say, North America versus domestic practice abroad. But many differences *also* occur between – and in some respects within – non-Western countries. And at the same time, there are many overlapping principles between practice within and outside the West. These, given the historic tendency to reify into "international" versus "multicultural" fields of interest, are either lost, or serve to reinforce a multicultural reference to one particular country, rather than trans-national structures.

Social work practice with Bedouin-Arab peoples: Three important cultural constructs

And so we stress our commitment to thinking about international practice in multicultural terms, and vice versa. To this end, three cultural constructs of Bedouin-Arab life bear emphasis. True, the specific ways in which they occur do differ from place to place. Beyond this consideration, it should also be noted, heterogeneity rather than homogeneity is probably the best analytical stance for considering the meaning of the following practices to individuals, communities and people. Comparable variance occurs over time. At the same time, the relevance to scholars and practitioners in the West and non-West is, in our view, equally strong, given in particular the growing diversity of Western nations and the continued need to push social work thinking beyond immediate national/parochial frames of reference.

The Bedouin-Arab people

Although originally intended to describe only those who herded camels, "Bedouin" has come to be known as the general name for all the Arabic-speaking, nomadic tribes in the Middle East.[11] Since much of this chapter concentrates on Bedouin-Arab practices in the Negev region, Israel, several comments arise.

The Bedouin have lived in the Negev region since before Christianity or Islam became established religions.[12] Today there are about twenty Bedouin tribes in the Negev, consisting of 120 000 people: 40% live in villages, and 60% live in unrecognized villages without basic infrastructure and social services.[13] Traditionally, the Bedouin economy has been based on rearing animals such as cattle, goats and sheep, although within the past 25 years, an increasing number in today's villages work in industrial or service industries. To a considerable extent, social status, safety from economic hardship and potential for personal development continue to be founded upon tribal identity; the larger the tribe, the more powerful it is in the Bedouin status hierarchy. Each tribe has a leader (sheik), and forums of male elders representing the several extended families that constitute the tribe[14] make major decisions. This process ensures that even within the context of a modern industrial state, the Bedouin adhere to a predictable set of practices suitable to nomadic life in the desert.[15]

There are three social strata in Bedouin society: "true" Bedouin of nomadic heritage, belonging to one of the five confederated nations (Qabials or Sfuf)[16]; peasants (Flahin, singular Flah), originally from

the cultivated areas bordering on the desert who worked the tribes'
lands; and slaves (Al-Abid) who originated from Arab and non-Arab
captives from Sudan and Egypt.[17]

The Flahin migrated to the Negev before the establishment of the
Israeli state, and lived among the Bedouin as laborers, working the
tribes' lands, shepherding the sheiks' flocks, but not being allowed to
own land. When the Israeli state was established, the Flahin were con-
sidered practically to be part of the "true" tribes. Work opportunities
from neighboring Jewish settlements have also blurred any economic
and educational differences between them; indeed, the Flahin have
often attained superior wealth and education.[18] *Nevertheless, the*
Flahin have retained their inferior status in the eyes of many "true"
Bedouin. A Bedouin man may marry a Flah woman, but the converse
is forbidden, even if the "higher tribal status" Bedouin woman wishes
it.[19] *This disjuncture between attainment and social stratum is an*
ongoing source of competition and tension between the two groups.[20, 21]

Finally, it is essential to emphasize that the social structure is
highly patriarchal. Gender roles are strongly adhered to, marriages
are frequently arranged and women rarely leave the home unescort-
ed. Gender segregation is intense, and the two spheres rarely inter-
sect, save for relationships in one's immediate family. The society is
high context;[23] that is to say, both a slower pace of societal change
and a higher sense of social stability predominate, and the collective
is emphasized over the individual.[22] Family honor is very important,
and tribal/familial social and economic relationships are quite interdependent.[24]

Blood vengeance

Much of the following considerations are from Al-Krenawi &
Graham.[25] We argue that blood vengeance, the obligation to kill in
retribution for the death of a member of one's family or tribe, is an
essential component in much of social work practice among
Bedouin-Arab peoples. As we point out, it is

a kind of collective guarantee provided by a given group to all of its
members in a society where communal duty is paramount.[26] *It*
evolved, in part, from the special needs of a nomadic, warrior people,
where living in tents, without benefit of solid walls in the sparsely
populated desert, makes one vulnerable to attack by others. It therefore
reflects the need for some system of justice in the absence of the formal

apparatuses, the legal specialists or the police forces that are common to Western societies.[27]

It arises when a misunderstanding occurs between one major social group and another, be it a family, a *hamula* or, as is usually the case, a tribe. The key point is its re-establishment of symmetry between social relations.

"Thus, unlike synonyms in the English language, such as spite, malice, vindictiveness, envy or rage, the Bedouin conception of vengeance is more than an emotional response to a perceived wrong: it is based on a perception of being in the right, of restoring symmetry to an imbalanced social exchange."[28] And so, if a man in one tribe is killed by someone from à different tribe, an affront is perceived to have been committed against that entire tribe. Blood vengeance would require that a member of the offending tribe be killed, in order to remove the assault on the *Ar*, or pride, of the murdered man's tribe. The concept of *Ar*, indeed, is key to understanding blood vengeance. Numerous rituals precede the carrying out of vengeance, and likewise there are rituals that can occur between tribal members to avert vengeance. These are beyond the scope of the current chapter but are covered fully in Al-Krenawi & Graham, 1997b. To that extent, social work may play a key role in arranging for locally-based responses to a vengeance situation.

It is likewise important to emphasize the significance of blood vengeance in the field of child welfare practice. Say, for example, that a man has been put on death row because a third cousin within his tribe killed a member of a different tribe. The aggrieved tribe seeks vengeance against the man, who with his family flees his immediate community and lives in the most extreme form of isolation and poverty. As we note, blood vengeance is, therefore, "a culturally-specific phenomenon putting Bedouin-Arab children at high risk of neglect." We examine one such family and conclude that vengeance creates "significant psychological and social implications of vengeance upon children." Also relevant, however, are children's coping strategies, including various games that they play, help they provide one another and strengths that they cultivate. The role of social work is particularly significant, and includes "non-authoritarianism, strategies to form a positive helping alliance, and culturally sensitive assessment and (in their various forms) intervention."[29]

Seven principles of child welfare intervention are particularly salient. The first is the capability of *not* being – and *not* being construed to be – an authority figure. In the case study we examine, a worker rightly concluded that immediate apprehension of the children would have done little to cultivate a working relationship with the family. Moreover, early apprehension would have ripped the children out of their familial and cultural contexts, especially given the problems of placing them in a Bedouin-Arab home, with all of the complex inter-relationships with vengeance that would have arisen. Such placement concerns could easily interfere with blood vengeance intra-tribal resolutions, exacerbate the children's at-risk status by placing them in greater public exposure and place the foster family and its broader hamula and tribal relations in jeopardy of involvement in the blood vengeance dynamic.

A second related facet is, therefore, striking a positive helping alliance based on acceptance, respect, trust and validation of the family's current situation. A third is cultural sensitivity in appreciating the ecological context, and significance to family members, of blood vengeance, as well as the family members' perception of their circumstances, problems and resources. Fourth, and relatedly: a worker is best not to impose culturally-inappropriate techniques, such as insisting that the family visit the social work office, as opposed to continuing worker home visits. A fifth and sixth principle is encouraging a worker to identify with, and strike a positive helping alliance with, children of vengeance families. To that end, playing games with children is a powerful way of connecting and establishing trust. A final principle, perhaps pre-eminent of all, is to provide concrete services for meeting the family's basic needs, including clothing, food, schoolbooks, toys and the family's access to monthly income security payments.[30]

Polygamy

These facets lead to a second aspect of Bedouin-Arab life: family structures. While most families are monogamous,[31] polygamous structures are also known to exist. These require culturally-sensitive considerations. Much of this discussion is taken from Graham & Al-Krenawi.[32]

Anthropologists typically define polygamy as "a marital relationship involving multiple wives." It includes three types, only the first of which is of concern to the present chapter: polygyny (one husband is married to two or more wives; hereafter referred to as polygamy), polyandry (one wife married to two or more husbands) and polygynandry (a group marriage scenario in which two or more wives are simultaneously married to two or more husbands). Of the three forms, the first is the most common world wide.[34, 35]

Several years ago, we examined student files of 25 Bedouin-Arab children born to senior mothers of polygamous families, and conducted interviews with their teachers and mothers. We found that mothers complained of somatic symptoms, economic problems, poor relations with the husband, and competition and jealousy between the co-wives and among the co-wives' children. Children had a variety of behavioral problems, and below average academic achievement. We compared learning achievements, social adjustment and family conflict among Bedouin-Arab children from polygamous and monogamous families. In a second study, of 146 boys and girls, aged 8 -9 (73 were from polygamous and 73 monogamous families), data likewise confirmed differences between the two groups. Children from polygamous families had a higher level of learning achievement than children of monogamous families, while those from monogamous families adjusted to the school framework better than those of polygamous families. The conflict rating of children from polygamous families was higher than their counterparts.[36]

Several principles of social work practice arise. Workers, firstly, should comprehend the cultural and personal significance of polygamy to family members. The transition from sole wife to senior wife, or from junior wife to intermediate wife, is traumatic. In the Bedouin-Arab community we examined, men tend to favor the most recent wife and her children. The man's provision of instrumental and emotional support varies accordingly. There are significant relationship implications between wives – who tend to live with their children in separate accommodations from the other wives and their children. Likewise, the children of different wives may often embrace mutual antipathy.

Thus, to think about a second theme, social workers need to appreciate the significance of polygamy to children's functioning. It is profoundly significant that from our admittedly limited study number, children of senior wives appear to have, on balance, fewer economic resources and tend, on balance, to attain weaker scholastic performance. The implications for personal, social and community development are extensive.

Thirdly, it is essential to select children as a target system for intervention. Children are, in fact, the common frame of reference between the father and his wives. Both parents' social status and future eco-

nomic well-being are strongly dependent upon the size of the family; family honor is closely associated with the number of sons and their future life successes. Thus, a social work intervention could feasibly be framed in the context of attending to the children's emotional, instrumental and relational needs. Motivation to address these aspects may be high, if a social worker can help the family to appreciate their relationship to the children's social functioning at school.

Moreover, in focusing on the children's difficulties, other familial systemic issues may also be addressed. This allows entry into considering differential allocation of economic and social support between the two sub-families. Improvements in sub-family, half-sibling and co-wife relations may be convincingly portrayed as interdependent. Junior and senior wives could be encouraged to perceive each other as partners, rather than opponents; half-sibling relations could improve in alike proportion.

Fourthly, the value base of such interventions could be reinforced by the cultural canons of Islam. The Koran clearly emphasizes the husband's imperative to treat his wives equally: "Marry women of your choice, two, or three, or four; but if ye fear that ye shall not be able to deal justly (with them) then only one."[37] Other Islamic ideals that are implicit to the interventions include harmony with others, peace in the family and ensuring children's well being.[38]

Traditional healing

A final consideration for social work practice is traditional healing, which remains profoundly embedded in Bedouin-Arab culture,

Healing rituals are fundamental to the community's cultural canon, are inextricably linked with its strongly Islamic basis of living, and are a non-stigmatizing and legitimized aspect of its natural helping systems and traditional forms of physical and mental healing. Most Bedouins who are illiterate or not verbally skilled might prefer traditional healing rituals to modern, more discursive counselling techniques. To many they have greater community sanction than Western forms of helping.[39]

The following comments are taken from Al-Krenawi & Graham 1997a, 1997b, 1997c,[40] 1996a, 1996b; and Al-Krenawi, Graham & Maoz, 1996.

Among rituals we've written about previously are *Zurah* (visiting saints' tombs), *Rahameh* (memorial ritual for the dead) and *Dhikr* (invoking God's name).[41] The *Zurah* occurs when individuals, or more usually groups of people (often family and extended family members) go to dead saints' tombs, which are considered holy places and are associated with stories of relieving personal anxiety, healing physical and mental ailments, and mediating requests to God. Visits to saints' tombs usually take place in a day, but may sometimes be over extended periods of time. The entire process – from departing to the tomb, visiting the tomb, the dinner that follows and then the return home – emphasizes group cohesion and support. "At the tomb Koran verses are read, candles and incense are lit beside the grave, and white cloth is hung on the tomb itself. Vows are meant to appease the saint's soul and special requests to prevent tragedy or illness from striking the supplicant, his/her children or property. Prayers are said corporately and individually."[42] *Rahameh*, a memorial ritual for the dead, involves the elaborate preparation of a meal, prayers and comparable group cohesion during and after a meal. Like saints' tomb visiting, it provides considerable solace to people in distress – in the case of tomb visiting, for a variety of anxieties; in the case of the *Rahameh*, in light of a close individual's death or anniversary of a death.

The *Dhikr* ritual, performed often by Bedouin-Arab healers, the *Dervish*, is especially significant to mental health practice. One becomes a *Dervish* following proscribed stages of initiation. The first is to have received a *Baraka* (a blessing, a gift from God) that is thought to be bestowed upon a devout person of positive qualities. This takes place usually in a dream, or sometimes in a conscious vision via a supernatural message bestowed by an angel. The *Baraka* itself is an actual encounter with the spiritual forces of good and evil, with the former ultimately triumphing over the latter. Once a *Dervish* determines that an individual has experienced a *Baraka*, the former becomes the mentor to the latter, who acts as an apprentice within a particular *Dervish* school of thought. Both genders may become *Dervish*, but one only apprentices under a same sex *Dervish*.[43]

The *Dhikr* occurs on Thursday evenings, a holy time beginning the Muslim Holy Day of Friday.

> *The sessions begin in silence, with participants sitting in a circle. The Dervish facilitates the group, initiating group conversation regarding members' problems and coping strategies. During the next stage the group stands, the Dervish enters the middle of the circle and initiates prayer. Prayer is ended with the Dervish singing a hymn, accompanied by two group members repeatedly beating large drums in loud monotonous rhythm. At this point, the transition is made to the group*

meditation stage in which members focus on the power of God and sway to the drum beat in a trance by repeating the phrase <u>Allah Hai</u> (God is alive). This stage often culminates in individual members reaching a state of physical and emotional ecstasy. The <u>Dervish</u> ends the ritual by leading a group prayer in which all members corporately ask for God's forgiveness. A silence is maintained, individual requests to God are made and the session ends with members silently departing from the <u>Dervish</u>'s home."[44]

From the vantage point of helping, the ritual induces a state of hypnotic trance, a process about which much research has indicated therapeutic value.[45] On an individual level the transition from the subjective reality of personal experience to the irrational world of the Divine leads to feelings of satisfaction, confidence, catharsis, psychological release, self-expression and, above all else, resolution to deal with one's problems. On another level group members give emotional support, universalization, as well as a network of support outside of the ritual. The ritual process itself provides a further sense of union with other members participating in that ritual, reinforcing greater group cohesion.[46, 47]

Other traditional healers, it should be noted, also exist in Bedouin-Arab society. They include the *Kayy*, who provide acupuncture treatment which is used to treat rheumatic and arthritic pain. The *Mujjabir* heal broken bones with splints, and the *Alaashp* are herbalists who treat various forms of pains. The *Hawi* are known for their skills in sucking the poison out of scorpion stings and bites of wild snakes. The *Fatah* are fortune tellers whom the Bedouin consult about the future or to discover the location of missing possessions. The *Khatib* (or *Hajjab*) produce amulets that are worn on the body to ward off evil spirits.[48] Limits of space preclude more extensive analysis of those healers.

Conclusion

Three points bear emphasis. The first is the common ground between indigenous phenomena, such as what the present chapter analyses, and social work. As we argue, in a comparison between traditional healers such as the *Dervish*, on the one hand, and one of social work's immediate precursors – late 19th century evangelical Protestant charity volunteers – there is much in common.[49] This includes gender inclusiveness in performing activities, overcoming women's marginalization in pursuing such activities, conceptualizing services in the context of a religious ethos, among other facets.

This work led us to write an article for the World Health Organization, in which we elaborated some of the common ground, and differences, between such modern helping professions as social work, and traditional healing activities in communities such as the Bedouin-Arab.

As we pointed out, to turn to a second theme, an

individual who receives treatment from a traditional Bedouin healer may do so on a variety of levels. Firstly, there is the need to address the precipitating problem, whether it is, for example, somatic, psychosocial, psychiatric or a combination of the same. But beyond this there are obvious resonances between a traditional healer and the person seeking help. Some are cultural, since the healing rituals incorporate familiar religious, community, regional or tribal praxes. Some are interpersonal in the sense that the healer is either known in person or by reputation. Some are normative, in that the healing rituals enjoy community sanction. Some are experiential, in so far as previous rituals have been directly observed and have provided evidence of a certain utility. And some, implicitly at the very least, are political, in the context of geopolitical/ethnic cleavages between a dominant Jewish population and a minority Muslim/Arab community in the Negev. Bedouin healers are of the same cultural background as those who seek their help and are therefore apt to be trusted. By the same token any encounter between a non-Bedouin modern practitioner and a Bedouin patient necessarily enters the two into the wider symbolic universe of Middle Eastern politics.

Likewise any dialogue between modern and traditional healers, in this cultural context, must be undertaken with great sensitivity to process. If members of another culture were to supervise a traditional healer's activities, for example, there would likely arise suspicions and hostility. Creating greater opportunities for mutual referrals, on the other hand, may well be productive: the patient would stand to experience higher quality care, and the practitioners, self-improvement. So too might informal discussions between modern and traditional healers have potential merit, particularly if the former were of a Bedouin, or at least a similar cultural background. One should emphasize, however, that mutual notions of collegiality might be a distant realization, although mutual respect is a valid objective over the shorter term. Finally, and perhaps foremost, the modern and the traditional healers both must recognize their own limitations. Modern practitioners, for example, may not be familiar with Bedouin cultural and religious beliefs; and traditional healers may be far more limited than their modern counterparts in dealing with psychotic illnesses, among other chronic or acute medical conditions.[50]

And so, lastly, to return to the theme of globalization, the Bedouin-Arab in many respects remain close to the cultural/religious values that differentiate them from the West. Such considerations are particularly important to the Bedouin-Arab community in the Negev, which is undergoing a remarkable period of change. Within a generation the community has been transformed from nomadism/semi-nomadism to settlement, and from a time-honored, agrarian economic base to growing participation in Israeli life. Surely, in this clash between totalizing globalization versus localization, social work has a role to affirm an indigenous community's lived destiny, however subtle and dynamic particular cadences between globalization and localization might be. But only if its knowledge base and practices cultivate sensitivity to, and knowledge of, those cultural aspects that are of enduring importance to the minority community in question.

Endnotes

[1]Fukuyama, F. (1992). *The End of History and the Last Man*. New York: Avon Books.

[2]Gutman, A. & Taylor, C. (Eds.). (1994). *Multiculturalism: Examining the Politics of Recognition*. Princeton: Princeton University Press; Hazlett, J.D. (1998). *My Generation: Collective Autobiography and Identity Politics*. Madison: University of Wisconsin Press; Sarat, A. & Kearns, T.R. (Eds.) (1999). *Cultural Pluralism, Identity Politics, and the Law*. Ann Arbor: University of Michigan Press; Stychin, C.F. (1998). *A Nation by Rights: National Cultures, Sexual Identity Politics, and the Discourse of Rights*. Philadelphia: Temple University Press.

[3]Potocky, M. & Rodgers-Farmer, A.Y. (Eds.) (1998). *Social Work Research with Minority and Oppressed Populations: Methodological Issues and Innovations*. New York: Haworth.

[4]Al-Krenawi, A. (1998a). "Reconciling Western Treatment and Traditional Healing: A Social Worker Walks with the Wind." *Reflections: Narratives of Professional Helping*, 4(3), 6-21.

[5]Al-Krenawi, A. (1998b). "Contribution of the Constructivist Approach to Professional Practice in a Multicultural Society," *Society and Welfare*, 18(2), 253-267.

[6]Graham, J.R. (1996). "A Practical Idealism: A Theoretical Values Conception for Northern Social Work Practice." In R. Delaney, K. Brownlee & J.R. Graham (Eds.), *Strategies in Northern Social Work Practice* (pp. 95-103). Thunder Bay: Centre for Northern Studies.

[7]Payne, M. (1997). *Modern Social Work Theory: A Critical Introduction.* Chicago: Lyceum.

[8]Turner, F. (1996). *A Wall Chart of Social Work Theory.* Toronto: Frank Turner.

[9]Devore, W. & Schlesinger, E.B. (1996). *Ethnic-Sensitive Social Work Practice.* New York: Allyn Bacon.

[10]Hokenstad, M.C. & Midgley, J. (1997). *Issues in International Social Work.* Washington: NASW.

[11]Kay, S. (1978). *The Bedouin.* New York: Crane Russak.

[12]*Hebrew Encyclopaedia.* (1954). Vol. 7, Tel-Aviv, Reshafim Press (in Hebrew).

[13]Al-Krenawi, A. (1996). "Group Work with Bedouin Widows of the Negev in a Medical Clinic." *Affilia: Journal of Women and Social Work, 11*(3), 303-318; Ben-David, Y. (1993). *The Bedouin Settlements of the Negev,* Jerusalem: Jerusalem Institute (in Hebrew).

[14]Al-Krenawi, A. (1998c). "Family Therapy with a Multiparental/Multispousal Family." *Family Process, 37*(1), 65-81.

[15]Reichel, A., Newmman, Y. & Abu Saad, I. (1987). "Organizational Climate and Work Satisfaction of Male and Female Teachers in Bedouin Elementary Schools." *Israel Social Science Research, 4,* 2, pp. 34-38.

[16]Al-Aref, A. (1934). *The Bedouin Tribes in Beer-Sheva District.* Jerusalem: Bostnai Publishers; Marks, E. (1974). *The Bedouin Society in the Negev.* Tel-Aviv, Reshafim Press (in Hebrew).

[17]Al-Krenawi, A. & Graham, J.R. (1997b). "Social Work and Blood Vengeance: The Bedouin-Arab Case." *British Journal of Social Work, 27*(3), 515-528; Lewando-Hundt, G. (1978). *Women's Power and Settlement: The Effect of Settlement on the Position of Negev Bedouin Women.* Edinburgh: Unpublished M.A. Thesis, University of Edinburgh.

[18]Ben-David, Y. (1994). *The Bedouin Education System in the Negev: The Reality and the Need for Advancement.* Jerusalem: The Floersheimer Institute for Policy Studies Ltd. (in Hebrew).

[19]Baar, A. (1985). *Bedouin, Flahin and Abid in Rahat: The Social Process Between These Social Classes.* Beer-Sheva: Arceon Toveahow, Ben-Gurion University of the Negev; Lewando-Hundt, 1978; Marks, E. (1974). *The Bedouin Society in the Negev.* Tel-Aviv, Reshafim Press (in Hebrew).

[20]Ben-David, 1994.

[21]Al-Krenawi & Graham, 1997b, p. 516-7.

[22]Hall, E. (1976). *Beyond Culture.* New York: Doubleday.

[23]Al-Krenawi, 1998c.

[24] Al-Krenawi, A. & Graham, J.R. (1998). "Divorce Among Muslim Arab Women in Israel." *Journal of Divorce and Remarriage, 29*(3/4), 103-119; Al-Krenawi & Graham, 1997b.

[25] Al-Krenawi, A. & Graham, J.R. (1999). "Social Work Intervention with Bedouin-Arab Children in the Context of Blood Vengeance." *Child Welfare, 78*(2), 283-296; Al-Krenawi & Graham 1997b.

[26] Jabbur, J. S. (1995). *The Bedouins and the Desert: Aspects of Nomadic Life in the Arab East.* New York: State University of New York Press.

[27] Al-Krenawi & Graham, 1997b, p. 517-18.

[28] Al-Krenawi & Graham, 1997b, p. 518.

[29] Al-Krenawi & Graham, 1999, p. 283.

[30] Al-Krenawi & Graham, 1999, p. 291-293.

[31] Al-Krenawi & Graham, 1998.

[32] Al-Krenawi, A. & Graham, J.R. (1997a). "Nebi-Musa: A Therapeutic Community for Drug Addiction in a Muslim Context." *Transcultural Psychiatry, 34*(3), 377-398.

[33] Low, B.S. (1988). "Measures of Polygyny in Humans." *Current Anthropology, 29* (1), 189-194; Kottak, 1978, cited in Low, 1988, p. 189.

[34] Valsiner, J. (1989). "Organization of Children's Social Development in Polygamic Families." In J. Valsiner (Ed.), *Child Development in Cultural Context* (pp. 67-86). Toronto: Hogrefe and Huber Publishers.

[35] Al-Krenawi, A., Graham, J.R. & Al-Krenawi, S. (1997). "Social Work Practice with Polygamous Families." *Child and Adolescent Social Work Journal, 14*(6), 444-458.

[36] Al-Krenawi, A., Lightman, E.S. (In Press). "Learning Achievement, Social Adjustment, and Family Conflict Among Bedouin-Arab Children from Polygamous and Monogamous Families." *Journal of Social Psychology.*

[37] Koran, Surah 4, v. 3.

[38] Al-Krenawi, Graham & Al-Krenawi, 1997, p. 454-5.

[39] Al-Krenawi, A. & Graham, J.R. (1996a). "Social Work and Traditional Healing Rituals Among the Bedouin of the Negev, Israel." *International Social Work, 39*(2), 177-88.

[40] Al-Krenawi, A. & Graham, J.R. (1997c). "Spirit Possession and Exorcism: The Integration of Modern and Traditional Mental Health Care Systems in the Treatment of a Bedouin Patient." *Clinical Social Work Journal, 25*(2), 211-222.

[41] Al-Krenawi & Graham, 1996a.

[42] Al-Krenawi & Graham, 1996a, p. 180.

[43]Al-Krenawi, A., Graham, J.R. & Maoz, B. (1996). "The Healing Significance of the Negev's Bedouin Dervish." *Social Science and Medicine, 43*(1), 13-21.

[44]Al-Krenawi & Graham, 1996a, p. 183; Al-Krenawi, Graham & Maoz, 1996.

[45]Cassanas, J. (1992). *"Le Cadre et ses Origines." Psychanalystes, 44* (fall), 29-42; Witztum, E., Buchbinder, J.T. & Van der Hart, O. (1990). "Summoning a Punishing Angel: Treatment of a Depressed Patient with Dissociative Features." *Bulletin of the Menninger Clinic, 54* (4), 524-37.

[46]D'Aquili, E.G. (1985). "Human Ceremonial Ritual and the Modulation of Aggression." *Zygon Journal of Religion and Science, 20* (1), 21-30.

[47]Al-Krenawi & Graham, 1996a, p. 184.

[48]Al-Krenawi, Graham & Maoz, 1996.

[49]Graham, J.R. & Al-Krenawi, A. (1996). "A Comparison Study of Traditional Helpers in a Late Nineteenth Century Canadian (Christian) Society and in a Late Twentieth Century Bedouin (Muslim) Society in the Negev, Israel." *Journal of Multicultural Social Work, 4*(2), 31-45.

[50]Al-Krenawi, A. & Graham, J.R. (1996b). *Tackling Mental Illness: Roles for Old and New Disciplines.* World Health Forum